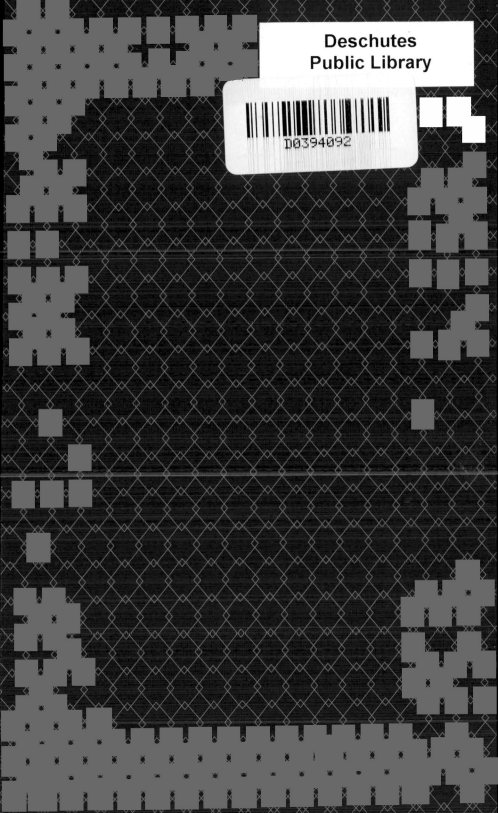

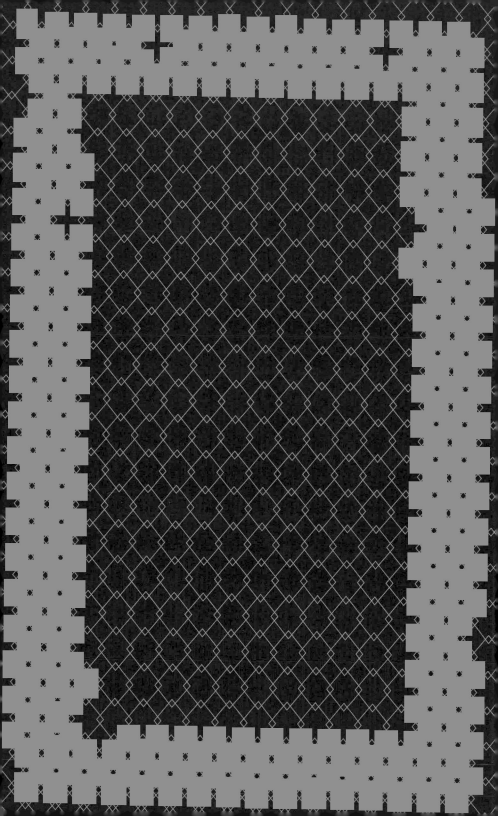

The
Storm-Tossed
Family

The
Storm-Tossed Family

How the Cross Reshapes the Home

RUSSELL MOORE

B&H
PUBLISHING GROUP

NASHVILLE, TENNESSEE

978-1-4627-9480-5

Published by B&H Publishing Group
Nashville, Tennessee

Dewey Decimal Classification: 306.85
Subject Heading: FAMILY \ DOMESTIC RELATIONS \
FAMILY LIFE

Cover design and illustration by Wayne Brezinka.
Cover photography by Randy Hughes.

1 2 3 4 5 6 7 • 22 21 20 19 18

For Taylor Eugene Moore, my son.
You surprised us in birth, and surprise us still, with joy.

Contents

CHAPTER ONE

The Storm-Tossed Family

THIS BOOK IS NAMED FOR a song I hate. And, Lord knows, I love songs. I grew up with the lyrics of songs all around me, the most vivid of which were those sung every Sunday in the little red-brick church I attended, multiple times every week. Many of those hymns I find myself singing at the most surprising of moments. I will find myself turning to them whenever I am at a moment of personal crisis—when I need to be reminded that God loves me "just as I am"—or at a moment of temptation—when I must remind myself that "I have decided to follow Jesus"—or at a moment of joy, when I want to sing out, "How marvelous! How wonderful!" There's one I never sing to myself; though, like the others, I could sing it by heart, if asked.

The chorus of the hymn goes: "Place your hand in the nailed-scarred hand." I would say that perhaps the hymn is too sentimental, but lots of them were, ones that I still treasure. I would say it's because the hymn starts off with a mixed metaphor of a question—"Have you failed in your plan of your storm-tossed life?" But it's hardly alone on that front either. I suppose it's because the song doesn't seem to make sense in terms of what it's saying with how it's sung. The chorus is exuberant and light, almost like a commercial jingle, and yet the words are about the gruesomely sober reality reaching out to a hand spiked over with bloody scabs. That doesn't seem to fit.

Even so, that hymn kept emerging in my memory as I wrote this book, and for a long time I didn't know why. At first, I thought it was obvious. This is a book about the family, but family in light of the cross. My subconscious was mining up this old hymn because I was talking about the cross. And yet, my mind is filled with cross songs about Jesus and crosses and blood—fountains filled with blood, being washed in the blood, finding power in the blood. It wasn't until much later that I realized: what I was grasping for somewhere in my hidden psyche was not the imagery of nails or scars, but that of the storm.

As with blood, my revivalist church tradition had plenty of songs about storms—about being lifted out of stormy waters, about lighthouses beckoning ships in from the storm, about houses built on solid rocks, able to withstand the gale of the winds and the rain. That makes sense. The Bible, after all, is filled with these images, of thunder and tumult and storms. The world of the Bible was, after all, an agrarian one, in which the survival of nations and tribes and villages and families was dependent upon rain. And the sea was the embodiment of chaos and disorder and peril. Those who sailed upon the water could harbor no illusions that they had control over the ocean, especially if they were battered back and forth by a suddenly emerging storm.

No wonder, then, that the ancient nations surrounding the people of God so often made idols out of storms. Many of their gods were fertility deities, who would bring forth rain if they were appeased enough. The storms that could arrive in that ancient Middle Eastern world could communicate all sorts of things about the idols. They could bring rain enough to save you from starvation, but the fire and thunder could also scare you into remembering they could kill you too. One would cry out to these gods for rain, but one could also be willing to sacrifice a human life to still a boat-capsizing storm (Jonah 1:11–15). Even in delusion, the nations could recognize something quite true: that bound up in a storm is both a blessing and a curse. And in both the blessing of rain, and the peril of the storm, we lose all of our illusions of control.

Family is like that too: the source of life-giving blessing but also of excruciating terror, often all at the same time. Likewise, this is also true of the cross. In the cross, we see both the horrific curse of sin, the judgment of God, and the blessing of God in saving the world (Gal. 3:13–14). At the cross, Jesus confronted both the "joy that was set before him" and at the same time was found "despising the shame" (Heb. 12:2). These families of ours can be filled with joy, but will always make us vulnerable to pain. And the joy and the pain are pointing us to the same place: the cross. Nothing can show you that you are loved and that you belong like family—and nothing can strip away your crafted pretensions and comforting illusions like family. Regardless of whether, as Jesus put it, one's house is built on sinking sand or solid rock, the storms that come with being part of families can make us feel as though we are lost to the howling winds around us. And, with family, just as in a tempest at sea, we inevitably realize that we are helpless to do anything about our plight.

For those of us in Christ, though, storms should be no surprise. They need not panic us, nor need they destroy us. The worst thing that can happen to you is not whatever you went through with your mother or father. The worst thing that can happen to you is not your sister who won't speak to you. The worst thing that can happen to you is not a spouse walking out on you, or cheating on you, or dying on you. The worst thing that can happen to you is not seeing your child rebel against you, or even attending your child's funeral, as awful as all those things are. The worst thing that can happen to you is dying under the judgment of God, bearing the full weight of the sentence of death and hell. If you are in Christ, that's already happened to you. You are not only a survivor; you are a beloved child, an heir of everything. Even so, it's hard to remember all of that when your life seems to be reeling back and forth on stormy seas.

Whatever your storms, though, you are not in uncharted waters. Psalm 107 speaks to this evocatively. "Some went down to the sea in ships, doing business on the great waters; they saw the deeds of the LORD, his wondrous works in the deep," the psalmist writes. "For he commanded and raised the stormy wind, which lifted up the waves of the sea. They mounted up to heaven; they went down to the depths; their courage melted away in their evil plight; they reeled and staggered like drunken men who were at their wits' end" (Ps. 107:23–27). But the psalm does not end there. "Then they cried to the LORD in their trouble, and he delivered them from their distress. He made the storm be still, and the waves of the sea were hushed" (Ps. 107:28–29).

The disciples of Jesus must have thought of this passage as they rocked back and forth in a sudden storm on the waters of Galilee. The panic in their minds and voices is palpable, especially in Mark's rendering of the moment. Jesus, though, was asleep on a cushion. The disciples cannot be blamed for resenting this, for crying out "Teacher, do you not care that we are perishing?" (Mark 4:38). Jesus woke up, but not with the adrenaline-pumping alarm that most of us would expect. He spoke to the storm: "Peace! Be still." And it was gone. Elsewhere, the same pattern would be repeated. The boat was in a storm, "beaten by the waves, for the wind was against them" (Matt. 14:24). Jesus, again, was preternaturally calm, walking out on the storm-tossed waters themselves. When Peter attempted to join him, though, he was knocked down, not so much by the storm as by his own panic. "But when he saw the wind, he was afraid, and beginning to sink he cried out, 'Lord, save me'" (Matt. 14:30). Jesus, of course, grabbed him by the hand. In this, of course, Jesus was doing what he would do for all of us. He would endure the sign of Jonah, go into the storm of sin and death and hell, and take us by the hand to pull us out, safely toward home. Jesus was not panicked by the storms around him because he was headed into another storm, the really scary one, at the cross. The more that I think of it, maybe the question, "Have you failed in the plans of your storm-tossed life" isn't loaded with a mixed metaphor after all. Maybe it makes more sense than I knew. Maybe that's why I couldn't write this book without humming that tune.

* * * *

Someone who chose the hymns in our church must have liked "The Nail-Scarred Hand," because we sang it so much. I never hear it now, and I can't really say that I miss it. The reason the song persists in my memory isn't the song, but two things that went with it: the message of the cross and the context of a family. The imagery in the song might be trite in some places, but the central picture is visceral—the hand that reaches out to us is scarred, and scarred not with abstractions but with nails. The other reason it lingers is because of who sang it with me—a church family of people I can see in my mind right now, and I could tell you exactly where most of them sat on any given Sunday morning. I probably muttered along with that song while on my mother's lap as an infant or playing with my father's watch as a small boy. That seems to fit because that's what this book is about. We are shaped and formed by family, in all sorts of routine and unexceptional ways that we may never even notice or remember. There's the joy, and there's the danger.

I don't know your situation. I do know, though, that you are part of a family—a past or present or future family, even if you don't know any of the names or faces of anyone in that family. Someone has shaped you. Someone is shaping you. Someone will shape you. And I also know this: sometimes whatever home you make for yourself will seem to be tossed about in an uncontrollable storm. To make it through, we must recognize why family is so important to us, and why family can never be ultimate to us. We must see the family clearly, but we must see beyond it. The only safe harbor for a storm-tossed family is a nail-scarred home.

CHAPTER TWO

The Cross as Family Crisis

IF YOU ASKED ME MY favorite holiday, I would probably say Christmas or Easter, but I wouldn't want to risk saying that while hooked up to a lie detector. The polygraph would probably jump around erratically until I blushingly admitted the truth: it's always been Halloween. I'm reluctant to admit that, because some of you will think poorly of me. I know I'm supposed to hate Halloween. Because I'm an evangelical Christian, of the more conservative sort, some of you will expect me to dismiss All Saints' Eve as "the devil's holiday." Many would expect to see me manning the bobbing-for-Bibles booth at a church Fall Festival, or helping blindfolded children at the Reformation Day gathering play "Pin the Theses on the Castle Door." Some would think that Halloween night would mean my family turning off all the lights and pretending not to be home, while the costumed children of our neighborhood find gospel tracts on our doorstep where a Jack O'Lantern should be. I'm supposed to hate Halloween, but I just can't do it. Since I was a very small child, Halloween brought to me, well, tidings of comfort and joy.

As a child, I took seriously what the old people said about the holiday as a "devil's night," about the veil between the spirit world and ours being especially, and dangerously, thin that night. That was what I liked about it. Halloween, it seemed, took seriously what I intuitively knew to be true: the world outside was terrifying.

The night also seemed to reinforce what I read in my Bible, that the universe around me was alive with invisible forces, some of which meant me harm. Halloween seemed to be the night when grown-ups would admit this, at least a little bit. It seemed to my younger self, too, that if there were scary realities out there, the idea of calendering out a night to recognize them for what they were made sense.

The best part of the night for me had nothing to do with candy or costumes, but was rather when the night was over, when I was tucked away in bed, knowing that my parents were asleep on the other side of that sheetrock wall. The night outside might be howling with witches and werewolves, but all was safe at home. That seemed far from pagan to me. It seemed, as a matter of fact, right in line with my biblical ancestors in ancient Egypt. The angels of death could lurk around outside the house all they wished, but the blood was on the doorpost, and all would be well.

There is another reason I couldn't pass a holiday polygraph, though. The lie detector wouldn't let me get away with saying that this is the sole reason for my love of Halloween. Some of it was because, unlike Christmas or Thanksgiving, there was never any family drama on Halloween. No one packed us up to drive to the house of some great-aunt or second cousin on Halloween. No one sat us down at a card table for a meal someone frantically stressed about getting just right. No one would compare this Halloween to the Halloweens of years past. No one would get his or her feelings hurt, or upend Halloween with a fiery dinner table discussion about how Uncle Ronnie drinks too much. No one had to pretend that this was the most wonderful time of the year. No one slammed a door and cried out, through tears, "You've ruined our Halloween!"

However scary headless horsemen and swamp things could be, sometimes a Christmas dinner or an Easter egg hunt or a wedding reception or a child's birthday party can be even more terrifying than a haunted wood. Family, though, is supposed to be a refuge from all that; it is supposed to be warm and tranquil and sentimental. That's certainly the image most of us project in our Christmas cards. To be sure, these presentations are usually true so far as they go—most people don't just make up that little Connor won the science fair this year or that Emma made partner in her law firm. Most people don't announce there that the rumors of the restraining order against Aunt Flossie are "fake news." But much goes unseen and unsaid, for obvious reasons.

Much of what goes on in our families is underground, whether that's the annoyances of emotional conflict or the very real trauma of some family secret. That's because, in our culture and in many others, family is often an arena for winning and displaying. Our family mirrors to the outside world the kind of person we want others to see us to be. If something is awry with our family, we are afraid that people will conclude that something is badly wrong with us. And so, despite the fact that family can sometimes scare us half to death, we smile our way through it. A friend of mine likes to say that he knew that parenting would be humbling; he just didn't know that it would also be humiliating. Even when all is going well, one never knows when a toddler will tell his Sunday school class the new words he learned when Mommy was yelling at Daddy last night. And that only increases. As a child ages, every day could bring word of a catastrophic pregnancy or a failed school term or a lost job or a broken engagement or a car wreck. And, it seems, there is nothing one can do about any of it, except look back on pictures at how sweet that baby used to be—and all the ways you failed as a parent.

The truth is, though, that it is not just parenting that humiliates. Virtually every part of life in a family becomes humiliating, if only because we ultimately reveal in our families just how dependent we can be. Being a husband or a wife, a brother or a sister, a son or a daughter, humiliates too. In relationship with people, we are bound to disappoint, and to be disappointed, to wound and to be wounded. As part of a family, it is almost impossible to maintain the image of ourselves we so carefully construct for the world, and for our own sense of meaning. Perhaps you, like me, have looked at all your family failures and wondered, "Why does this have to be this hard?"

If you are like me, you have searched for information to learn how to navigate all of this in a way that isn't humiliating. What I tend to want is a list of surefire principles to help me navigate life in a family—and I always have, no matter what stage of life I was in, no matter my place in the family at the time. As a boy, I wanted a foolproof guide to get my parents to understand how hard Algebra was for me—that a "C" really was good enough—and to show me how to meet the way-too-high expectations of my grandmother next door. As a teenager, I wanted a list of principles that could guarantee I could resist sexual temptation or, better yet, show me a loophole that would allow me to yield to it and stay a good Christian. More truthfully, I wanted principles that would show me how to get a girl to like me enough that I would have temptation options to actually overcome. As a young man, I wanted a step-by-step guide to choosing the right kind of wife. After marriage, my wife and I both wanted a list of steps that would ensure we wouldn't end up like other couples we had seen—in divorce courts scrapping it out with each other or, somehow even worse, lying together in middle-age, in a loveless, sexless, resentment-filled bed. I wanted a list of all the things expected of a Christian husband, from which chores I should do to how I could make sure my wife feels loved enough that she will never seek the attention of some soccer-dad in the produce aisle of the grocery store.

On into our marriage, I wanted the exactly worded prayer to cause us to conceive children when that turned out harder than we expected. After the children came, we wanted to know whether to schedule-feed them or to attachment parent, whether to schedule preschool violin lessons or roller-derby instruction. I wanted a comprehensive guidebook for how to keep my children from getting drunk in high school, drug-addicted in college, or divorced in a mid-life crisis. I'm sure one day I'll want explicit directions on how to guarantee that I will relate well to my future grandchildren as they soar above me on their hovercraft, communicating telepathically with their artificially intelligent cyborg friends. At every stage, I want an exhaustive list of steps for how to stop comparing everyone else's shiny, happy lives with what seems, for me, like my keeping just one step ahead of disaster, every second.

There are many reasons, of course, why family is so difficult. The most important reason, though, is one we rarely talk about. The stakes are high; that much most of us know. Some people rage against their parents all their lives, even after the mother and father are long dead. Others spend years resenting their children for all the trouble they put them through. We often see the stakes as high but we don't often see why. Family can enliven us or crush us because family is about more than just the life cycle of our genetic material.

Family is spiritual warfare.

* * * *

The family is one of the pictures of the gospel that God has embedded in the world around us. Through a really dark glass, we can see flashes in the family of something at the core of the universe itself, of the Fatherhood of God, of the communion of a people with one another. Not every personal being likes what it sees in that. Even more than Halloween, the Bible tells us the truth about what's out there. If the Scriptures are right, then ancient cultures were right that there are invisible and hostile powers afoot in the cosmos, and these powers rage against the picture of the gospel, wherever it is found, because the gospel is a sign of the end of their reign, of the crushing of their heads. That's why the fall of humanity, presented in the earliest pages of Scripture, is not simply a story of personal guilt or shame. The Fall immediately splinters husband from wife, brother from brother, father from daughter, uncle from cousin—all just in the opening chapters of Genesis. If the family is not wrecking you, it's only because you don't know what is going on.

Into all of that, the Bible does not give us a family manual. The Bible gives us instead a word of the cross. By "the cross," I don't mean shorthand for Christian principles or "family values." By "the cross" I mean the tangled mess of a murder scene outside the gates of Jerusalem.

The Bible says much about family, but it does not do so from the warmth of the hearth, but from the Place of the Skull. As a matter of fact, the most important truths about life in the family are not found in the passages we think of as "family" passages—those we are likely to hear preached on Mother's Day or Father's Day or at a wedding ceremony. The most important passage related to the family is probably in the account of Jesus, "bearing his own cross, to the place called The Place of a Skull" (John 19:17), where, in the agony of execution, Jesus would cry out, "My God, my God, why have you forsaken me?" It would be easy to conclude—as those standing around no doubt did—that this was the complaint of one who was rejected and utterly abandoned by his God. But Jesus here was not spontaneously venting a complaint to the empty skies. He was quoting a lyric from a song.

Every account of the crucifixion in the Gospels is riddled with references to Psalm 22, a song of David, from this cry of anguish to the soldiers gambling for his clothes to the agony of thirst. Psalm 22 is a song meant to be sung by the worshipping people of God, a song that tells a story, from seeming desolation all the way through to a realization of the steadfast love of God. This song from the cross has everything to do with the family.

One of the hardest things for us to grasp as family members—whether as sons or daughters, husbands or wives, mothers or fathers, even as spiritual brothers and sisters within the church—is just how complicated it all is. I don't just mean the mechanics of getting along with one another, of modeling good marriages or good parenting, of honoring our father and mother. I mean the unique mixture that comes with family of joy and terror, of beauty and brokenness. A new study will come out every once in a while that shows that parents are happier than those who have no children, or that married people are happier than people who are single. And then another study will come out that will show the reverse, that parents are more depressed than those who have no children, or that married people have more anxiety and regrets than their non-married peers. Families grow us up, and make us stable, one study will show. Families destabilize us and drive us crazy, the next study will show. I suspect that both sets of data are true. Family is awesome. Family is terrible. As Christians, we already have a category for that. The cross shows us how we can find beauty and brokenness, justice and mercy, peace and wrath, all in the same place. The pattern of the Christian life is crucified glory—this is as true for our lives in our families as in everything else.

As he is crucified, Jesus is, on the one hand, utterly alone. The sign above his head reads, "The King of the Jews." This is a sarcastic reference, seemingly contradicted by the very fact of its location. The sign demonstrated that he was rejected by the Roman Empire around him, and by his own people, right down to his tribe and his village. He seemed cast out and doomed by his family, his people, his God. The song on Jesus' mind tells a different story, though.

David there in Psalm 22 did indeed sing of his godforsaken state, but he didn't stop there. He remembered his family history: "In you our fathers trusted; they trusted, and you delivered them" (Ps. 22:4). And he remembered his own immediate family story: "Yet you are he who took me from the womb; you made me trust you at my mother's breasts. On you was I cast from my birth, and from my mother's womb you have been my God. Be not far from me, for trouble is near, and there is none to help" (Ps. 22:9–11). Even as Jesus' disciples fled from him in shame, he could cite Psalm 22 while looking out from the cross at his mother. In the moment of his greatest desolation, Jesus could see the invisible outline of God's mercy and presence there in the one from whom, in his human nature, he learned to trust a fathering, nurturing God. He learned that from his mother. And there she stood. Jesus said, echoing his ancestor David, "I can count all my bones" (Ps. 22:17; John 19:36). The horror of the scene was not the whole story. And Jesus knew the whole song.

As she watched her son ripped apart by nails, struggling to gasp for air, Mary no doubt remembered the words of the prophet Simeon, in the first days of her baby's life at his eighth-day dedication at the temple. Simeon foresaw that the child would be "appointed for the fall and rising of many in Israel, and for a sign that is opposed" (Luke 2:34). Looking at Mary, the aged prophet said, "A sword will pierce through your own soul also" (Luke 2:35). She could hardly have imagined this soul-rending sword would be a Roman cross. And yet, she was not alone in the collateral damage of the crucifixion. Jesus said that all of us must carry the cross. We can only find our lives by losing them, by being crucified with him. We will be broken too.

I am not sure what your family situation is, as you read these words on the page. Maybe you dread another Thanksgiving with some aunt asking, "So are you seeing anyone special?" Even worse, you dread the day she stops asking, because that will mean she's given up on you ever finding someone. Maybe you're newly married, and you're scared. You look at the smiling faces in your wedding pictures, and you can't help but notice the same sorts of smiles in your parents' old wedding photographs. You know those smiles didn't last but degenerated into hatred and acrimony. You are in love—but so were they. You've made vows—and meant them—till death do you part. But so did they. Or maybe you resent every baby shower invitation you get, because you keep seeing month after month that one pink line on the pregnancy test instead of two. Or maybe you sit in church hoping no one will know that your daughter is in prison or that your son is on a sex-offender registry. Or maybe you're just lying on a bed, in a room smelling of ammonia, asking the nurse one more time if anyone called for you, knowing from her wincing, forced smile that the answer is no. You can tell she feels sorry for you, and that she fears ending up like you. All of that can be scary and exhausting.

On the other hand, you might have the family that others around you envy. Maybe your parents are exactly the ones you would have chosen. Maybe your marriage is affectionate and growing in intimacy as you age together. Or maybe your children are well behaved, successful, and constantly in touch. And maybe, then, you wonder how long this can last. That can be scary and exhausting too.

Family is hard because family is unpredictable. You cannot plan out your life. You cannot choose your parents, or your genes, or your upbringing the way you choose your career path. You cannot know everything about your future spouse, or fit your children into some preexisting life plan. Family means vulnerability. You can be hurt. You will be hurt, and you will hurt others. You will learn to love others so much that you wish you could protect them from what's out there: being bullied at the bus-stop, that fiancé who breaks the engagement, a bone-marrow transplant in an oncology ward. And family also exposes who we really are, stripping us of our pretensions and our masks. Family will, sooner or later, reveal that we are not the person our families need us to be. We are naked before our illusions, and those closest to us eventually learn that we do not have it all together. In the fullness of time, we will feel not only the cross on our back, but the sword through our soul.

And yet, from the Place of the Skull, Jesus joined his song to that of David. He knew not only the dark passages of that song but the whole thing. When he sang of what he learned from his mother, he could see her there, and not just her. The psalm ends with David announcing, "I will tell of your name to my brothers; in the midst of the congregation I will praise you" (Ps. 22:22). There, Jesus could see from his cross the disciple he loved, John. Even from the cross, Jesus was occupied with family matters, arranging an adoption, handing responsibility for Mary's care over to John. "Woman, behold your son!" he said to his mother, and to John, "Behold your mother!"

(John 19:26–27), and from that hour, John recounts, he took her into his own home. In something as seemingly mundane as arranging care for a parent, Jesus demonstrated that the little burdens of family matter and that they are part of a larger burden of a cross. Moreover, he was showing us that we need one another. We cannot be families if we are not disciples first. We must recognize the joys and responsibilities that come with being part of a family formed not by the blood of biology but the blood of crucifixion.

The church has often failed at this point. In too many cases, we have turned congregations into silos packed with countless minivans full of individual families, coming to receive instruction and then return to their own self-contained units. The end result, especially in a rootless, hyper-mobile American culture, is the reality of mothers who are lonely and fear they're failing but who don't want to say anything for fear of being judged or starting up the Mommy Wars, or fathers who are lonely but who aren't supposed to signal that they don't know what to do about their son's pornography addiction or their daughter's anorexia. Our churches are often filled with unmarried or divorced or widowed men and women who believe that they are without family because there is no one to stand beside them in the church directory picture. And yet, the cross shows us that we need one another. We will never be godly families until we are brothers and sisters to one another.

Years ago, I was serving as a minister in a church and would lead our Wednesday night Bible study through a time of taking prayer requests. One night a woman came up after the service was over and said, "I didn't want to say this in front of everyone, but can you pray for my daughter?" She looked furtively over her shoulders, as though scouting out the presence of enemy spy drones, and whispered, "She's gone away to college and become an atheist." I promised to pray but asked why she was whispering. "Oh, I don't want everyone to wonder what we had done to make our daughter an atheist," she said. "I didn't want to embarrass my husband like that." Something has gone terribly wrong when a Christian feels she must protect herself from her church, for fear that her daughter's spiritual crisis will be discussed as part of a debate over whether she should have breastfed longer or whether they should have chosen homeschooling over public school. That's especially true when literally every family in Scripture, without exception, has prodigals, including that of God the Father.

* * * *

Family is humiliating, yes, which is one reason I hesitate to even write this book. Family discloses sooner or later that we are not the experts we think we are. When my oldest sons were just learning to read, they would sound out the words on the billboards we would pass in the car where we lived at the time in Louisville, Kentucky. One day we passed an advertisement for Budweiser beer, with just the words of the abbreviation "Bud Light." My son Ben asked, "What is Bud Light?" Not really wanting to get into the whole discussion of alcoholic beverages and all that comes with that, I just said, "It's a drink some people drink." A few weeks later, I saw a gaggle of senior adults at a church where I was preaching, gathered around my little son. He had, I learned, just announced to them, "You know what my Dad's favorite drink is? Bud Light!" Now, I do not drink even a thimblefull of beer or any other alcohol, and I serve what is perhaps the most anti-alcohol church communion in the world. I was tempted to just go ahead and form a committee to investigate myself. Parenting only became more humiliating from there, with many moments where I've wondered, as I have with marriage, whether I am competent to do this. But if it were not so, we would not need to seek the power of one another, or of the Lord in prayer. God told his children in the desert wandering, that he had humbled them, made them to hunger, and disciplined them as a man disciplines his son, so that they might know "that man does not live by bread alone, but man lives by every word that comes from the mouth of the LORD" (Deut. 8:3).

If family were easy, we could do it in our own fleshly self-propelled willpower. If we could do it on our own, we would not bear a cross. And if we are not bearing a cross, then what we are doing would not matter in the broad sweep of eternity. Family matters. That's why it is hard. As the songwriter Rich Mullins once put it, "I can't see where you're leading me unless you've led me here, where I'm lost enough to let myself be led." Family will do that, but not with our pride and self-sufficiency intact. Thanks be to God.

Family can be humiliating, but what's more humiliating than family is being naked, covered in blood, hoisted on a pole, while people gamble for one's clothes. And yet, we've all been there, in Christ. Once we've been crucified, and survived to tell the tale, one would think we could admit to one another that we need help in the spiritual warfare that comes with life together in our families. One would think we could humble ourselves and confess to one another, to ask for forgiveness, when we hurt or fail one another. One would think we could deal honestly with the pain of our own childhoods without fearing that we are predestined to live out our parents' mistakes or to live our lives performing for their approval for whatever they expected of us.

Jesus could count all his bones. Everything else was falling apart, but no bones were broken. At first glance, that seems to be cold consolation. After all, what difference does it make if one has an intact skeletal system if one is executed in the most torturous method possible? Jesus did not have bones made of titanium steel. He was not surrounded by a force field. His bones would have snapped, just as easily as did the legs of the crucified murderers and terrorists on either side of him. Why did, and why does, this matter?

The lack of broken bones there at the cross was a sign to Jesus, along with the face there of his mother, that whatever happened could not go any further than God's purposes, and that God's purposes were good. Whatever the soldiers were doing, their actions were not random and chaotic. The veil of the temple was ripped asunder, but the seam in Jesus' garment was not, nor were the bones in his legs. God might seem to be absent at the cross, but he was not. He was there, as elsewhere, providentially ruling, even through the most wicked actions imaginable. Your skeletal system is the last identifiable piece of who you are, or who you were, the last to decay away into dust. That's why a skull can be so startling to see. Jesus could count all his bones because of the mystery of God's providence, which works behind, and through, even the most awful things that happen to us. God handed him over to the curse, to judgment, to death. But, even then, God did not utterly break him. Jesus' intact skeleton was a sign that no matter how much it seemed that he had been abandoned, the steadfast love of God would not depart. God was still there.

Being a part of a family—whatever the part, and whatever the family—is essential to our flourishing as people. And being part of a family—whatever the part and whatever the family—is difficult. That should be neither surprising nor dispiriting for a people of the cross. All of us are failures at family. That's because all of us are part of families, and all of us are fallen. The cross shows us that the family can be an arena of God's mercy and God's glory. Being a child can point us to our dependence on our God, a dependence seen most perfectly in the helpless figure of a crucified Christ, committing his spirit to his Father. Our sibling relationships can point us to the joys—and the difficulty—of being part of a bustling band of brothers and sisters in the church. Marriages can point to the union of Christ and his church, a union sealed at the cross. Parenting can point to the Fatherhood of God, a Fatherhood seen in the darkest moments of the cross as well as in the vibrant moments of resurrection and exaltation. All these seemingly mundane relationships then are not just about what it means to be happy. They all are, in some way or another, part of the training ground for our ultimate destinies as joint heirs with Christ, and heirs of the universe.

We need practical wisdom on the family. The Bible gives it to us. We need to know how to honor our parents without being enmeshed with them. We need to know how to honor marriage without idolizing it. We need to know how to discipline the next generation in a way that is neither harsh nor negligent. But before all of that, we need to see the vulnerability of family within the prism of cross-bearing.

I don't know about you, but I don't want that. I would rather protect myself from the possibility of hurt, with a hard, exterior shell, not the soft vulnerability of breakable bones. Nothing opens one up to more potential for hurt, for more vulnerability, than being part of a family. Parents can nurture you, but they can also reject you. A spouse can love you but can also leave you. Children can bring joy but just might one day ask for that inheritance early and head off for a pigsty of rebellion in a far country. I don't mind working hard for my family, but I wince at the thought of one day needing my family to empty my bedpan and wipe my drooling mouth. And yet, that vulnerability is what God uses to conform us to Christ. He does not make us holy through Pharaoh-like exercises of power but through the hidden dynamism of the cross. That sort of vulnerability means, of course, that bad things are possible. Your parents might disown you. Your spouse might find someone else. Leukemia might ravage your child. The gospel doesn't hide any of this from you. The gospel doesn't promise you prosperity and tranquility. But the gospel does promise you that you are never outside the reach of the fatherly providence of God, a providence that fits you with a cross not to destroy you but to give you a future. Your skeleton is safe, even at the Place of the Skull.

* * * *

That cross brings the freedom to be family. And freedom is precisely what we need. Because family is an aspect of spiritual warfare, it can seem crushing. Because family is an aspect of cross-bearing, it can seem excruciating. We often seek an exit. Some find an exit through evading the responsibilities of family altogether. Think of the child of a contentious divorce who is forever fearful of commitment, to avoid getting hurt the way his parents did, or the way they hurt him. Some find that exit by a kind of stoic resignation, that concludes whatever will happen with one's family will happen. Some find that exit though self-medicating with some addiction or self-sabotaging through an affair, or even by walking away from one's family altogether. Still others find that exit by binding up their identities with their families, so that their life consists in a blur of soccer games and debate competitions, one extracurricular activity after another to ensure that the next generation is a little better off in opportunity so that parents will be able to face themselves as having been "good enough." None of that is freedom. It is instead soul-deadening and heart-defeating. Those who neglect their family responsibilities and those who deify them end up in the same place, at giving up. That's no freedom at all.

We have a different sort of freedom, a crucified freedom. Our families are important but not ultimate. The devil doesn't mind marriage experts or parenting experts. The devil doesn't mind class valedictorians or a mantle full of trophies. The devil does, though, tremble at a cross. The end result of our mission as families is not to impress our peers that our kids are well-behaved enough not to keep us awake at night, but that they are, like us, crucified with Christ. To go back to Jesus' cross-hymn from Psalm 22, the end result is to be that "it shall be told of the Lord to the coming generation; they shall come and proclaim his righteousness to a people yet unborn, that he has done it" (Ps. 22:30–31). That he has done it; not that we have done it. Family humbles us. Family humiliates us. Family crucifies us. That's because family is one of the ways God gets us small enough to fight the sort of battle that can't be won by horses or chariots but by the Spirit of the Lord.

Our families shape us. We shape our families. The cross should shape both.

* * * *

Glory shows up in broken places. The psalmist tells us that "the heavens declare the glory of God" (Ps. 19:1; 8:3–4). Looking into the night sky can fill us with a sense of God's creative power and wisdom, along with our own smallness before his cosmic reach. And yet, most of the stars visible to us in the night sky above us—or above David as he wrote that psalm—are dead, their light reaching us long after they have burned out. They declare glory nonetheless. This should not surprise us when we look at our own lives. Our outer self is wasting away, the Bible tells us, and yet in the middle of such weakness and death, there is hidden the glimmers of an "eternal weight of glory beyond all comparison" (2 Cor. 4:17). We have the treasure of the gospel in these jars of clay, "to show that the surpassing power belongs to God and not to us" (2 Cor. 4:7). We then carry death with us, but from this death comes life, for us and for the world (2 Cor. 4:11–12). And the cross takes us right back to Halloween.

If you stop by my house come Halloween, you might see me walking around our neighborhood, with my sons in their costumes. I can predict that, just like every year, the neighbors down the street will have homemade chili and root beer on their porch, with enough for everyone. I can also predict that my youngest son will tense up and grab my hand when we pass this one particularly creepy house around the corner, the one with the lit-up skeleton on the porch. He will be scared, and I will too. I'll be scared of a different sort of skeleton, my own, of what will happen after all my life of perpetual motion is over. Will my wife know that I loved her? Will my children see something in the way that I fathered them to point them to the Father God who always loves, who never leaves, who comes with both authority and mercy, both truth and grace? My son will be afraid the skeleton on the porch will eat him. I'm afraid that the skeleton in my future casket won't measure up to the image I project right now, even on this very page. And that my family will know it.

But on that autumn night, I will take him in my arms, again, and I will say, "Don't worry. I'm not going anywhere. And I'll protect you from that skeleton. It can't hurt you." In that moment, I will remember what I, as a child, loved most about Halloween. The fear will be there, not hidden away, not rationalized out of existence, not avoided in polite conversation. But behind the fear will be the kind of safety that comes only with a parent's protection. The monsters are out there, and in here, but they will not win. That's just one night of the year, but that's what a Christian vision of the family is about all year long.

The family isn't really summed up in Halloween alone, and the family isn't summed up in Christmas, at least not the way we celebrate it in our sanitized culture. The family is summed up in Good Friday. Your family can teach you that your intuitions are right. You want peace in your home. You want a legacy that outlasts you. A cross-shaped life in a storm-tossed world shows us that we will never get there as experts but only as sons and daughters. You can find family only by entrusting it to the One you can trust with your very soul.

Family takes you to the cross. If you are in Christ, everything in your life leads you there eventually. But from there you can see an empty tomb. Family shows you, once again, that the only way you can gain your life is to lay it down, that the only way you can win is to lose. The wisdom of God and the power of God are hidden there, in the place of crucifixion, in ways that can terrify us. The cross exists to disturb and disrupt the perilous quiet of our lives. "The cross is the safest of all things," Martin Luther wrote. "How blessed is he who understands!"[1] Family takes you to the Place of the Skull but shows you there that though you can take nothing with you, not even your clothes, not one of your bones is broken.

Your skeleton is safe.

CHAPTER THREE
The Family as Spiritual Warfare

BORN AND REARED ON THE West Coast, my student had never before been in the Deep South. Travelling with me to my home state of Mississippi for a speaking engagement, he was seated next to a courtly southern pastor. The pastor, knowing that the student was interning at the time in my office, assumed there might be a Mississippi connection, maybe even a family connection to a fellow minister in the state. Speaking in a low voice so as not to compete with the announcements from the podium nearby, the pastor leaned over to my student and drawled, "Who's your Daddy?"

My student sat silently for a half-moment, wondering if this was some southern cultural way of greeting, along the lines of "How are you?" Not knowing what response would be expected, my student just guessed and said, "Um . . . you are?" The pastor stared back at him, and then looked over at me and asked, "What's wrong with him?"

The conversation turned out to be a good one, but that initial banter did not work. In order to understand one another, these two would have needed to understand that "Daddy" in a southern context can refer, often, to a grown man's father, not just to that of a small child. They both also would have needed to understand that, in a Mississippi context, asking who one's relatives are, or what one's hometown is, is far more than just small talk. It's another way of asking, "Who are you?" The wording couldn't transcend regional cultures, but the basic principle, in many ways, does and always has. Your family background and family connections tell much about you. That will not, of course, be as immediately recognizable if you live in an urbanized area with lots of people coming and going, where people are less likely to know your family, than it would be if you are from a small, rural town. But, even in the most cosmopolitan place, much of what makes you "you" comes from all sorts of family connections, only some of which you are conscious of at any given time. We often don't know where our genetic predispositions or our cultural practices have come from; they are just there, and they inform for us what seems "normal" or "right." There's much mystery there.

For some, that idea is comforting. They take pride in their family, and see in their connectedness a kind of solidarity and belonging. This is the kind of person who might keep a detailed genealogy on hand or put a family crest on the wall. For others, their family background is troubling or even smothering. They don't want to think they might end up making the decisions their parents or grandparents or others have made. Either way, we naturally discover who we are in terms of our families. Some people do this by their similarities to their families, prizing their family heritage, or their family business, or their family religion. Some people define themselves over and against their families—spending a whole lifetime proving that they are not their fathers or their mothers. "Look at how different I am from them," their lives seem to say. "I am my own person." For some, to "be myself" means to distinguish themselves from their families. The ways their family backgrounds still shape who they are can be disorienting or even terrifying. Regardless, the family persists, and has a great deal to do with who we are, how we perceive ourselves, and how we evaluate the present and plan for the future. That's why family matters—and not just for those who consider themselves "family people."

But, behind that, there's another reason why family matters, to all of us. Family is spiritual warfare. Such language makes some of us uneasy, sounding like the hyper-dramatic incantations they have seen in the exorcism services of some Pentecostal sect. In reality, though, the unseen subtext of the world around us is intrinsic to the thought of the Bible, and only seems antiquated or outlandish in our secularized Western context. Every ancient culture—and most cultures outside of the First World even now—has held that there are mysterious realities afoot in the cosmos, including personal beings who mean us harm. In our scientific era, we could conclude that we know better than they, that we have moved beyond their superstition. And yet, our scientific age should demonstrate to us, even more, that even with all we know about the universe, we learn every day how much we do not know. Scientific progress has not eradicated mystery but revealed mysteries we previously never even knew how to name.

The gospel does not shy away from this reality. The apostle John wrote straightforwardly: "The reason the Son of God appeared was to destroy the works of the devil" (1 John 3:8). If we accept Jesus' reading of the cosmic story—and I do—then we must reckon with his teaching that the world around us is like the house of a strong man that Jesus has bound and whose pirated goods Jesus is now plundering (Mark 3:27). We must further recognize that the way these "principalities and powers" (as the Scriptures call them) rule is through accusation and death (Rev. 12:10). At the cross, Jesus defeated the accusing spirits by breaking the deception they have over the human image-bearers (2 Cor. 4:4–6) and by absorbing in his sacrifice on the cross the just penalty for our rebellion against God. In the crucified Christ, God has "forgiven us all our trespasses, by canceling the record of debt that stood against us with its legal demands. This he set aside, nailing it to the cross" (Col. 2:13–14). In this way, he "disarmed the rulers and authorities and put them to open shame, by triumphing over them in him" (Col. 2:15). By sharing our human nature, and through his sacrifice on the cross, Jesus set out through his own death to "destroy the one who has the power of death, that is, the devil, and deliver all those who through fear of death were subject to lifelong slavery" (Heb. 2:14–15). When the kingdom of God comes, in Jesus, the old order is torn down. The kingdom of Christ means cosmic regime change, and the powers-that-be fight back against that reality.

* * * *

So what does spiritual warfare have to do with the family, in general, or with your family in particular? First of all, it matters because in order to understand the gospel we must see that something has gone badly wrong with the universe, something Christian doctrine calls "the Fall." When our ancestral humanity opted to align with a snake-god rather than with their Creator, their mission was derailed into exile from God's life-giving presence. That meant catastrophe for everything connected to image-bearing humanity. And the family, among the first of God's creation structures, bears much of the weight of this calamity. As soon as the man and woman sin, their one-flesh union is disrupted. They are ashamed in the presence of each other, and start blaming each other for their insurrection. Their marriage now is riddled with distrust and disharmony and rivalry (Gen. 3:16b). Their vocations are then directly frustrated. The woman as "mother of all living" (Gen. 3:20) now suffers pain and anguish in childbearing (Gen. 3:16a). The man's calling to till the ground from which he came is frustrated by a cursed creation that no longer recognizes him as God's representative (Gen. 3:17–19). Eastward from Eden, the biblical story shows us families splintering apart in virtually every kind of breakdown. We see brothers envying and murdering each other (Gen. 4:1–16), polygamy (Gen. 4:23), father/son division (Gen. 9:18–27), rape (Gen. 19:1–11; 34:1–31), incest (Gen. 19:30–38), vigilante tribal honor killings (Gen. 34:1–31), sexual blackmail (Gen. 39:1–23), even a husband willing to prostitute his wife for political influence (Gen. 12:10–20). Again, this is, mind you, all just in the first book of the Bible. The wreckage continues throughout the canon, and beyond. The peace of Eden for the family is no more.

This is important for us to recognize because in order to work toward healthy families we must grapple with the fact that all of us are part of a dysfunctional family, because all of us are rooted in the family history of Adam. Part of what our family background does for us is to embed in our psyches what we deem "normal" or "abnormal." When a couple marries, for example, they must work to merge all sorts of habits and temperaments, and that's hard enough. But often the ways we do things are picked up, without a rational decision, from the way we saw our parents do things.

When my wife and I married, one of the things I maintained from day one was that I would never want a dog in the house. I really didn't have an argument beyond, "That's nasty." Looking back, this is probably because my parents carried an unspoken attitude that an animal in the house was always unclean and because the people I knew who did have pets in their home tended to confirm that (as they usually had an entire menagerie of them). Now, over twenty years later, I type these words while sitting at my feet is our dog Waylon. I had not thought through the question of dogs; it just didn't fit my definition of "normal," until I learned to see otherwise. Sometimes this grid through which we see the world is benign, but often it is not. That's true not just for some of us, at the micro level, but for all of us, at the macro level.

The gospel informs us that we cannot understand the world around us rightly without distinguishing between those aspects that are "from the beginning," and thus good, and those aspects that are part of the curse of the reign of death. I once heard a man justify the fact that he cheats on his wife with multiple women because it is "natural." Monogamy is rare among mammals, he reasoned, and our evolutionary history has designed men to seek to "spread their seed" as broadly as possible. People are killed every day in mudslides and crocodile attacks, too, so should we conclude that because this is "natural" we should allow murder? We know from God's Word that nature has gone awry. Things are not the way they are supposed to be, and much of that distortion shows up in family life.

The family is not only part of the problem, though, but part of the solution. Yes, humanity experiences difficulty and travail in childbearing, but the grace there is that humanity does in fact go forward into the future. In fact, from the very beginning, God threatened the serpent with the prophecy that its skull would be crushed by the family. The "offspring of the woman" would be the undoing of the dark rulers of this age, though not without pain and distress: "He shall bruise your head, and you shall bruise his heel" (Gen. 3:15). That's, of course, exactly what happened. Through the human family, and specifically through the house of Abraham and Sarah, God brought to us a child through whom everything is reconciled, "making peace by the blood of his cross" (Col. 1:20).

* * * *

Family is difficult because we live in a fallen world. Our psyches are shaped by early childhood, and we bring that glory and brokenness into every other relationship in life. But family is also difficult because family is a staging ground for a universe in the throes of regime change. Family is difficult because family represents far more than just genetic lumping. The demonic powers care about the family not because they are in revolt against "family values" but because they are in revolt against God. These powers are intimidating in their ancient craft, but they are a relatively cowardly lot. When the incarnate Jesus walked into their presence, they would shriek in terror, often begging him to send them away (Mark 5:7–13). Why? This is because, in the sign of Jesus, the principalities and powers see their own inevitable future destruction. "What have you to do with us,

Jesus of Nazareth?" they cry out. "Have you come to destroy us? I know who you are—the Holy One of God!" (Mark 1:24). Of course, that's exactly who Jesus is, and *not* exactly what he has come to do.

The Bible tells us that this visible depiction of Christ and the gospel is not limited to Jesus' physical presence in any given space and time. God created everything after the pattern of Jesus Christ, summing up everything, seen and unseen, in him (Eph. 1:9–10). He is the pattern and blueprint for everything. Everything is created through him and for him, and in him everything "holds together" (Col. 1:16–17).

What this means is that God has embedded pictures and analogies of this ultimate truth of the cosmos in the creation itself. None of these pictures exhaustively show us the purposes of God or the gospel, but they point in that direction. Family is no exception. We long to belong, to have and to hold, not out of some random, evolutionary accident but because God is "the Father, from whom every family in heaven and on earth is named" (Eph. 3:14–15). Marriage is not just about companionship or procreation but is a mystery, pointing to the one-flesh union of Christ and his church (Eph. 5:32). Parenting is not just about human flourishing (although it is that), but a reflection of the Fatherhood of God (Matt. 5:7–11; Heb. 12:5–11) and the motherhood of the Holy City to which we belong in Christ (Gal. 4:26).

It is no accident, then, that the old serpent seeks, in every generation, to disrupt the peace of the marriage covenant, of the integrity of the sexual union, of the parent/child bond, of the unity of the church as the household of God. These are organic icons of the mystery of Christ, the very reality that crushes the skulls of the old order. Family points beyond itself and beyond nature to the truth about humanity: that the end of our lives is not intended to be the silence of the casket but the clinking of glasses, not a funeral but a wedding feast (Rev. 19:6–9). That's why the demonic powers rage in fury against the family order. The destruction of a family that images and announces the gospel is just as sacrilegious as desecrating a holy place. The powers aligned against God always wish to display trophies of their presence on his ground. The Philistines wanted the ark of the covenant in the temple of their god (1 Sam. 5:2). Babylon did not wish to simply raze the City of David, but to carry back the holy vessels of the Lord with them (2 Kings 24:13). The spirit of Antichrist seats itself in the temple of God himself (2 Thess. 2:4). Those counter-kingdom powers delight in doing the same by defacing the visible sign of gospel reign in marriages, or parenting, or extended families, or—perhaps most of all—the unity of the household of the church.

This warfare is not just cosmic or social but decidedly personal. In the Proverbs, a father warns his son that adultery could appear to "just happen" when in reality it is a strategically conceived plot, the coaxing of a hunted prey into a slaughterhouse (Prov. 5–7). Perhaps you have noticed this in your own life. Just when it seems that your family situation is what you would like, or what God would like for you, something unhinges. It would be easy to blame this on the external pressures and temptations around us. We can say that technology is too difficult to navigate, that the culture is too sexualized, or that "people just don't respect the family like they used to." The Bible allows no such nostalgia, however, showing us the perils to the family in every generation outward from Eden.

We have different points of vulnerability, not just in our internal lives but also in our families. For some, the pull is to abandonment. For others, the pull is to infidelity. To others still, the pull is to selfishness or negligence. There are powers at work who know your vulnerabilities and those around you. You cannot fight such battles with your intelligence or your willpower. Such spiritual warfare must be met, at every point, with the gospel. The gospel informs our place in the family because the gospel redefines two points at which the devils rage the most: our identity and our inheritance.

When Jesus taught us to pray, the first words on his tongue were "Our Father." That is, before anything else, a statement about who we are. Jesus is the son of the Father, language that situates him in his eternal relationship to God (John 5:18–23), but also situates him as the true Israel of God, God's firstborn son (Hosea 11:1; Matt. 2:15) and as the heir of the throne of David (2 Sam. 7:14; Ps. 89:26–27). Like most evangelical Christians, I conclude most of my prayers with the words "in Jesus' name." Jesus told us, "If you ask me anything in my name, I will do it" (John 14:14).

In my younger days, I took this to mean that those words would especially get God's attention, so I would pepper them all around requests that were of particular importance to me. "In Jesus' name, please let me pass Algebra, in Jesus' name, in Jesus' name, in Jesus' name." That's not what Jesus was telling us to do and is, in fact, the exact opposite. Before teaching his disciples to pray, he taught them how *not* to pray. He taught us not to use prayer as a way of public display, to seem pious to those around us. But public display is only one of his concerns.

He also said we shouldn't "heap up empty phrases as the Gentiles do, for they think that they will be heard for their many words" (Matt. 6:7). That was certainly true of virtually every other people on the earth, who thought of their gods as distant, impersonal figures who, at best, regarded human beings as their servants. With gods like that, a people would need to learn how to find ways to gain an audience. Think of the priests of Baal cutting themselves and screaming into the sky: "but there was no voice. No one answered; no one paid attention" (1 Kings 18:29). The prophet Elijah, on the other hand merely prayed, and the fire fell (1 Kings 18:36–38). Of those who feel the need to manipulate their god with their constructed phrases or magical incantations, Jesus said, "Do not be like them, for your Father knows what you need before you ask him" (Matt. 6:8). There are two crucial parts of that statement; "your Father" and "what you need": identity and inheritance.

Our family backgrounds are meant to tell us something about who we are and, more importantly, what we are not. We aren't self-creating, self-sustaining gods. We are part of someone else's story—backward into the past and, perhaps, forward into the future. You and I are each the product of a near-infinite series of decisions that other people made. If your great-great-grandfather had not emigrated from his homeland, you might not be able to read the language on this page. If my grandmother had not decided to disregard her parents' wishes and elope as a teenager with that older man, I would not exist. I would not want anyone else to repeat her decision, and can only imagine my dismay if one of my own children were to do likewise, but, nonetheless, I am glad I exist.

A sense of identity is marked out in many ways, starting with our names. Think of how much of the Bible is taken up with genealogies. I was once horrified to hear a preacher reading through a text of Scripture, skipping over a list of "begats" with the words "yada . . . yada . . . yada" before starting back up with the narrative. Setting aside this man's thoughtless handling of the Word of God, one can understand something of why the preacher did not want to get bogged down in a series of names as "the father of . . ." and "the son of . . ." one another. It doesn't seem relevant. But it is. Note how often the Bible refers to figures as "Joshua, son of Nun" or "Saul, son of Kish" or "John, the son of Zebedee." Even in our individualistic cultural moment, we haven't quite transcended this.

You probably don't know anything about my relatives, but if you know me you are confronted immediately with at least something about them when you learn my name. "Moore" tells you who my father's family is, and, if one wanted, tells a story that could be traced back to, I'm told, the moors of England. Even if that proved not to be where my name came from, the family lore of it would still tell you something about us: that we're the kind of people that would like to be from the moors of England. I suppose, if I wanted, I could seek to individuate myself by rejecting my family name, and just be "Russell." That too, though, would point back to my family. The fact that my name is "Russell" and not "Sergei" or "Moon Unit" is because my parents were neither Russians nor hippies.

In fact, even if I were to rename myself, the people around me still would have tied my name to my family: "That's Ozymandias, Gary and Renee's little boy . . . something's wrong with him." Far deeper, though, than the relative superficiality of our names is the way that we learn who we are, very early on, from our interactions with our families. Psychologists tell us how our personalities can be shaped lifelong by the ways that our parents "mirrored" back to us who we were as individuals and as those who belong in the larger family structure. Identity is rooted in family.

Inheritance is a concept Western people, at first glance, find even harder to relate to their lives. We tend to think of inheritance as a transfer of assets. As I write this, I have just heard of yet another family torn apart by grown children bickering over a newly dead parent's belongings, fighting one another tooth-and-toenail over quilts and ceramic cats. That's not what an inheritance is about, in the biblical understanding of the word.

An inheritance wasn't so much a transfer of money and property as the cultivation of a way of life. The original humanity was created to cultivate a garden. Within the bounds of Israel, God gave detailed instructions on how to care for the ground, maintaining cycles of crops, for example. The inheritance of a farming family would be not just the land but the lifetime of working that went into it, along with the received practical wisdom of agriculture. Simon Peter would have inherited nets and fishing supplies from his father, but along with that he would have inherited the expertise of knowing when to cast a net, how to sail a boat, how to spot a storm. Indeed, the Old Testament idea of Jubilee is rooted in the idea of inheritance. Because families were connected economically through the generations, one person's financial woes were not his own individual problem. As Christopher Wright argues, "The economic collapse of a family in one generation was not to condemn all future generations to the bondage of perpetual indebtedness."[2] The Jubilee is not just a pattern of old covenant law. Jesus' inaugural sermon, announcing his kingdom, was a lyrical ode to the concept of Jubilee, a release from debt and captivity for all of those for whom God has favor (Luke 4:18–19).

When Jesus taught us to pray "Our Father," this comes with inheritance language too. "Give us this day our daily bread," we cry out, knowing that our Father knows what we need. This is not a storehouse of bread in the future (although we certainly have a future inheritance waiting for us) but the ongoing, everyday supply of bread. Inheritance is not about merely receiving but being invited to participate. The family is meant to teach us this, to teach us what it means to function in an economy, in an order. This is to be seen in the ways we live our lives in the now, as well as in the fact that we will one day be part of a vast cosmic order (with different kinds of callings) in the kingdom of God.

* * * *

The cross is a crisis of identity and inheritance. The jeering crowds around Jesus weren't especially cruel or sacrilegious compared to everyone else. They just knew their Bibles. They could see that Jesus was hanged on a tree and therefore, according the book of Deuteronomy, he was cursed by God (Deut. 21:23). This was a family matter. The language of this curse starts with a question of family identity. The Bible says, "If a man has a stubborn and rebellious son who will not obey the voice of his father or the voice of his mother, and, though they discipline him, will not listen to them, then his father and his mother shall take hold of him and bring him out to the elders of the city at the gate of the place where he lives, and they shall say to the elders of the city, 'This our son . . . is a glutton and a drunkard'" (Deut. 21:18–20). Jesus was indeed charged by the elders with being a drunkard and a glutton (Matt. 11:19). He was indeed charged with being a rebellious son; one who, they said, would dishonor the Sabbath and even threaten to tear down the temple of God itself. The book of Moses said what would happen to such a man: "Then all the men of the city shall stone him to death with stones. So you shall purge the evil from your midst, and all Israel shall hear, and fear" (Deut. 21:21). Jesus' kinsmen had already dragged him outside the borders of their town and attempted to stone him with stones (Luke 4:29–30; John 8:59). At the end, though, they went even further, hanging him on a tree in crucifixion, the ultimate sign of the curse of God.

This has everything to do with both identity (is God with us?) and inheritance (what will God give to us?). Moses said, "And if a man has committed a crime punishable by death and he is put to death, and you shall hang him on a tree, his body shall not remain all night on the tree, but you shall bury him the same day, for a hanged man is cursed by God. You shall not defile your land that the LORD your God is giving you for an inheritance" (Deut. 21:22–23). Jesus' crucifixion meant, those standing around would have reasoned, that he was rejected as God's Son and that he had forfeited his inheritance. That's why the cross was a scandal, both to Jews and to Gentiles. Who could follow a God-cursed, humiliated criminal? And how could a crucified man ever give a kingdom to his followers, when he could not even escape execution himself?

The entire New Testament unpacks this reality. That's why the apostle Paul claims that he knew "nothing among you except Jesus Christ and him crucified" (1 Cor. 2:2). This seems, at first glance, to be untrue. After all, the apostle Paul gave instructions on all sorts of things—many of them discussed in these pages—such as what criteria there should be for financial support of widows or how often married couples should have sex with each other. This is not inconsistent. The entire Christian life is lived by those who have been crucified with Christ, and who therefore now live through him (Gal. 2:20). We are cursed with Christ at the cross. There we have experienced death and hell. That means the accusing powers have no say over us anymore. We cannot be re-cursed, re-damned, re-crucified. And, joined to Christ by the cross, we have a new identity and a new inheritance. The cross happens "so that in Christ Jesus the blessing of Abraham might come to the Gentiles, so that we might receive the promised Spirit through faith" (Gal. 3:14).

The gospel means then that all of us, no matter what our background or origin, are all now children of God, and if children then heirs, in fact joint-heirs with Christ (Rom. 8:16–17). We know that we are in Christ because we cry out, often in pained groaning, "Abba! Father!" (Rom. 8:15), and we find in so doing that Jesus is himself actually crying out through us (Gal. 4:6). Jesus does not merely instruct us on how to pray to "Our Father." We often do not know how or what to pray (Rom. 8:26–27). He actually then prays through us by the Spirit. The Lord's Prayer coming from our lips is quite often literally the *Lord's prayer*. It is by means of this cross-rooted reality that we do warfare against the principalities and powers that stand against us.

Before a long period of silence from God, the prophet Malachi said that God would send the prophet Elijah "before the great and awesome day of the LORD comes" (Mal. 4:5). The prophet "will turn the hearts of fathers to their children and the hearts of children to their fathers, lest I come and strike the land with a decree of utter destruction" (Mal. 4:6). Jesus identified this spirit of Elijah with his cousin, John the Baptist (Matt. 17:10–13). John's preaching in the wilderness attacked the presumption of identity and inheritance the people had. John confronted the Israelites who presumed upon God's favor simply because they were biological descendants of Abraham. God's axe was at the root of that family tree (Matt. 3:9–10). The question was, where was the faithful remnant God had promised? Where was the son to whom God would offer the ends of the earth as an inheritance? Right there at those waters, Jesus submitted to baptism—signifying the judgment that would come upon him for his people later at the cross (Luke 12:50; Rom. 6:4). As he came up out of the water, a voice boomed from the skies above, "This is my beloved Son, with whom I am well pleased" (Matt. 3:17). The heart of the Father was turned toward his Son; the heart of the Son turned toward his Father.

We not only learn who we are; we often gain an inheritance through the family. We gain patterns of life, expectations, models, and wounds from our families of origin. Our life stories show us that we are part of a larger story—a story brimming with other characters. No matter how much we want to believe that we have shaped and formed ourselves, that we control our own personality and destiny, we all come from somewhere, and, more to the point, from some people. For many, this inheritance is good. Maybe you can see with gratitude all the things you carry with you from your family—how to bake a cake or how to change a tire or, much more importantly, how to trust Jesus, and how to pray. For some, the inheritance is mixed, or even quite dark. Even those who wish to cut themselves off from their families are often frustrated at how difficult this can actually be to accomplish. One can leave home and never speak to one's relatives again, make the opposite of all of their religious, political, and career choices—and still see one's father's eyes in the mirror or hear oneself saying the sort of thing one's mother used to say.

Many of you learned in the training-ground of your families a distortion of identity and inheritance. Perhaps a parent told you, explicitly or implicitly, that you would never amount to anything. Perhaps a parent saw you as just an extension of himself or herself. Maybe you inherited a biological disposition toward crippling depression or addiction. Or maybe you inherited a family system filled with strife and trauma. Perhaps your family background left you with limited economic and social means to escape a situation filled with despair or even violence. The good news is that Jesus not only taught us to pray "Our Father," but followed those words with these, "in heaven, hallowed be your name" (Matt. 6:9). There's an analogy between what we are intended to experience in our family formation and the Fatherhood of God. But the Fatherhood of God, even in the best circumstances, infinitely transcends those earthly categories. God is "Father," near to us, but he is also "in heaven," distant from us. We know the name of our God (nearness) but that name is holy (distance). This God asks: "To whom will you liken me and make me equal, and compare me that we might be alike?" (Isa. 46:5). You can come out of the best or the worst of family backgrounds and still come to know, and to teach others, what it means to call out to God as Father.

* * * *

We should pursue every opportunity to cultivate healthy families because what goes on in our families shapes our consciences and personalities and souls. Family is more than food and shelter. It ripples out through generations, transforming how countless people see God, the gospel, and themselves. We must work, if we are parents, to discipline our children in the nurture and admonition of the Lord, that they might see a reflection of something of what God is like.

But you don't have to come from a good family, or even know who your parents were, to experience the Fatherhood of God. In reality, every family is, to some degree or other, a broken family. If you've come from a terrible situation, God is not surprised by this. After all, Jesus loves *you*; the Good Shepherd came out searching for *you*. You are not just that collection of cells, or that bundle of DNA. You are also your memory, your experiences, your story. An essential part of who you are is the story of where you came from. The fact that you know that something was wrong is itself grace. The fact that the gospel has come to you means that God, fully knowing your background, offers you, right along with the rest of us, a new identity and a new inheritance. As the prophet Daniel said of God, "he knows what is in the darkness, and the light dwells with him" (Dan. 2:22).

We see this throughout the Scriptures, even through horrible family patterns of which God does not approve. It's hard to imagine a family more dysfunctional than a band of brothers beating their little sibling to near-death, and then selling him into a human trafficking racket. Early in Israel's story, though, that's precisely what happened to Joseph. God condemned this for what it was: wickedness. At the same time, though, God was at work, turning this awfulness around, to save Israel by Joseph's providing grain in a time of nation-threatening famine. Joseph said to the brothers, "You meant evil against me, but God meant it for good, to bring it about that many people should be kept alive, as they are today" (Gen. 50:20).

Unlike Joseph, we don't have direct revelation, to see exactly why God permitted you to go through the awful things back in the background that some of you have experienced. In some ways, you might be able to look back and see how God was with you, even in the valley of the shadow of death. You might be able to see how the scars you bear made you into who you are or prepared you to minister later to others. Or you might not be able to make sense of any of it at all. Our family stories demonstrate, from the very beginning of our existences that we are part of a plotline, but that plotline can often seem confused and mysterious and unseen to us. We know this, though. We know that God is just and will call every evil to account. We know that you cannot go back in time and undo those things. You can fantasize about an alternative reality where you had better parents or where you were a better parent, where you had better children or where you were a better child. But those fantasies cannot force those alternative universes into existence.

You are not your genealogy. You are not your family tree. You are not your family. After all, if you are in Christ, you are a new creation. You are not doomed to carry on the dark family traditions that would harm you or drive you away from God or other people. That will entail the sort of ongoing prayer and effort the Bible refers to in spiritual warfare terms. That's not just a task for those who come from "dysfunctional families" but for all of us, just in differing ways. The religious leaders around Jesus were quite proud of their family tree—a family tree we call "the Old Testament." And yet, Jesus reminded them that, like their ancestors, they were not above killing the prophets among them (Matt. 23:29–36; Luke 11:47–51). Stephen the martyr told his fellow Israelites much the same, that they were repeating the errors of their ancestors by stifling the prophetic word (Acts 7:51). The apostle Paul warned a Gentile congregation that they should not "walk as the Gentiles do" (Eph. 4:17). And the apostle Peter reminded another Gentile band of new Christians not to go back to the "futile ways inherited from your forefathers" (1 Pet. 1:18). That means that they should overcome their natural backgrounds by following Christ. This is not done by sheer willpower. It is done by clinging to the gospel, remembering your new identity and your new inheritance in Christ. You are ransomed from your old inheritance "not with perishable things such as silver or gold, but with the precious blood of Christ" (1 Pet. 1:18–19).

Do many of you have good, stable family backgrounds for which you should give thanks? Yes. You should not therefore boast as though this makes you better than another; "What do you have that you did not receive?" (1 Cor. 4:7). Do many of you have wounds that you carry throughout life? Yes. Must you unlearn old patterns and models? Yes. Are you then hopeless? Are you predestined to repeat the disappointments or traumas enacted upon you? By no means. Your inheritance is not just your future reward in the world to come. Your inheritance is also a new Spirit and a new community, able to overcome through you all of the snares of the Evil One.

Family dynamics have consequences, to be sure. If you are a parent, you cannot assume that your refusal to stay married or to keep a job, that your alcohol abuse or drug addiction or cutting words, will have no influence on your children—or, for that matter, your grandchildren and great-grandchildren and great-great-grandchildren. You will give an account. "For it is necessary that temptations come," Jesus said, "but woe to the one by whom the temptation comes" (Matt. 18:7). If you are downstream from that, though, the important thing is that you recognize the good—the longing for home, say—and the bad that comes to you from your situation. The dangers for you are not the patterns you can see and identify but those that you do not see at all. Yes, many children of absent fathers grow up to abandon their own families. Yes, children of alcoholics grow up to drink their lives away too. Yes, the children of violent people sometimes grow up to be just as violent when they are in a place of relative power. That happens, but usually in people who do not see their own vulnerability.

When I talk to someone who fears repeating his or her family's dysfunctional patterns, I almost never worry for their future. They see the problems there and are thus armed to go, by the power of the Spirit, in a different direction. Some of the best marriages I know of are people who lived through their own parents' divorces. Some of the best parents I know are those who had absent or abusive or negligent parents. Some of the most compassionate advocates for children I know were emotionally or physically or sexually abused themselves as children. They survived, and spend their lives making sure no one else will go through the same trauma. The danger is for those who don't even think about how their family's yelling of profanities at one another or serial adulteries or string of divorces is simply accepted as the way things are. Often, those who lived through such things are more proactive than their peers at putting good practices in place ahead of time. A person who grew up with a family given to screaming at one another, for instance, might map out ahead of time that he will take a walk during a time of intense stress, to calm down and pray before dealing with a controversial family matter. In some instances, he may ask his spouse from a more even-tempered family background to handle a situation. That's not weakness but grace.

That's where there is peril, not the presence of brokenness itself. As a matter of fact, counselors tell us that they worry when they encounter someone who describes a completely idyllic golden age of a childhood. Often, they find the opposite to be the case. The person idealized his or her backstory because he or she couldn't bear to live with the actual story. That's where the danger is.

Some of you might struggle to believe that God loves you because of the ways you have rebelled in the past—your alcoholism, your abortions, your sexual history, your relationship breakups, your prison time, or whatever. Some of you live then in fear, cringing as though God were angry with you, looking to punish you. Some of you maybe have lived that way so long that you've just given up, choosing just to rebel because you've concluded that's just who you are.

My situation is in some ways the exact opposite from that, but it just might be even more dangerous. I laughed to myself when I noticed that I referenced in this chapter, in an aside, my teenage fears about passing Algebra. That's very telling because, in some ways, it seems that my whole life is an exercise in taking a report card in to my father, for his approval or disapproval. I've always been the one who has to do everything right—to be the well-behaved one, the well-mannered one, the hard-working one, the smart one, the pious one, the one who does everything he is supposed to do. I was in church virtually every time the doors were open when I was a child. I was the one who, from the age of five, made sure that my grandmother's yard was mowed, her garden tilled, and who, inexplicably as one who was just out of toddler stage, counseled her through the loss of her husband and even stood in the backseat as she was learning late in life to drive a car, telling her she could do it. I preached my first sermon at twelve. I was running communications for a United States congressman's campaign before I was twenty. I later earned a doctorate and was, before I knew it, dean of my theological seminary at age thirty-two. None of that is because I am particularly talented, but because I am perhaps unusually driven. I realize now how much of that drive came from believing I could only be loved if I earned my keep, if I behaved and performed better than anyone else around me. The fears and insecurities I picked up as a child were the devils I would run from to this very moment.

I would like to say that that has gone away, but it hasn't. A newspaper wrote an article one time about some people who criticized me, really sharply, for not taking political stands they would want me to take. I was crushed by this, to the point that I wondered sometimes if I could even get out of bed in the morning. I wondered why. I really was not worried about what those people thought of me. I believed what I believed. I was not worried about some bad consequences for me or for my ministry. Most people were affirming and supportive, even more than ever before. I slowly came to realize that what I was feeling was not regret or fear but shame. The main thing I worried about was my father seeing that article, or a sort of surrogate father-in-ministry seeing it, and concluding that I was a failure. I was worried that my children would see it, and think that I had failed them. I was standing there with the report card. Again.

Like the older brother in Jesus' parable of the prodigal, I too often believe I can earn my place in the house, my future inheritance, by doing the right thing—by behaving and performing and being deemed useful and likable. And like the returning exile in that story, I too often believe that I should be a hired hand, not a welcomed son, in the Father's house (Luke 15:19). My drive to succeed is really not ambition but a drive to belong, to hear the words, "You are my beloved son, and with you I am well pleased." Behind virtually everything I do, from teaching my children dinner-table manners to writing this book, there's a little boy looking behind him for his parents, to see if they're looking, to see if they're proud of him. That's brokenness. But that's not my identity, and that's not my inheritance. The gospel has to interrupt me constantly, taking me away from my futile whirling dervish-like performance right back to that sky above the Jordan River.

Many of you are in a similar place. Whether you hide behind your athletic skill or your intellectual caliber or your artistic brilliance or your spirituality and morality, those who perform for a Father's recognition will find themselves failing. Performing for your identity and your inheritance does not lead to holiness but to exhaustion, bitterness, and ultimately, death. To do otherwise is spiritual warfare. And it's hard.

* * * *

When we learn to say "Our Father," we enter into battle. As dependent children, we look to our parents for, among other things, the basic needs of security: provision and protection. Jesus asked, "Or which one of you, if his son asks him for bread, will give him a stone? Or if he asks for a fish, will give him a serpent? If you then, who are evil, know to give good gifts to your children, how much more will your Father who is in heaven give good things to those who ask him!" (Matt. 7:9–11). No matter your family background, you are not an orphan in the cosmos. The same Jesus who taught us to call God our Father also taught us to look to him for provision ("Give us this day our daily bread") and protection ("Lead us not into temptation but deliver us from evil"). These are not separate requests. The devil came to our Lord in the desert and asked him to turn stones into bread. The devil was not just trying to tempt Jesus; he was trying to adopt him. Family is meant to teach us, among other things, that we are creatures, that we cannot, ultimately, provide for and protect ourselves. We are dependent in our infancy, and dependent again in our old age. That sense of need is the first step to overcoming, in a war-torn universe in which the family is often ground zero.

In this, Jesus is not absent from us or ashamed of us. He is with us. He finds his identity in his Father's blessing (Matt. 3:17). He watches his Father's vocation, and finds there his own (John 5:19–21). He also, at the cross, finds himself "a stranger to my brothers," and "alien to my mother's sons," because the zeal for his Father's house "consumed" him (Ps. 69:8–9). The cross informs what it means for us to be a family, and our lives in our families are meant to drive us back to the cross. The kingdom is breaking through. The family is a sign of this kingdom, and that's one reason why the powers of darkness want to rage against it. That's not true only for "The Family" in abstract but for your family, in particular. Whatever your family background, you can be faithful to your family. Whatever your family situation, you can be a part of the family of the church. You can fight this battle. But you can only do so if you know who you are, and if you know where you're going. No matter what—the call to be family is a call to hardship, to suffering, to combat in the spiritual realm. And sometimes the only weapon you can find is the battle cry, "Jesus loves me, this I know." Through it all you will hear a persistent question from the defeated powers of this age, from the nagging fears in your own psyche. The question is, "Who is your Father?" You have an answer to that question.

The answer is shaped like a cross.

CHAPTER FOUR

Family Is Not First

A LONG TIME AGO HE was a psychic. The man standing there in front of me in the church lobby made it clear that he had never been a real telepath, back in his pre-Christian days telling fortunes. He was just scamming people, he said, by pretending to be able to peer into their futures. He said the pay hadn't been all that impressive, but it was the easiest job he ever had. He could convince people he could see into the spirit-world, first of all, by using the same methods one would see in a horoscope or a fortune cookie: broad generalizations that could apply to anyone. "I can see that you have had a surprising development in your life" or "You've had some sadness" or "I'm seeing someone in your life with an 'r' somewhere in their name." More importantly, though, he said the secret to getting repeat customers was to make sure the future he foresaw wasn't nuanced or complicated at all. One could gain a happy client if one would "see" something really good, telling the person what he or she wanted to believe. "You will find love" or "I see a lot of money in your future."

But one could also gain a repeat customer if one prophesied something catastrophic, while maintaining that the only way the client could avoid this disaster was if he or she employed the psychic to help keep it from happening. He was ashamed of his past, and he shrugged his shoulders, wondering if this was the first time I'd ever heard of such a thing. I assured him it wasn't. I've seen prosperity gospel evangelists do the same maneuvers on television for years.

Witchcraft is witchcraft, whether it comes with a Bible or with a crystal ball.

The ex-psychic told me that the surprising thing to him was that most people really did not want dramatic things for themselves. Of course, very occasionally he would meet someone who wanted global fame or a private jet with his name on the side (again, probably a television evangelist, come to think of it). Most people didn't want a penthouse on Park Avenue or vacations in Switzerland. Most people just wanted a basic sense of security, a reassurance that everything was going to be all right. They wanted to know that they could count on someone to love, that they would be able to meet the obligations of those who depended on them. If they had children, they wanted to know that they would be happy and cared for. They either wanted a very minimal Promised Land, or a very avoidable Armageddon—that's all.

What embarrasses me is how often I am just like those who flock to roadside psychics or health-and-wealth preachers. I don't want a fleet of sports cars or a private Caribbean island. I just want security too. I just want to know that my family will make it through life all right, and that I will do well at getting them there. Like the Canaanites looking to fertility religions promising rain for the fields and fertility for the wombs, I sometimes want a gospel just natural enough to let me run my own life but just supernatural enough to give me what I need to get there. I want a sign that my life-plan will work out, or, if not that, then whatever voodoo it takes to fend off disaster.

When Jesus taught us not to be anxious, we too often interpret that through a highly individualistic grid, as though Jesus were simply telling us to avoid the psychological distress of selfish desires. The worry Jesus spoke against though is far more than just individual. He told us not to ask, "What shall we eat?" or "What shall wear?" (Matt. 6:31). For those in a kin network (as virtually every one of his hearers would have been), those are questions not just about personal security but family security. And Jesus did not dismiss those concerns ("Your Father knows you need these things"). He commanded us though to "seek first the kingdom of God and his righteousness (Matt. 6:32–33).

The kingdom is first; the family is not.

* * * *

When many people think of North American Christianity, one of the first words that comes to mind is "family." Part of that is good, necessary, and unavoidable for a church on mission. If we are going to disciple people, we must teach them to keep themselves from idols (1 John 5:21), and many of the idols of our age come under the rubric of allegedly freeing people from the "constraints" of family responsibility and even family definition. When the outside culture valorizes sexual promiscuity, gender confusion, a divorce culture, and the upending of marriage, then the church must work hard to articulate a different vision. For the most part, there's nothing unhealthy about this. There is a danger, though, that comes with any mission, and this one is no exception.

The outside world is interested in order and stability. In that sense, the world can see the value, in most cases, of "The Family" in a way that it would not see the value of, say, the doctrine of justification by faith. Churches could talk about the family, then, in ways that seemed immediately relevant even to their most metaphysically disinterested neighbors. With the secularizing of Western culture, many churches find that their neighbors simply aren't asking questions like, "What will I say when God asks me, 'Why should I let you into heaven?'" They find they are asking, though, "How can I find sexual fulfillment if I'm not married?" or "How can I stop arguing so much with my husband?" or "How can I relate to my kids during the teenage years?" For many churches, the family then becomes the point of contact with the outside world, and the incentive for some to investigate the church in the first place. When they find that the church has a vibrant youth ministry or a Sunday school that children enjoy, they often stay around. A church might not be equipped to talk about the problem of evil or the Trinity but can offer therapeutic tips on discipline or potty-training or couples' date nights to keep the sizzle in the marriage. Some of this focus is due to genuine missionary commitment; some is due to the marketing and entrepreneurial focus of so much of the North American church.

Of course, teaching family values and faith in Jesus side by side in church is, by no means, all cynical. Children and family are one way (though not at all the only way) that God awakens people to the world outside themselves. Some people profess faith as a sense of obligation to their parents, but many people genuinely meet Christ through the witness of their parents or grandparents (think of Timothy's mother and grandmother; 2 Tim. 1:5). By the same token, some people go back to the church out of some superficial sense of obligation to their children, being a "good Christian" in order to be a good parent. Many others genuinely find Christ as part of their struggle to make sense of what it means to be a mother or a father to a living human being. Because this happens so often, it is easy for some to conclude that "religion" is one more accoutrement of being a family, something one adds the way one adds an infant seat to the car. Thus, many think "family values" immediately when they think "church." To some degree that is positive and unavoidable, but often this categorization wrongly makes the family the fundamental point of contradiction between the church and the world. The gospel, though, does not see the primary distinction as our being "pro-family" and "anti-family" people but between crucified and uncrucified people. A church that focuses on the family is in line with the Bible, but a church that puts families first is not.

As a matter of fact, a Christianity that puts family first will soon find itself uncomfortable with Jesus. If we were to hear the words Jesus spoke on the family coming from anyone else, we might quickly conclude that person is not one of us. Jesus taught us, "Whoever does not bear his own cross and come after me cannot be my disciple" (Luke 14:27). That part is uncontroversial among today's Christians, largely because we don't understand what Jesus is saying. First of all, we don't, like Jesus' contemporaries, walk down roads with the sight of people writhing in torture on actual crosses along the way. We see "cross" as a safe metaphor for spiritual devotion. Sometimes we see it as a metaphor for the stresses of life, the way an office-supply store manager once told me of yearly inventory as "my cross to bear." Jesus was teaching here, though, specifically about the context of the family. "If anyone comes to me and does not hate his own father and mother and wife and children and brothers and sisters, yes, and even his own life, he cannot be my disciple," he said (Luke 14:26). Most people would not want that as the theme verse of their church's summer children's camp, much less written in frosting on a wedding or anniversary celebration cake. When we hear this verse referenced at all, it usually is mostly in terms of what the verse does not say, reassuring people that "hate" here does not mean hostility or disrespect but priority of affection. That's true enough, and needs to be said.

Regarding this verse, C. S. Lewis was, no doubt, correct in saying it is "profitable only to those who read it with horror." As he put it, "The man who finds it easy enough to hate his father, the woman whose life is a long struggle not to hate her mother, had probably best keep clear of it."[3] Still, we rarely spend much time exploring what Jesus *does* mean, especially in light of the fact that this is hardly an isolated text. Why does Jesus make these shocking statements that seem to marginalize the family?

Jesus is the Prince of Peace, who told us that the peacemakers are blessed as the sons of God. He came to bring "peace on earth, goodwill toward men," as the angels sang at his birth (Luke 2:14 KJV). And yet, Jesus said: "Do not think that I have come to bring peace to the earth. . . . I have come to set a man against his father, and a daughter against her mother, and a daughter-in-law against her mother-in-law. And a person's enemies will be those of his own household" (Matt. 10:34–36). This is not some obscure diversion from his main teaching, but the introduction to one of the most important sayings of Jesus on the cross-shaped life in a storm-tossed world: "And whoever does not take his cross and follow me is not worthy of me. Whoever finds his life will lose it, and whoever loses his life for my sake will find it" (Matt. 10:38–39). This mentality manifested itself not just in Jesus' words but even in the way he chose his disciples.

Recently I hired an impressive new staff member, who asked if he could delay his taking the position for some months in order to complete the adoption of his new child, a process that would require him to stay in residence in his state until the paperwork was all completed. I never even considered for a second saying, "Do you want to work with me or not? Let the babies take care of their own babies." First of all, the new staff member would (rightly) have turned down the job, and would have (rightly) concluded that I am a hypocrite with my activity on adoption and foster care. He also would have thought, if not said, "Who do you think you are?" I know I would have. Delaying a new mission because one must put in order the affairs of a recently deceased parent would seem not simply reasonable but commendable. Jesus, though, responded to the man who said, "Lord, let me first go and bury my father," with what seems preternaturally cold and devoid of empathy: "Leave the dead to bury their own dead. But as for you, go and proclaim the kingdom of God" (Luke 9:59–60). One would hardly think ill of someone who, before he took off with the Air Force, went to say goodbye to his family. And yet, when another prospective disciple of Jesus asked to "say farewell to those at my home," Jesus would have nothing of it. "No one who puts his hand to the plough and looks back is fit for the kingdom of God," he said (Luke 9:61–62). Again, if anyone but Jesus were to say this, let's be honest, it would sound at best harsh and at worst evil.

This was not a temporary aberration from Jesus' recruitment of his band of followers, either. When one is training people to recognize cults, one of the first details explained is that a cult typically seeks to isolate people from their families. A group that tells new adherents to cut off contact with their mother or father or siblings is usually suspect as a scary sect out to do harm. No wonder, then, that this is exactly the way many in first-century Judea viewed the Jesus movement. Everyone in the first century would have paid attention when the Gospels tell of Jesus speaking the words "Follow me," prompting the fishermen-apostles to immediately drop their nets and come with him. James and John, Mark recounted, stopped mending their nets and "left their father Zebedee in the boat with the hired servants and followed him" (Mark 1:20). We wrongly interpret this as the equivalent of a young Christian couple leaving their extended families to go on the mission field to a faraway country. Jesus' hearers would have understood this as much more than that, as a repudiation of the family. The fishermen walking away from their nets are not the equivalent of a modern person taking a job in another city. When they walked away from the nets, they were walking away from their inheritance. They were cutting themselves off from the heritage of their ancestors, who cultivated this seafood business over probably many generations. They were also sacrificing the means of living for their future offspring, and their offspring, on down through unseen generations to come. This seemed not just shockingly anti-family, but a violation of the command of God to honor father and mother.

Jesus was no hypocrite. He not only taught these things, but also lived them. He was never married and never had children. He seemed to disrespect at almost every turn his immediate and extended family. Once when Jesus was teaching, a woman in the crowd yelled out, "Blessed is the womb that bore you, and the breasts at which you nursed!" (Luke 11:27). As someone who teaches often, I have had people yell things out at me, occasionally, but never to compliment my mother. If someone did, though, I'm sure I would stop and say how great my mother is, and how much I owe her. Jesus did not do that. He said, "Blessed rather are those who hear the Word of God and keep it" (Luke 11:28). When Jesus' family stood outside one of his teaching venues asking to see him, Jesus responded with the words, "Who are my mother and my brothers?" And answering himself he said, "Here are my mother and my brothers! For whoever does the will of God, he is my brother and sister and mother" (Mark 3:33–35).

I once heard a friend tell me of the experience he had coming back to his blue-collar hometown after being away at an elite university. He started back up where he left off, with his brothers and sisters and friends, laughing and joking around. He made a comment about their town, that he had made uncountable times with them as they grew up. He noticed everyone stiffen up. They said, "We can say that, but you can't. When you do it, now, it's like you are looking down on us." My friend realized that, suddenly, he wasn't an insider joining with other insiders making fun of one other. He was now, in some way, an outsider making fun of them. Those are two very different realities, with two very different reactions. How much more incendiary would be Jesus' attitude toward his hometown (Luke 4:24-30). A celebrity who "makes it" in, say, the music industry, must either cultivate a close attention to his hometown, performing free concerts there, for instance, or else risk hatred from those who see him as having gotten "too big" to see where he came from. No doubt this was the reaction of many to Jesus; he even told them he knew this was on their minds ("Physician heal yourself"). But beyond even that, Jesus went further in marginalizing his own immediate family in ways that would be startling in virtually any context and any culture. Indeed, for many, Jesus' attitude toward natural family attachments might have been the most controversial thing about him. And given the near-constant controversies Jesus was sparking, that is saying something.

On the other side of the ascension, we recognize (correctly) that Jesus is always right. Sometimes, though, our sense of "sweet Jesus" can obscure for us some of the tension found in the text itself, which is meant to convey just how strange the way of the kingdom Jesus was offering actually was. The horrified reaction of Jesus' family and tribesmen is not crazy. Jesus was going against something universal in human nature. Jesus hardly seemed to be a good family man. In fact, he didn't seem even to be a good mammal.

After all, scientists tell us that kinship bonds are powerful, between all creatures, because of the drive for life toward species survival, the protection of one's own genetic material. Many mammals, in particular, exhibit survival-oriented behaviors in relationship with their mates and offspring. This is why we do not require spouses to testify against one another in court, or children to testify against their parents. Such tears against something primal in our nature. One need not see natural selection as the primary driving force of the universe in order to see this, though.

In fact, Jesus' model and instruction on the family not only seem out of step with biology, but out step with the Bible. The biblical story starts with a family—a man and a woman charged with being fruitful and multiplying across the face of the earth (Gen. 1:27). Childlessness is a recurring problem in the Old Testament, but not simply because of the personal grief that comes with infertility. God's promise was that he would make Abraham the "father of a multitude of nations" (Gen. 17:5), that his descendants would be as numerous as the sands of the shore and the stars of the sky (Gen. 15:5). God's promise to David is that God would establish a royal dynasty for David, that one of his sons would sit on his throne forever (2 Sam. 7:4–17).

What it boils down to, ultimately, is that Jesus did not make the family as important as his culture did. Ironically enough, this is how Jesus saved the family. We need not flinch when we read Jesus tells us that the one who follows him must "hate" mother and father, brothers and sisters. In the same breath, Jesus said that the one who follows him must hate also "even his own life" (Luke 14:26). Is Jesus mandating suicide upon conversion? Obviously not. Instead, he is putting one's life in the context of the cross: "Whoever does not bear his own cross and come after me cannot be my disciple" (Luke 14:27). In the economy of the kingdom the way to find one's life is to lose it (Mark. 8:35). Likewise, the way to reclaim the family is to crucify our family values.

* * * *

Novelist Walker Percy is an unlikely person to suggest that the cure for depression is to kill oneself, since he spent a whole life reeling from the suicide of his father. But that's precisely what he did. By suicide, Percy, rightly, did not mean the literal taking of one's life. That solves no problems, though suicidal people mistakenly believe it will. What happens, though, he mused, if one considers suicide but decides not to go through with it? The result is freedom. "You are like a prisoner released from the cell of life," he wrote. Knowing that you could have not existed, you are now free to exist without all the expectations that once crushed you in their disappointments. You are free to see life as a gift. There's a huge difference, Percy suggested, between a "non-suicide"—someone who has not killed himself—and an "ex-suicide"—someone who counts himself as already dead, and thus is free to live. "The ex-suicide opens his front door, sits down on the steps and laughs," Percy wrote. "Since he has the option of being dead, he has nothing to lose by being alive. It is good to be alive. He goes to work because he doesn't have to."[4]

That's what the cross does for family, and it is there that we face the primary arena of spiritual warfare. The dark powers would have us to idolize ourselves and by extension our families, by which usually we mean the image we've cultivated of ourselves and our families. We clamor for security, for our lives to turn out the way we expected, the way we think we deserve, with our families and otherwise. But if we receive family as a gift, and not as the singular defining feature of our lives, then we are freed to love our families as they are, not as idealized extensions of ourselves. We need not force our families to conform to an image that only exists in our imaginations, or resent them for falling short of our idolatrous ideal. The intellectual father need not resent his developmentally disabled son because the child is his child—a gift—not the man's hope for a "legacy." Our grasping for security for our families is often a cover for our own self-exaltation, as when Saul lashed out at his son Jonathan for showing friendship with David: "For as long as the son of Jesse lives on the earth, neither you nor your kingdom shall be established" (1 Sam. 20:31).

Most of us do not have literal monarchies to protect, but family can stand in for whatever idol we seek to guard—be it economic security or reputational acclaim. The fact that family can be a temptation is no more a sign that family should be discarded as food or clothing because Mammon is a temptation. Following Jesus requires us to reorder our priorities.

If we seek first the kingdom, we are better able to seek the welfare of our families. If we love Jesus more than family, we are freed to love our families more than we ever would have otherwise. If we give up our suffocating grasp on our family—whether that's our idyllic view of our family in the now, our nostalgia for the family of long ago, our scars from family wounds, or our worries for our family's future—we are then free to be family, starting with our place in the new creation family of the church.

Family is a blessing, yes. But family is only a blessing if family is not first.

Chapter Five

The Church as Family

A FRIEND ONCE TOLD ME that she spent her Sundays, in the weeks before she became a Christian, sitting in a coffee shop, watching people across the street from her walk from their cars to the church. At the time she was an atheist and had believed the concepts of God and "traditional" concepts of marriage and family were all alike rooted in oppressive patriarchy. She believed in sexual freedom, and found Christian moral norms suffocating. But to her surprise, she found herself drawn to Jesus, and started to believe his claims about himself. But before she committed herself to Christ, she wondered if she could ever fit in and find belonging as a Christian. She sat there watching moms and dads walking from their minivans, babies in arms and children by the hand. And she pondered, "Could I ever be one of them?"

That we miss this too often cannot be seriously disputed. Unmarried Christians often feel as though they are deficient (which would mean that our religion itself is deficient since Jesus himself never married). Even more than that, our churches too often mirror the loneliness of the outside world. One of my former students,

who came to Christ after years in a street gang, tells me he is happy
to give up the violence and the drugs but says he misses every day
the community and the sense of belonging that came with his gang
membership. I've heard much the same from those who have come
to Christ out of everything from the pornography industry to the Ku
Klux Klan. They do not, for a minute, look longingly back at their
former sin, but they have found no comparable sense of camaraderie,
of belonging, of family. What an indictment.

* * * *

There are serious consequences of losing a sense of family within the
church. Some studies have shown that laboratory rats isolated from
one another are more likely when presented with mind-numbing
drugs to become addicted. Other studies have shown that much of
the trauma that comes to returning soldiers is due not only to the
memories of horrors on the battlefield but also to the lack of connection that comes, suddenly, with civilian life. We assume that the
nuclear family can meet this need, and yet some of the loneliest, most
isolated people in our communities are married with children, often
so frenetically busy with childrearing and/or caring for aging parents
that they have lost touch with old friends and no longer know how
to make new ones.

The church is not a collection of families. The church *is* a family. We are not "family friendly"; we are family. We learn the skills
within the church to be godly sons or daughters, brothers or sisters,
husbands or wives, fathers or mothers, and the reverse is also true.
We learn dynamics within the family that we then live out within
the church. The pastor is required biblically to "manage his own
household well" (1 Tim. 3:4). That's not because people with chaotic homes are worse people than anyone else. It's because the skill
set to lead a family and a church is the same. "[I]f someone does
not know how to manage his own household, how will he care for

God's church?" Paul asked (1 Tim. 3:5). As the church, we grow up together, and, as such, we need one another.

The new covenant promised to Israel looked forward to a future for the people, an ongoing kingdom of priests to mediate God's blessings to the nations. That's why we come across what seems strange to us in accounts of, say, Onan, who is rebuked for the fact that he did not complete the sexual act with his dead brother's wife, but spilled his seed "on the ground" (Gen. 38:9). Over the years, some have interpreted this as a warning against masturbation or barrier methods of birth control. I've even heard one preacher use this text to lambast "self-focused" churches that don't do enough for missions. The warning against this premature evacuation, though, is about the requirement of a brother-in-law to continue the family line, to "raise up offspring for your brother" (Gen. 38:8). In order for God to be faithful to his promises, Israel must survive. Thus, the sign of the covenant was the cutting away of skin, not on a finger or a toe, but on the organ of generation. The twelve tribes of Jacob must reproduce.

That's why the exile of the people of Israel into a foreign land, the destruction of the temple, the evacuation of the Davidic throne, it all seemed like the end of the world. God had worked to make Israel distinct, not just morally but also through signs of the covenant and through the prohibition against their intermarrying with the nations around them. In order to bless the nations, Israel could not be absorbed into the other nations and cease to exist. Jeremiah said of the faithless King Jehoiakim, "Thus says the LORD: Write this man down as childless, a man who shall not succeed in his days, for none of his offspring shall succeed in sitting on the throne of David and ruling again in Judah" (Jer. 22:30). This was not just a judgment of a royal house that played around with idols and mishandled foreign invasion; this was an act of judgment, it seemed, against the whole world. The line of David seemed to be over, and with it the only hope of redemption. And yet, God consistently promised that out of the wreckage of that family tree a branch would sprout (Jer. 23:5; Isa. 6:13). This hope was always future. Through Israel was to come "the Christ, who is God over all, blessed forever" (Rom. 9:5). Any generation could be just one generation away from the Messiah, from the sweeping away of the debris of Eden. And yet, every generation ended in death. The kings, even the good ones, all proved broken, and most were followed by sons who outdid them in their sin and rebellion. Israel could not procreate itself out from under the curse of the Fall.

In the midst of all of this there was the promise of a sign, something as everyday as a woman giving birth to a child (Isa. 7:12–14). The baby—one who would be "God with us"—would come from a remnant of Israel that seemed incapable of providing a future. In the virgin birth of Jesus, there was both continuity and discontinuity, both threat and promise. God works through the chosen bloodline but at the same time disrupts it. Salvation would come through "her offspring" (Gen. 3:15), through the line of Abraham and David. At the same time, the infant would be born "not of blood nor of the will of the flesh nor of the will of man, but of God" (John 1:13). From the womb of a mother who had never known a man, Jesus was a sign that nature alone could not save us. Family was important, but family was not enough. In Psalm 110, one of the most oft-quoted Old Testament passages in the New Testament, the coming deliverer is shown to be of the family of Abraham and David, fully qualified to be king, and yet David called him not "my son" but "my Lord" (Ps. 110:1; Mark 12:35–36). He is rooted in the family line of Israel, and yet he is not the sum of his genealogy. He is priest not by inheritance but in the way of the mysterious old figure of Melchizedek who is "without father or mother" (Heb. 7:3). We do not know Melchizedek's background, and we could not find his natural heirs. He seems to come out of nowhere. Jesus is not a priest because he is of the family of Israel; the family of Israel is a kingdom of priests because of him.

* * * *

When Jesus taught the kingdom of God to the Rabbi Nicodemus, the old man was confused by Jesus' insistence that one must be "born again" in order to inherit God's new order. Nicodemus saw this literally, in terms of physical obstetrics and gynecology. Jesus was pointing to something new that God was doing, that he had announced beforehand. Abraham had laid his son on the table of sacrifice, knowing that, were he to be killed, the entire hope for the future, all of God's promises, would be gone (Gen. 22:1–14). He trusted God to overturn death itself to keep those promises. We are heirs then, the children of promise in Christ (Gal. 4:26–28). The promises were never made to DNA lines or to marked-out skin, but to a faithful remnant. That remnant turns out to be one man, Jesus of Nazareth, who joins in himself God and God-imaging humanity. Flesh and blood gave us our physical existence, but flesh and blood cannot inherit the kingdom of God. We must be born again (John 3:3). All the family trees of the Bible thus look forward to the tree of Golgotha. The triumphant Christ, having offered his life as a sacrifice at the cross and having overturned death in his resurrection, is now seated at the right hand of God, announcing, "Here I am, and the children God has given me" (Heb. 2:13 NIV). Our identity is found in him. His story is now our story. His bloodline is now our bloodline. His inheritance is now our inheritance. And his family is now our family. If we are in Christ, we have a new Father, a new ancestry, and a new household bustling with brothers and sisters. We have a church.

In the church, there is a startling upending of our understanding of family. The prophet Isaiah foresaw that God would rescue the remnant of his people, and resettle them in the land of promise. But he saw more than just that. He promised that this remnant would include many people that didn't look much like ethnic Israelites. "Let not the foreigner who has joined himself to the LORD say, 'The LORD will surely separate me from his people'; and let not the eunuch say,

'Behold I am a dry tree,'" wrote the prophet (Isa. 56:3). Why would God in a word of hope about taking his people out of exile from the foreign nations speak this way about the inclusion of foreigners? And why would he single out eunuchs—those castrated, often in order to serve pagan kings without the distraction of family? The eunuch's lament certainly seems reasonable. He has no future in front of him, the way one could map it out on a family tree.

Every time I read this passage I remember being invited to speak at a men's conference for a friend of mine. Not knowing the church, I assumed the participants would be like those at other men's conferences I had attended, young married men. I came prepared to speak on sexual temptation and the necessity of sexual joy in marriage, of "rejoic[ing] in the wife of your youth" (Prov. 5:18) with lots of material from the Song of Solomon. When I arrived, I found that there was not a man in the room under the age of eighty-eight years old. Now, I recognize that some people are able to maintain vibrant sexual relationships right up to and beyond the centennial mark, but as I taught my material it became obvious none of these men thought they could live up to Solomon in that way. Afterward, one ancient brother-in-Christ stepped forward on his walker, and said to me, "Bless your heart, son, you're like Ezekiel trying to say to these dry bones 'live.'" I was stupid, and yet, even so, my geriatric sex conference was infinitely more realistic than God saying to eunuchs that they should not see themselves as infertile. Of course they are. They lack the equipment to consummate a marriage or to procreate children. So how could God say this?

God promised that those foreigners who joined themselves to him would be genuinely a part of his people. He promised that the faithful eunuchs would have "within my walls a monument and a name better than sons and daughters; I will give them an everlasting name that shall not be cut off" (Isa. 56:4–5). One could hope for a family line to go forward, carrying one's name into the future. In the gospel, God has given us much more than that—he carries us, personally, into the future, through the everlasting life of resurrection from the dead. That's true even for those who are without citizenship or family or, in the case of the eunuch, without even testicles. "My house shall be called a house of prayer for all peoples," God announced, because he gathers together the outcasts of Israel, and declared, "I will gather yet others to him besides those already gathered" (Isa. 56:7–8). God revealed all of this right after he revealed to us a servant who would be "crushed for our iniquities" and would bear our sin (Isa. 53:5). God redefined for us who the "our" would include. In one of the few times we see our Lord Jesus angered in the Gospels, we see him quoting this passage, as he drives the moneychangers from the temple: "My house shall be called a house of prayer for all the nations" (Mark 11:17). After his resurrection, Jesus sends forth the Spirit to do just that, to join to his people those who are of every tribe, tongue, nation, and language. One of the first we see is an Ethiopian eunuch, reading the scroll of Isaiah. By joining himself to Christ, he is no longer a "foreigner" but a "fellow citizen with the saints." He is not a "dry tree" but a member "of the household of God" (Eph. 2:19).

We naturally have a drive to belong. In the church we belong to one another, as brothers and sisters with a common future. Even using the language of "brother" and "sister" can seem overly metaphorical to us, like "brother" in a fraternity or "prayer warrior" in Christian parlance. This metaphor rocked the ancient church, though, as the people discovered just what it meant to share a storyline in the past, and an inheritance in the future. They knew that brothers and sisters have obligations to one another that they do not have to the outside world. That's why the early churches are described as caring for the needy among them financially, and as holding accountable fellow church members for their sins. We are not isolated in walls of privacy, but belong to one another. We bear one another's burdens because we are family.

* * * *

As the father of five sons, I have had to have "the talk" repeatedly, with my children, about what to expect in puberty. I don't want them to be, as I was, taken off guard by the startling changes—to feel in a haze and guilty. I repeat then, sometimes over and over, "Here's what will happen. Don't be scared. It's normal. You're not a freak." Usually when I first start having these conversations, the son with whom I'm talking will assume I am exaggerating. He cannot imagine having (those kinds of) thoughts about girls, much less all the rest of it. I will just repeat myself and say, "I'm telling you now so that you will know that you can talk to me when it happens." As I do this, sometimes, I wish there were someone doing the same for me, with all the other life changes that come along. "Here's what a mid-life crisis looks like" or "Here's what can happen in your marriage in empty nest years" or "Here's how you deal with the stress of an aging parent in another city who wants to keep all of her hoarded stuff when it's time to move into a retirement village apartment." I often need someone to say to me, "This is normal; don't panic," and I would imagine many more people need to hear that from me. The church is here to prepare one another spiritually for the changes that come with our pilgrimage to Zion. And, as we go, the church is a household economy, where all of us use our gifts for the sake of the mission. The fact that every person has a gift for the upbuilding of the rest of us is one more way of God signaling to us that we belong. We are wanted. We are loved.

Part of what it means, then, for conservative Christians to have "family values" is to see that our vision of the family is bigger than that of Darwinian biology. This may mean having an extra bedroom in our home where the AIDS victim spends his final years, a spot on the living room couch in front of the television for the woman whose parents kicked her out of the house when they discovered she was pregnant, a spot at the breakfast table for the man who fears that if he spends the night alone in his house he would end up finding that whiskey bottle again. A Christian opening his home to an unwed mother or an unemployed man or to a struggling teenager in the foster care system is not an act of charity or heroism. In this, we simply do what people do for their families, with no sense of obligation in return. We are family. That means no Christian lives alone, and no Christian dies alone. There's no such thing as a "single" Christian.

The family nature of the church is also why the Scripture speaks on family matters not to families only but to the whole church. The admonitions to husbands and wives, to children and parents, in Ephesians 5 and 6 or Colossians 3 are not written merely to those in the presenting situations but to entire churches, to be read all together. My marriage is my church's business. My fellow church members' struggles with matters unique to singleness are not his issues alone but mine too. We belong to one another. Beyond that, issues of family are not simply for those who "have families" as we define it. We all have come from some sort of family union, even those who don't know the names or faces of those involved (which brings with it its own challenges). Much more than that, though, we are all called to, for instance, parenting and being parented. That's not just for those who are married with children, which may be the most common reality in the North American church but is hardly what the New Testament defines as the "normal Christian life." Marriage, not celibacy, is the exception in the New Testament, the concession to frailty (1 Cor. 7:7–9).

You are called to be a father or mother, a brother or sister, whether you have any natural or legal family at all. The apostle Paul wrote to Timothy as his "true child in the faith" (1 Tim. 1:2). He called himself not only a father to many but also like a mother, laboring in pregnancy on behalf of the churches, "until Christ is formed in you" (Gal. 4:19). To one troubled church, Paul wrote, "For though you have countless guides in Christ, you do not have many fathers. For I became your father in Christ Jesus through the gospel" (1 Cor. 4:15). That's not just the case for apostles and prophets but for all of us. "Do not rebuke an older man but encourage him as you would a father, younger men as brothers, older women as mothers, younger women as sisters, in all

purity," Paul wrote to Timothy (1 Tim. 5:1–2). This is pivotally important for us to grasp if we are to follow the way of the cross, a way in
which from the cross Jesus hands a new mother to her new son as he
established a church. We are to have spiritual mothers and fathers, leading and nurturing others within the church. In this way, the church
connects the generations.

* * * *

Often I will hear older people within the church blame younger generations for not honoring the wisdom of the aged, of only wanting to
listen to their peers. Sometimes, of course, this is true. The kingdom
of Israel splintered partly because Solomon's son Rehoboam "abandoned the counsel that the old men gave him and took counsel with
the young men who had grown up with him" (1 Kings 12:8). Long
story short: it did not go well.

I don't sense this attitude, though, in most of the younger
Christians I encounter. Instead, I find that the question I get most
often is, "How do I find a mentor?" When one presses these young
Christians, you will find they do not want a "mentor" the way the
corporate world describes it—someone to pass on skill sets and to
help shepherd them up the ladder of success. Instead, what they
describe they want is less like a corporate coach and much more
akin to a father or mother. They don't know how to seek out such
relationships. Making friends, after all, is itself difficult once we get
past the childhood playground. One cannot, without making oneself
especially vulnerable to rejection, walk up and say, "Will you be my
friend?" It's even harder to imagine walking up and saying, "Would
you be a mother to me?" Or, "Would you be my spiritual father?"
And yet, this is a crucial aspect of spiritual formation. We learn both
by word and by imitation. "That is why we have cooking classes and
cooking demonstrations, as well as cookbooks," one social scientist
observed. "That is why we have apprenticeships, internship, student

tours, and on-the-job training as well as manuals and textbooks."[5] In redemption, God has given us both—a written and proclaimed Word to guide us, and the one-on-one apprenticeship of the body of Christ.

Jesus said bearing the cross would mean a willingness to walk away from father or mother, brothers or sisters. The early church was filled with people who had done just that. They were rejected by their parents and families for embracing a weird Middle-Eastern cult, for stepping outside of a culture where respect for the gods was an important part of patriotism. In any healthy church that is on mission, we should be seeing many more people who also have faced such rejection in their families. This does not mean they are without family, but that they have found a new one. When Peter said to Jesus that he had left everything to follow him (which certainly seemed to be true), Jesus responded, "Truly, I say to you, there is no one who has left house or brothers or sisters or mother or father or children or lands, for my sake and for the gospel, who will not receive a hundred-fold now in this time, houses and brothers and sisters and mothers and children and lands, with persecutions, and in the age to come eternal life" (Mark 10:29–30). We should expect persecution in this age, but we should also expect to find within the community of the cross a "hundredfold" the family we may have left behind.

That's in this present age. We have even more waiting for us in the life that is to come. Jesus' saying that in the resurrection there would be no marrying or giving in marriage but that we would be "like angels in heaven" (Mark 12:25) can yield a great deal of confusion. In fact, it can cause us to squirm, if we are honest. We want to go to heaven, but we see it as an uprooting of what really matters to us—friendships, family, relationships. That was what Jesus was undoing in his controversy with the Sadducees, in which he made the "no marriage in heaven" comment. These religious leaders, who did not believe in bodily resurrection, sought to trap him with a ridiculous scenario of a woman who married one brother after another, each dying. Will she be the wife of seven husbands in the new creation, they asked? They presupposed a view of the future that is not resurrection life but a kind of zombie existence—an extension of this age's priorities and callings into eternity. The calling of marrying and populating the earth will be over, because Jesus will have presented to his Father the full number of his human children. The universe will be alive with human life and human rule. Our impoverished view of the supernatural leads us to conclude that "angelic" existence means a lonely, passionless, static boredom. The angels, though, are ruling beings, "principalities and powers," who carry out a mission from God (Heb. 1:14). Our mission will change, but this change leads us into even more blessedness, not less. The family can be a vehicle for us to see Jesus, but Jesus is not a means to the end of family.

* * * *

Natural allegiances are strong, and strong for reasons designed by God. The pull of a fallen universe is to make those natural allegiances even stronger, into religions. There's a parallel here with patriotism, since the word *patriotism* comes from the root of the word for *father*. It is natural to love one's homeland. Patriotism is a good recognition of gratitude to God and to others for the blessings one has inherited as part of a country. Patriotism or nationalism when made ultimate, though, is ugly, violent, and even satanic. Those who are the best citizens of any earthly country are those who recognize that their citizenship in that country is not ultimate. There is a higher allegiance over the state. The problem with putting the nation—any nation—first, over the kingdom of God, is not just that such is idolatrous (the most important problem) but also that it is not, in fact, patriotic. Any state or tribe or village must have principles that transcend the body politic, and hold it accountable for its own ideals and aspirations. Where that is lost, one loses patriotism and sees it replaced with a cult.

The problem with putting family first, over the kingdom of God, is that we, first of all, replace a living God with the worship of ourselves, and, second, we lose the ability to be the kind of people who can love our families. The same is true with family. Love for family is not only good but also biblically mandated. When love of family becomes ultimate, though, it becomes, at best, Darwinist and atheistic.

If my friend, watching the churchgoers across the street from her coffee shop window, had heard that she would be welcome only if she were part of a nuclear family, she would have heard something other than the gospel of Jesus Christ. Fortunately, that church knew to offer her the gospel and nothing else. There are many like her, though, perhaps even now watching the church from a safe distance. Will they hear from us the good news that Jesus invites them, and us, into a family we never could have imagined, a family united through not the blood in our veins but the blood shed from his?

CHAPTER SIX

Man and Woman at the Cross

GROWING UP, I FOUND ESCAPE from the drive to achieve, perform, and behave in comic books. I resonated with superheroes, mostly because I longed for a fortress of solitude or a lair in an underground cave, for a secret identity where no one could demand my attention with a signal in the sky. I could identify with Kal-El of Krypton and Bruce Wayne of Gotham. Wonder Woman, though, I wanted to marry.

Looking back on that, my infatuation with the Amazon princess makes perfect sense: she is beautiful. She is undressed just enough to give the thrill of the forbidden to a Baptist adolescent, but not so much that he would feel guilty about it. I wonder, though, if there wasn't more to it. Unlike many of the real-life, grown-up women around me, she didn't demand anything from me—whether good grades or Bible memorization or a mowed lawn. She didn't need me to help her or protect her. She didn't need me at all. She was tough enough to take care of herself. That being the case, I was exactly the kind of boy for which Wonder Woman was created in the first place.

Wonder Woman was imagined by prominent psychologist William Moulton Marston, a progressive, early pioneer of feminism, with expertise in the mythologies of Greece and Rome. He thought comic books were morally damaging to children because of their "blood-curdling masculinity."[6] Maleness was domineering and violent, he argued, but boys could be given another option. "Give them an alluring woman stronger than themselves to submit to," he wrote, "and they'll be proud to become her willing slaves."[7] The result was Diana, a princess brimming with the mythos of Greek and Roman deities, a woman who lived on an island of powerful women, with no men, and thus no bloodshed or war. She was sent out into the world of men, to curb all the violence caused by that blood-curdling masculinity, with strength, wisdom, and a golden lasso that, like Marston's other invention, the polygraph, could make liars tell the truth. Unlike other women in comic books, she wasn't the wife or girlfriend or long-lost cousin of some male hero. She wasn't a stereotypical fainting weakling in need of rescue by a strong man. She hardly needed protecting, and was, in fact, here to protect men from what was scary about their own maleness.

I outgrew my infatuation with Wonder Woman, though I still admire her. Boys and girls (and men and women) do indeed need models of strong, dynamic, self-assured women. On that, Marston and the later feminists were right. Still, one would have to conclude that Wonder Woman sends some mixed signals. It's hard to imagine Wonder Woman as overweight or unattractive by the standards of Madison Avenue. In that sense, she seems to reinforce the cultural message that a woman's value is, at least in part, in whether she seems physically attractive to men, that the supermodels shall inherit the earth. Moreover, Wonder Woman almost couldn't exist if not for gender wars. Many men were indeed willing to become her slaves, if for no other reason than her ability to relieve them of the burdens culture puts on men to bear responsibility for the provision and protection of women. And women could, thankfully, see a picture of a woman who did not buckle under the sort of predatory male behavior that is, even after all these years, still ubiquitous in workplaces, and even in their own homes. Even in the twenty-first century, we still cannot find a Warrior Princess to fight for us, or an island to escape from the tensions and divisions that often show up between men and women, especially when those men and women are married to each other.

The apostle Paul knew about Wonder Woman. Or, rather, he knew about the mythological goddesses on which she was based, including a Greek deity named Artemis (or Diana). Ephesus, in Asia Minor, was renowned for a temple to this goddess. She represented both what were considered to be "hard" masculine qualities of hunting and war and the "soft" feminine qualities of fertility and childbearing. She was also quite useful to the male power structure in that seaport city. The gospel disrupted Ephesus because of the market instability of a silver industry that made figurines of the goddess, Artemis (Wonder Woman action figures, I guess one could say), which one would purchase seeking her blessings. The men leading this business knew that the kingship of Jesus would be a threat to the fertility cult, and thus a threat to their marketing strategy. Fearing the demise of the renown of the city, based on the temple's presence there and the worship of Artemis, the silversmiths whipped the crowds to chant over Paul's proclamation of the gospel, "Great is Artemis of the Ephesians," until the whole city was "filled with confusion" (Acts 19:28–29). In a culture like that one, perhaps just blocks away from that famous temple, the words of Paul's letter to the Ephesians—which he wrote to them from a prison cell sometime after his confrontation with the silversmiths—would have been read aloud probably by candlelight to a small gathering in some borrowed room.

Christians have rightly understood that the fifth chapter of Ephesians is crucial for understanding marriage, even when they have disagreed about precisely what the text means for husbands and wives. That's why verses from that chapter are read so often in wedding ceremonies. What we don't as readily perceive is that this chapter is about much more than marriage, and, in fact, is much bigger than just men and women.

Ephesians fits into a broader framework, one that the Ephesian silversmiths were right to see as a cosmos-rattling message. Part of our confusion is that we are accustomed to reading the Bible in chapters and verses. This is a helpful structure, enabling, for example, me to quickly reference a verse and for you to find it almost immediately. The letter read at Ephesus, though, would not have been chopped up into separate chapters and verses. We can unwittingly assume that the early chapters of Ephesians are the "deep" sections, dealing with such issues as predestination and God's sovereignty over the course of history and the plan of salvation, while the later chapters are the "practical" ones on everyday matters such as marriage and parenting. This is not the case. Ephesians did not come as disconnected "episodes" of teaching (". . . and that concludes tonight's study on Jew/Gentile unity. Join us next week as we turn to chapter four and talk about spiritual gifts."). Instead, the entire letter is one unfolding argument, about what the apostle called "the mystery of Christ" as the key to the meaning of the world. In this letter, God is disclosing something monumental, something Paul said had been hidden from previous generations and was now unveiled. The mystery is this, that God's purposes are seen in Christ, "as a plan for the fullness of time, to unite all things in him, things in heaven and things on earth" (Eph. 1:9–10). This mystery is further explained in the makeup and mission of the church, "that the Gentiles are fellow heirs, members of the same body, and partakers of the promise in Christ Jesus through the gospel" (Eph. 3:6).

In this mystery, we see that the gospel is not an afterthought rescue operation, but the point of all of created reality, from the beginning. Jesus is not a "Plan B" to set the universe back on track, but the blueprint and the end goal. And the divisions between Jewish and Gentile believers weren't just a miserable way to live together; those divisions preached an alternative gospel. The reconciliation of Jew and Gentile reveals the mystery of God's plan to save and unite his people in Christ. Paul told the congregation what this meant for marriage and, therefore, something about the way men and women should relate to one another.

The sentence above might prompt you wrongly to conclude that this assumes the text is teaching that marriage is normative. It is not. The apostle elsewhere tells us, as we have noted, that marriage is the concession in this age, and that celibacy is the default for those serving the church. You might also assume that discussing men and women in terms of marriage would imply that masculinity and femininity are defined only in terms of marriage. Again, this is not so. Men who never marry are men, and women who never marry are women, both in every sense of the word. In the first sight of a new baby, whether by ultrasound technology or in person, we say, "It's a Girl!" or "It's a Boy." We do not say, "It's going to be a woman one day if she finds a man," or vice versa.

Marriage informs us about something of the meaning of men and women not because it is intended for everyone but because this union is the one, first of all, where we see most intimately the relatedness of male to female. For example, in a passage obscure to most modern Christians, the apostle Paul discussed "head coverings" for women within the church (1 Cor. 11:1–16). As scholars of this era have argued, these coverings at that time culturally signified marriage, that a woman was not available for pursuit by some other man. The neglect of this symbol was forbidden by the apostle.

This would hardly seem relevant to our age since head coverings do not carry such a meaning (although other symbols do). But, at first glance, it would seem irrelevant even to those in the original context, who were not married, or for whom the symbol would otherwise not apply. And yet, even here, the teaching was about something much more broadly applicable and counter-cultural: the dependence of men and women on one another. We are not independent of one another, "for as woman was made from man, so man is now born of woman" (1 Cor. 11:12). The old slogan that a "woman needs a man like a fish needs a bicycle" is just not true.

The persistent myth of male superiority is undone by the fact that even the most bigoted misogynist first found life in the reproductive system of a woman, found his first habitat in the uterus of a woman. We need each other. That's not only true for married people, but marriage demonstrates it to everyone because all of us, whether ever married, come from a marriage or marriage-like union. When Jesus reminded us that "from the beginning of creation, 'God made them male and female,'" he was doing so in the context of a controversy about marriage (Mark 10:1–12), appealing to the first biblical reference we have to male and female, which is in the context of a marriage union.

* * * *

Marriage means something for the rest of the church, and for the world. Sometimes this highlights the goodness of both male and female and sometimes it highlights specifics of the marital covenant that should *not* be applied more generally to men and women. The typical way that these foundational New Testament texts on marriage are preached would, in fact, exclude the rest of the church, as they are presented as tips for happier, healthier "relationships." There's much more here.

The mystery of Christ, Paul revealed, explains why Genesis told us that "a man shall leave his father and mother and hold fast to his wife, and the two shall become one flesh" (Eph. 5:31). A person need not even accept the authority of Genesis to see that the principle here is true. Every generation thinks through sex education, in some form or another, for the next. But usually, this is not about convincing the next generation to have sex for the sake of the future of the human race. There's a powerful force at work, driving people toward sexual union, a force that sometimes makes us feel as though we are going crazy.

Human cultures through the millennia have had different cultural notions of what marriage should look like, but human cou-
pling is assumed in every culture everywhere. Every culture has love
songs. There's clearly a great "mystery" at work here, with mystery
not meaning something incomprehensible but instead meaning a
larger, cosmic force at work beyond mere individual companionship
structures or orgasm maintenance. Many in our day would explain
this "mystery" in terms of impersonal Darwinian drives for natural
selection. The Bible explains this mystery differently: "This mystery
is profound, and I am saying that it refers to Christ and the church"
(Eph. 5:32). We all know (to some degree) the "what" of marriage,
and believers know the "Who" behind it, but the mystery of Christ
tells us also the "why" of it all.

Christ and the church are not here presented as an illustration of
men and women in marriage. To say this would be as absurd as if I,
as a Baptist, were to argue with my friends who christen by sprinkling
that Jesus was crucified, buried, and raised from the dead in order
to teach us the proper mode of baptism. The argument is backward.
If not the other way around, it makes no sense at all—we baptize
because of Jesus' saving work, but he did not die so that we might
practice baptism.

The same applies to marriage. Christ and the church don't
illustrate marriage; marriage illustrates Christ and the church. God
embedded this sort of "one-flesh union" in nature not simply so that
humanity would proceed. He could, after all, have designed us to
individually subdivide like amoebae. He embedded it here as an icon
of a more foundational one-flesh union, that of the gospel. Critically,
the text here, as do others in the New Testament, addresses the entire
church, and then addresses specifically "wives" and "husbands" (not
husbands on how to make decisions for their wives). And the Spirit
did all of this in terms of the cross.

This is important because if we do not start with the truth of
a common humanity in the creation and in the crucifixion, we will
end up deifying gender distinctions in ways that harm one another

and lead us to worship a different God. In teaching the Galatian churches about our union with Jesus in the curse he bore and the life he gives from the cross, Paul concluded, "There is neither Jew nor Greek, there is neither slave nor free, there is no male and female, for you are all one in Christ Jesus" (Gal. 3:28). This does not mean that the cross obliterates the created order, an order that both Jesus and Paul elsewhere affirmed. Rather, this text defined the meaning of inheritance. The text continued: "And if you are Christ's, then you are Abraham's offspring, heirs according to promise" (Gal. 3:29). That's precisely what Paul argued was so shocking about the mystery of Christ. Whoever is in Christ is now a full recipient of the promises of God. Gentile Christians are not receiving anything less than Jewish Christians because they both receive the promises on the same basis: they are united to Jesus, as a head to a body, and thus "co-heirs" with him.

The same is true for both men and women (perhaps an even more shocking claim in a first-century context). Both Jews and Gentiles, both men and women, are considered "sons" in the context of inheritance. An inheritance, of course, went from father to son, usually the first-born son. A woman's share of an inheritance was derived from her marriage, which is why widows were especially economically threatened. In Christ, though, women as well as men will rule and reign in the new creation awaiting us. That's in harmony with the Old Testament witness, as both male and female are created in the image of God. This means not only that they bear equal dignity and worth (although that's clearly true), but also that they share the mission God has given to humanity over the creation. At the cross, God was reclaiming a mission and an inheritance for humanity, not just for men with their dependents brought along with them. Jesus did not offer his life-sacrifice for angelic beings, but only for human beings (Heb. 2:16). The division, in terms of the reconciling power of the gospel, is not between men and women, but between human and non-human.

In making a distinction between "wives" and "husbands" in Ephesians 5, and between "men and women" elsewhere in the Bible, the Scripture assumes that, along with our common humanity and our common destiny, there are some unique contributions of men as men and women as women. That can be controversial in some quarters, though it really should not be. Virtually everyone recognizes that there is some uniqueness to mothering as opposed to fathering. That's why earth religions of every age will appeal to the "Divine Feminine." They recognize something is distinct from a mother, and virtually always this is with some emphasis on life-giving and nurturing. The same principle shows up when political commentators speak of a "Daddy Party," emphasizing issues of national defense and personal responsibility, and a "Mommy Party," emphasizing a social safety-net and help for the vulnerable.[8] Even those who would argue that gender is merely a social construct make similar concessions. Setting aside the ethics of the transgender debate for a moment, the very claim that one is biologically male but truly female, or vice versa, with the need to present oneself as such, presupposes that there is some difference, beyond just social convention, to maleness and femaleness. And, however politically perilous it can be to make even the most basic of such claims, any doctor knows that injecting a woman with testosterone or a man with estrogen will have certain predictable results that map out along the lines of male and female differences.

In terms of the complementarity of male and female, Christians may disagree about exactly what this means in a variety of situations, but we should all recognize a complementarity in the creation mission, if for no other reason than that the "fruitful and multiply" command is fulfilled by both men and women—indeed they cannot undertake it without one another—though in different ways in the act of procreation. This is why the Bible refers to the primal woman as "helpmate" to the man. We tend to see this in a modern corporate sense, as though the woman is somewhere on the office flow-chart as Assistant to the Regional Manager. This is hardly the case. She is his helpmate not because she is below him but because he cannot carry out the mission before him alone. He must be joined to another, one who comes from his side. And there she is.

In every culture, there is the temptation to idolize or exaggerate male/female distinctions. Ruth was both a wife and mother and an agricultural worker. David was both a warrior and a harpist. The idea of men as exclusively "wild" or "warrior-like" or of women as exclusively "sensitive" or "relational" does not bring about gospel order but the opposite. One can often see this tendency in churches where, in some regions, the "men's ministries" are almost exclusively geared toward "wild-game dinners" celebrating hunting and "women's ministries" are almost exclusively geared toward how to set table-settings and plan tea parties. Is there a place for emphasizing both? Of course. But we must compose our categories of what it means to be a man and woman from Scripture not from cultural stereotypes. In some sectors of Christianity, Nimrod and Lamech would be categorized as 'masculine" while the command to turn the other cheek when struck would be deemed "feminine." In such cases, masculinity and femininity are defined by idols, not by the cross. A cross-shaped masculinity walks not with Esau's swagger but with Jacob's limp. A cross-shaped femininity comes not with the glamour of Potiphar's wife but with the Bible-teaching prowess of Eunice and Lois.

* * * *

There are differences between men and women that are tied up with the differences between mothering and fathering—and remember, all Christians are called to at least some aspects of spiritual parenting, within the church even when not within the family. We see this in our first parents. Adam is created from the earth, and his name signifies his origin in the dirt (Adam means "earth" in Hebrew). He is called to work the ground, but the curse frustrates his aspect of the mission at precisely this point. As Adam aims to cultivate the ground, it will bear thorns and thistles and produce only by the sweat of his brow. Conversely, Eve is created from the side of humanity, and she is named for the giving of life. Yet again, the curse frustrates her aspect of the mission by impeding the nurture of new life. Even here in the curse, we see patterns emerge that teach us about their callings as man and woman, and mother and father. But these reflect general patterns of giftedness and calling, not zero-sum categories. Ask yourself: Are men nurturing? Yes. Jesus is a man and compared himself to a mother hen gathering her chicks. Likewise, the apostle Paul was a man and compared himself to a woman in labor and a nursing mother. Are women called to provide and to protect? Yes. One would be advised not to tangle with Jael if unprepared to take a tent peg to the side of one's head. Moreover, the Proverbs 31 mother is not presented as receiving breakfast in bed on Mother's Day but as out making real estate deals.

Poet and essayist Wendell Berry notes the difference between sexual difference and sexual division. Often, we cannot tell the two apart. "A sexual difference is not a wound, or it need not be; a sexual division is," Berry writes. "And it is important to recognize that this division—this destroyed household that now stands between the sexes—is a wound that is suffered inescapably by both men and women."[9] Berry commends an idea of "husbandry" and "housewifery" that he argues can hardly be understood in a post-industrial world in which the words themselves hardly make sense. Berry is right that in a pre-industrial world it would be impossible to separate cultivation from nurturing in the work of a man, since his primary calling would be the husbanding of the earth or of livestock. Likewise, what Berry means by "housewifery" is far from a 1950s caricature of a woman isolated from the work of her husband and the rest of the family. This "degenerate housewifery," to use his term, is wrapped up in consumer culture, whether in the "traditional" woman whose value "lay in the wearing out or using up commodities" or in the woman who pursues the same sort of soulless careerism to which men long ago submitted themselves.[10] In a pre-industrial culture, though, "housewifery" was a complicated task of managing a household, more akin to a project manager than to an amateur interior decorator. I hold no illusions of returning to an agrarian economy, but we must understand what one looks like in order to see the actual differences in the household economy of the biblical world rather than embracing or reacting against a modern model that we might see as "traditional."

Very few people want to return to caricatured and exaggerated ideas of "roles" in marriage, but the loss of a sense of order and economy has been more costly than we would like to admit. Rigid patriarchy benefits men and hurts women; on that we can all agree. But it turns out that virtual matriarchy also turns out to benefit men and hurt women. A Christian social worker in a large Asian city told me recently about the hostility toward men she faces in working with women. The reason is that in her area male unemployment is widespread. Often, she said, the women work to support their families, entirely, while the men do little. The result is a kind of simmering rage among many of the women there. In many contexts, the idea of the "breadwinner" man replaced by the "breadwinner" woman results in the women doing almost everything they would do in a "traditional" arrangement while also bearing the burden of financial responsibility. Male unemployment is itself not a family crisis. The man who redirects his energies into finding new work is still displaying service and leadership, maybe even more than before. When male unemployment comes to be seen as routine, though, a crisis develops. In such situations, many women not only grapple with unimaginable stress but sometimes come to see a husband and a father to their children as just another dependent that few can afford. As she asks women in working class areas ravaged by male unemployment why they do not marry the fathers of their children, author Hanna Rosin found that many of them responded not with moral rejections of "family values" but with a shrug: "He would just be another mouth to feed."[11] Men in the modern age are often not viewed as leaders or as servants but as consumers—of food, beer, video games, or whatever. They are seen that way because, in many ways, that's what they have become. Without a revelatory compass to find identity, more and more men have surrendered simply to satisfying their urges, and staying out of the way.

Instead of flattening these aspects of vocation out, the Bible refers to them in general patterns. Do fathers generally emphasize one aspect of raising up the generation, and mothers another? Yes. That's typically true even in the non-human animal creation. Does this mean a man is not masculine when he cries with his daughter? By no means. Does this mean that a little girl is not "feminine" if she prefers riding a dirt bike to playing with dolls? Again, absolutely not. The distinctions in emphasis in the general calling of mothers and fathers in Scripture is similar to the differing gifts that God grants to the church in the New Testament. One person has the gift of evangelism, and another the gift of mercy. Does this mean that those without such gifts should not share their faith or leave the hurting to die in a ditch? Not at all. The one with the gift of evangelism not only complements those with other gifts; he also equips them to be evangelists. The one with the gift of mercy would bear special responsibility for organizing acts of mercy but would not do so alone but by, in some sense, equipping the rest of the church to show mercy. Likewise, in mothers and fathers, spiritual and literal, God embeds signs of a general pattern of the need for both male and female influence.

These distinctions are seen in the way the Bible, while usually addressing us generally as followers of Christ, will sometimes include specific instructions to men or to women, to mothers or to fathers, to husbands or to wives. Often these are speaking directly to temptations more common to one sex or the other—for example, for men to avoid brawling and quarreling (1 Tim. 2:8) or women to avoid seeing their worth in terms of costly apparel and external beauty (1 Tim. 2:9–10; 1 Pet. 3:3–4). This is not at all to say that there are not men who do not define themselves by their appearance to others; there certainly are. Nor does it mean that there are not women who are given to physical brute violence. I once attended a funeral where the ex-wife of the deceased could not attend by court order, because at the visitation the night before she had beaten the second wife senseless, right in front of the casket.

The Scripture does not dismiss these realities but addresses the general patterns of the way our callings as men or women can be twisted in one way or the other. Men are warned not only against passivity and refusal to take responsibility (1 Cor. 16:13), but also from the sort of hyper-masculinity that leads to aggression. Women are warned not only against signifying a lack of need for the male but also against the kind of hyper-femininity that sees a woman's worth in her sexual attractiveness to men rather than in cultivating "the hidden person of the heart . . . which in God's sight is very precious" (1 Pet 3:3–4). In all of this, God's ultimate goal is not to make us "real men" and "real women" so much as it is to drive us away from the self and toward one another, toward the cross. It is here that the writings of Paul for wives to "submit to your own husbands as to the Lord" and for men "to love your wives as Christ loved the church" are of key importance, not only in the economy of a marriage but for the whole church to grasp the meaning of the gospel.

* * * *

The language of submission in reference to wives is controversial, and not just for those outside the church. I once heard a Christian react negatively to a statement that was more or less a direct quote of Ephesians 5:22 as a "Neanderthal idea" (thus holding to, I suppose, an early dating of the New Testament epistles). Part of this is because we tend to define what the Bible calls *submission* and *headship* in terms of power rather than in terms of the cross. Throughout the Scriptures, we are told that we will "reign with Christ." In the cosmic unveiling of Revelation 20, we see thrones of those who rule with the ascended Messiah. Sometimes this is jarring for people when they first recognize what it means to be "joint-heirs with Christ," as though somehow the uniqueness of Jesus is eclipsed by that reality. And yet, the message that we, as redeemed sinners, will reign with Christ is all about what it means to have been conformed to him through the sanctifying of our minds, our souls, our affections, our wills. The reign of believers with Christ is not akin to that of a city council meeting, with debates and filibusters and compromises. The Head is seamless from the body. We share the mind of Christ (1 Cor. 2:16). His purposes are now our purposes; his priorities are now our priorities. This differs, of course, from the sort of unity we see in a marriage, because Jesus is the sinless Lord, and none of us are. We do not have dominion over one another, even when we are responsible to lead. The point though is that this sort of joint-reign is possible because of organic unity. Hierarchy and mutuality are not opposed to one another. Submission, then, in Ephesians 5 and elsewhere is not presented in terms of unblinking obedience but in terms of seeking to respect and to cultivate the spiritual accountability of one's husband. The controversial part of this passage to those who first heard it would not be submission and headship but rather how the gospel radically redefined those terms, and limited them. First of all, Paul used the language of "wives" here, as did Peter elsewhere (1 Pet. 3:1). He does not, as did many others in the Roman ecosystem, view wives as the property of their husbands. Moreover, the Scripture demolishes the idea that women, in general, are to be submissive to men, in general, an attitude that too often persists both within the church and without.

In saying that wives should be submissive to their own husbands, Paul is not creating some new category of submission but rather demolishing a myriad of other categories of submission. Women are to submit to "their own husbands." Submitting to men in general would, in fact, render it impossible for a woman to submit to her own husband. Every act of submission includes at least one other act of refusal to submit. Eve's problem was not that she was unsubmissive, but that she was *too* submissive, submitting her future to the direction of the Serpent. Mary announced herself to be submissive to God's

will, which meant she refused to submit to Herod. The freedom of
the gospel means that we submit "to one another out of reverence for
Christ" (Eph. 5:21) and, at the same time, means that we "do not
submit again to a yoke of slavery" (Gal. 5:1). Women are never called
to submit to "guys" or to "boyfriends" or "lovers," or to men because
they are men. Rather, a wife rejects all other claims in order to cleave
to her own husband. A cross-shaped marriage is one in which a wife
cultivates a voluntary attitude of recognition toward godly leadership.
This is not docility or servitude. Abigail's refusal to empower her
"worthless" husband Nabal in his sin against the House of David is
presented in Scripture as fidelity to God (1 Sam. 25:14–42). A woman
once told me that her husband read Ephesians 5 to her in seeking to
persuade her to open their marriage up to a three-way sexual encounter. This would be laughable if it were not such a tragic twisting of
Scripture for self-pleasure. This wife's responsibility would be to call
him to repentance—following all the steps of Matthew 18 should he
not.

Likewise, "headship" in Scripture is not defined in terms of
Pharaoh-like rule but Christlike sacrifice. Men and women are given
dominion, over the creation around them, but they are never given
dominion over one another. A wife submits to her husband, Paul
wrote, "as the church submits to Christ" (Eph. 5:24). In order then
to know what that means we must look not to sociobiology or to
gender-war power struggles but to the way Jesus leads the church.
"Greater love has no one than this, that someone lay down his life
for his friends," Jesus said. "No longer do I call you servants, for the
servant does not know what his master is doing; but I have called you
friends" (John 15:13, 15). Headship does not refer to power but to
responsibility. A man who accepts the calling of husband and father
bears a special accountability for the spiritual direction of his future
family. This does not mean that a mother bears no responsibility (far
from it), any more than it means a father does not nurture. Rather,
the father is to be a visible sign of responsibility. As historian Robert
Godfrey puts it, humanity in a biblical rendering of the world has a

representative function which often seems odd to us in our ecosystem of individualism, but which "promotes a culture in which leaders represent and are responsible for the communities they lead."[12]

A husband's headship is not "Woman, get me my chips," nor is it, in a more sanctified version, "Blessed wife, please get my chips and then let's pray." In fact, it is the exact reverse of that. Headship is about crucifying power and privilege in order to love one's wife "as Christ loved the church and gave himself for her, that he might sanctify her, having cleansed her by the washing of water with the word, so that he might present the church to himself in splendor, without spot or wrinkle or any such thing, that she might be holy and without blemish" (Eph. 5:25–27).

How does Christ love and lead his church in these ways? He does so by laying down his own life to the point of crucifixion. A husband's leadership is about a special accountability for sabotaging his own wants and appetites with a forward-looking plan for the best interest of his wife and children. Headship is not about having one's laundry washed or one's meals cooked or one's sexual drives met, but rather about constantly evaluating how to step up first to lay one's life down for one's family. Headship will not seem often to the outside world to be "being the head of one's house" at all. Headship will look, in many cases, like weakness. So does the cross.

As a matter of fact, God prepared his people for this aspect of the cross by revealing himself over and over again as someone quite different from Baal. Rabbi Jonathan Sacks rightly notes the way that "Baal" meaning "master" was connected to, among other things, the idea of husbands "ruling" over their wives by the domination of force. God revealed to Hosea that he would not be called "Baal" by his people but instead would be called "my husband." The difference is profound: "For Hosea, at the core of Baal worship is the primitive idea that God rules the world by force, as husbands rule families in societies where power determines the structures of relationships," Sacks argues. "Against this, Hosea paints quite a different possibility, of a relationship between marriage partners built on love and mutual loyalty. God is not *Baal*, he-who-rules-by-force, but *Ish*, He-who-relates-in-love, the very word Adam used when he first saw Eve."[13]

Now, to be sure, this requires genuine leadership. Some Christian men passively watch all that goes on around them in their homes from the comfort of a reclining chair, and deem themselves "servant leaders," as though "servant" in Scripture means disengagement. Jesus gives himself up for his church. Jesus washes his church with water. The church did not, initially, see the need for either. When Jesus set his face for Jerusalem, Simon Peter, a foundation stone of his church, objected, saying that never would he allow Jesus to be handed over to crucifixion (Matt. 16:22). When the time came for the trek to Skull Place, Peter sought to fight it off with a sword (Matt. 27:51). Jesus responded to these events not with an exercise of dominion but with teaching of why the cross was necessary (Matt. 16:21, 24–28; 27:52–54). The "washing of water" language in the text arises from the prophetic promise that God would "sprinkle water" upon his people, cleansing them for life in the new covenant (Ezek. 16:9; 36:25), a priestly act anticipated in the ceremonies of the sacrificial system (Lev. 8:6–7). When Jesus bathed his church with water in the upper room before his death, once again the church did not see the need. Simon Peter objected to washing, but Jesus did not respond passive-aggressively, walking away resentfully. Nor did Jesus respond with raw sovereignty, pushing Peter's feet into the water. Once again, he gently taught (John 13:5–12).

A man does not exercise headship by giving directions and serving himself but by planning to pour himself out for the best interest of his family. A man is "head of his household" not when he "tells" his wife what to do but when he, for instance, crucifies his pornography addiction, seeking help to do so, not simply because he is looking out for his own soul but also because he loves his wife and wants what's best for her. One of the clearest examples of headship I ever saw was a husband who recognized that his wife was depressed because she wanted children but could see no way forward to be a mother. She was nearing the biological limits for conception, and she had a massive student debt from medical school. She could pay off the debt but only by years of round-the-clock work at her profession, leaving her with little time, in her mind, to be a mother. Her husband did not come up with orders for her. Rather, he listened to her fears and hopes, and worked to bear the burden on himself, to come up with a plan to pay the debt while empowering his wife to be the mother she believed God was calling her to be.

The fact that we see this language of headship in Scripture as being about "who is in charge of whom," instead of what it is, a question of where the primary burden of self-sacrifice falls, tells us much more about our own selfish inclinations than it tells us about the gospel. All leadership in Scripture is different from that of the world—instead of Roman "benefactors" who give orders, Jesus said, the heirs of the kingdom serve one another, and lay down their lives for one another (Luke 22:24–30). We have, after all, been purchased by a cross and are walking forward by the power of the cross.

We also sometimes misunderstand why the Scripture speaks in this way, wrongly assuming that the Bible is caught in a retrograde, patriarchal way of seeing the family. If by patriarchy one means the rule of women by men, then the household codes of the New Testament are decisively anti-patriarchal, and much more anti-patriarchal than the secularized atmosphere around us in the modern age. For instance, sociologist Rodney Stark demonstrates that first-century Christianity was so empowering of and attractive to women that in 370 Emperor Valentinian issued a decree to the pope demanding that Christian missionaries stop evangelizing in the homes of women. This was because, Stark argues, women were most likely to convert to the new faith since, among other reasons, "within the Christian subculture women enjoyed far higher status than did women in the Greco-Roman world at large."[14]

Our society has made in many ways great strides in recent years in recognizing the equality and dignity of women. Note, for instance, the different attitudes, at least in terms of ideals, toward sexual harassment now as opposed to even just a few decades ago.

And yet, look at the ways in which women are brutalized in repressive regimes around the world, and sexualized and objectified even in the most so-called "progressive" societies. What has gone wrong when a major malady facing young women are eating disorders and the quest to look as thin as the models in popular media? Is it really empowering to women when young girls are pressured toward the sort of sexual availability previously demanded by the worst manifestations of masculinity? What is wrong when an era is characterized by sexual assault, trafficking of women and girls, and a popular culture in which the boasting by men of their sexual prowess over women is tolerated and even celebrated? This is a predatory patriarchy worthy of a Bronze Age warlord.

* * * *

In this present darkness, *masculinity* is often defined as "winning"—whether in terms of sexual conquest or physical domination of another or economic advancement. This is hardly new, but goes all the way back to Lamech's prehistoric song boasting of his many women and the vengeance he enacted on his enemies. A wounded and insecurely held sense of masculinity often becomes a weaponized masculinity, as one seeks to prove one's "manhood" against all challengers, to "win" at all costs. And yet, Jesus does not "win" at all by such a definition. He loses. He does not, though, lose intentionally. "No one takes it [my life] from me, but I lay it down," he said (John 10:18). Unlike the fragile masculinity of those who overcompensate with theatrical toughness, Jesus had full confidence in his identity and his future, enough that he could plan to win by losing, by offering himself up for his church. A man who keeps his vows to his wife, who prays with his children, who visits the lonely, who shelters the poor, who serves his church, is more masculine than someone who can outfight everyone in the bar or out-orgasm his fraternity with countless women.

It would be bad enough if the exploitation of women by men were simply happening "out there" in the world outside. But such exploitation of women happens often within the church itself. The apostle Paul warned about wolf-like men who creep into the church, using women for their own carnal whims (2 Tim. 3:1–9; 2 Pet. 2:21–22). The sexual abuse of women and children by men within the church is one of the most horrific scandals in the history of Christianity. Those who cover up or remain silent in the face of such terror are not just accomplices to injustice but also are those who have embraced a different gospel from the gospel of Jesus Christ. A man who would say that a woman should "submit" to his abuse or exploitation, whether married or not, is akin to a government that exalts itself to godhood in harming the people (Rev. 13) and like such a regime should be resisted. The church should teach girls from a very young age that such abuse should result in, where possible, a leaving of the situation and the reporting of any misconduct to both the church and to the civil authorities. Jesus does not abuse or exploit his church. Any claim that such is an aspect of "headship" points to the devil and not to the gospel.

That's precisely why the Scripture speaks the way it does about the relationship between men and women, as highlighted in the covenant of marriage. In every culture, everywhere in this fallen world, the relative physical strength of men and the biological demands of childbearing and nurturing, have meant that when men are not intentionally self-sacrificial, women and children will be the hardest hit. That's what the apostle Peter meant when he wrote to men: "Likewise, husbands, live with your wives in an understanding way, showing honor to the woman as the weaker vessel" (1 Pet. 3:7). This does not mean inferiority, nor does it refer to the stereotypes of women as exhibiting emotional or mental fragility. Weakness is, remember, not a negative characteristic in a cross-shaped perspective. Vulnerability is not inferiority but is instead right at the heart of the most powerful reality in the universe: the crucified Christ who triumphs through vulnerability and leads us to find strength in our weakness (2 Cor. 12:9–10; 13:3–4). What Peter refers to here is also not saying that every woman is physically weaker than every man (which is obviously not the case). Instead, he means what we have outlined here, that women can be especially vulnerable to physical, sexual, social, or economic harm.

This also does not refer to some sort of chivalric noblesse oblige on the part of men. How often in churches do we hear men praised as having "married up," or hear phrases like "Thank goodness their baby looks like his mother" in ways we would never hear in reverse? In many cases, this turns out not to honor the woman in view but instead patronizes and condescends. The Bible, though, says that a man who shows honor to his wife does so "since they are heirs with you of the grace of life" (1 Pet. 3:7). Once again, the point goes back to the common mission men and women share in the image of God, and to which we are destined in the age to come. We relate to one another, then, neither in a way that flattens out our differences nor in a way that overinflates them. We are created for cooperation and for complementarity. We do this not through the will-to-power but through the way of the cross.

The mystery of Christ is seen in that, in marriage, the man and the woman are to be "one-flesh," united as a head is with a body. Christ and his church at the cross are not a contractual transaction but a covenant union. When Jesus appeared to Saul of Tarsus on the Damascus Road, his question was not, "Saul, Saul, why are you perse-cuting an organization that affirms my doctrinal principles?" or "Saul, Saul why are you persecuting a coalition that upholds my values?" His question was, "Saul, Saul, why are you persecuting *me*?" (Acts 22:7, emphasis added). The self-sacrificial love of a husband for his wife is not especially heroic since "he who loves his wife loves himself," since "no one ever hated his own flesh, but nourishes it and cherishes it, just as Christ does the church, because we are members of his body" (Eph. 5:28–30). No one is going to be commended for being so sensitive to his stomach's rumblings that he provides it with nutrition. "Look at how this man so cares for his belly! Like a mother bird, he took a hard crust of bread, tore it apart with his mouth, mashed it up, and plunged it through his esophagus in order to get nutrients to his bloodstream!" No one would applaud someone for taking a shower. "Look at how tenderly he caressed his skin with the soap, wiping away all of the grime!" No. He was hungry and he ate. He was dirty and he bathed. To do anything else would be self-loathing and self-sabotage. That's exactly the point. To say that a husband and wife are like a head and a body is not to say "head" as we typically think of "head of state," but, more literally, as a head with a body. Marriage, then, is not to be a Darwinian power struggle with the man asserting himself and the woman going along, or vice versa. Again, this is not a business model or a corporate flow-chart or a political arrangement, but rather an organic unity—"one-flesh." The more a husband and wife are sanctified together in the Word, the more they, like the nervous system and the limbs and organs of a human body, will move and operate smoothly, effortlessly, holistically. In so doing, the marriage will point away from itself, toward the blueprint after which it was modeled, the gospel union of Christ and his church.

That's one of the reasons marriage is important to everyone in the church, not just to those who are or who will be married. You would not refuse to read a Bible-verse banner on the wall of your church just because it wasn't addressed by name to you. Marriage is a picture to the whole church of what it means to see Jesus and his people joined by the cross. Not everyone will be a mother or a father but everyone will be called to model mothering or fathering within the community of the kingdom. Not everyone is called to marriage, but everyone is called to the gospel. Marriage matters then for everyone because marriage is not just about marriage. Marriage is about the cross.

* * * *

Years ago, a newspaper columnist known for his many marriages, divorces, and remarriages announced that he was giving up, at long last, on matrimony. He said he wasn't going to look for another wife, but rather would cut out the middle-step and save himself the time and trouble. "I'm just going to find a woman who hates me and buy her a house," he quipped.[15] This comment elicited the expected laughter, despite the obvious tragedy of his personal life, because the words rang true to a culture rife with conflict between men and women.

The seeming universality of these tensions is seen in their most innocuous form in jokes, present in almost every culture, about women who are late for everything or about men who can't clean up after themselves or whatever the stereotype of the moment is. But these tensions run into much, much darker territory, territory that often is whistled past with humor. The divorce culture is one obvious example of men and women in conflict, as marriages are ripped asunder and the custody of children fought over in law courts in virtually every city, town, or village on the planet. Even beyond this, though, many of the mores of the Sexual Revolution—meant to liberate us—are really thinly veiled self-protecting mechanisms for men and women who, at best, don't trust one another and, at worst, want to exploit one another. Far from merging into some sort of unisex utopia, men and women often find it near impossible to give themselves fully to the other, and, as sex distinctions are said to be meaningless, sex distinctions become all-consuming badges of identity. Even worse is the violence and devastation, present again in virtually every culture, that causes many to wonder if there is, in fact, something inherently dangerous about a "bloodcurdling masculinity."

Is it any wonder that whether in ancient Ephesus or modern El Paso, our imaginations can sometimes long for an occasional idealized mythic figure who can not only fend for herself but also represent the dignity and equality of women? Is it any wonder that we sometimes long for a hero who can represent the best ideals of masculinity and femininity, alone, without the often-grueling work of community? In such a scenario, women would not be vulnerable to hurt from men, and men would not be burdened with responsibility outside of themselves. This is not, though, the answer. Our lives as men and women should remind us that we need another. Our lives as men and women should remind us that Christ and his church are not in competition with one another, not hiding from one another, protecting themselves from one another. Our lives as men and women should remind us that all of history is moving toward the church, coming down from heaven "as a bride adorned for her husband" (Rev. 21:2). The universe is hurtling toward not a corporate boardroom or an amusement park but toward a Wedding Feast.

Chapter Seven
Marriage and the Mystery of Christ

OUR HONEYMOON WAS A DEBACLE. I should have sensed some trouble coming when I woke up on our wedding day with severe laryngitis. I felt powerless and frustrated. I kept practicing the words, "I Russell Moore, take thee, Maria Hanna . . ." but to no avail. I croaked them out with the wheezing rasp of an emphysema patient in an oxygen tent. Normally, Maria would have been the one to reassure me through something worrying me, but I'm a stickler for tradition. I wasn't going to see the bride before the wedding. I went through boxes of throat lozenges and endless cups of herbal tea, and just in time for the ceremony, my voice came back. It seemed that all was now made right, but then there was the honeymoon.

If social media had existed at the time, now over twenty years ago, I am quite sure that most of our friends would have assumed we were having an idyllic time from the photographs we would have posted. But we were miserable. First of all, we were both exhausted. The hubbub of the wedding was frenzied enough, but then the day of the rehearsal a guest had her feelings hurt and threatened to "get sick" and boycott the wedding. Moreover, we were both starting new jobs the Monday after the honeymoon. We were moving into a rented house together the same week. But, most of all, we were exhausted because the honeymoon meant way too much to us. We were both sexually inexperienced and very much in love so, well, I will just say this was not just a trip for us. My new wife expected that this would be something akin to a scene from the final narrative arc of a romantic comedy. I expected it to be akin to a scene from a documentary about mating rabbits. But then we both fell sick—not "sick" as in the theatrics of our family member, but sick, for real.

I had picked up a virus while Maria had some sort of allergic reaction (not to me) that became serious enough to land her, for a time, in the emergency room of a local hospital. As I waited in line at a pharmacy for antibiotics for us both, I started to grow resentful. We spent a lot of money that we really couldn't afford for this trip. But more than that, my mood was darkening because I saw this as a ruined start to a life together. Yes, we had consummated the marriage, but not frankly to the degree that I expected. There was only so much togetherness one could hope for when one of us was in a hospital bed. I kept ruminating on how this was going to ruin all the memories we were supposed to be making. Wouldn't we want, when we were celebrating our silver or golden anniversaries, to remember moonlight walks and gondola rides, instead of watching one another vomit? "If this is the honeymoon," I said, "what will the marriage be like?"

My spirits lifted somewhat as we were distracted by our unromantic plight and I focused on solving some basic problems. She was much sicker than I, so I tried to care for her, bringing her a can of chicken soup and then trying to find a way to open it without a can-opener, and to serve it without a spoon. By the end of the trip, we were laughing about how we had failed at the easiest part of marriage. It would all be up from here, we joked. This turned out to be, in fact, the case.

In the years since, we have faced far more serious crises, of course, than a pratfall of a honeymoon. We weathered infertility together. We ventured to a Russian orphanage to adopt two sons together, not knowing what to expect there, or afterward. We reared five sons. We've listened as some people railed at me as a "right-wing extremist" and others blasted me as a "closet liberal." We've grieved at the graves of loved ones. And we've faced things I wouldn't even want to write about it here because they are still too emotionally raw. But we have never gone through any of this alienated from each other.

Somehow we came up with an unspoken rule that we would not both go crazy at the same time. When Maria saw me sinking into a depression or buckling under anxiety, she achieved a kind of preternatural calm, and I did the same for her. Sometimes we would exchange places as the stable one in a matter of seconds. I credit that cursed honeymoon for all of that. The opening days of our marriage served, despite our best efforts, not as an escape from our lives but as a prelude to our singular life as a married couple. I expected the honeymoon to be about becoming one flesh, but I subconsciously defined this merely in terms of sexual acrobatics when it turned out, by God's good providence, to be a baby step toward a far more comprehensive joining of psyches and affections, not just bodies. Our honeymoon was ruined, and that just might have saved our marriage.

* * * *

When it comes to marriage, the idea of honeymoon haunts the modern consciousness, whether we know it or not. Some streams of the Sexual Revolution assumed that marriage was an outmoded social construct or, even worse, an oppressive institution serving to repress humanity's sexual freedom. In some ways, of course, marriage has declined dramatically in recent years. Cohabitation rates have gone up, and the median age of marriage seems to be older every year. At the same time, though, note what has happened to the wedding industry and to the cultural norms associated with weddings. Proposals are now often much more dramatized than a man getting on bended knee with a ring. Instead, the proposals are often choreographed, with family and friends hidden away to surprise the new bride-elect with a party after the ask, all with a photographer in tow. In the classes that can afford it, it's not uncommon to see "destination weddings," in which family and friends are expected to travel to some exotic locale for the perfectly photographable event.

It is quite common to hear ministers (and I am one of them) who will say that they would rather do a funeral than a wedding. This is because no pastor has been vilified at a funeral by the mother-of-the-corpse. Weddings are often fraught with tension precisely because they are so idealized. If something goes wrong at the wedding, the idea is that the one perfect day that frames one's entire life is jeopardized. This idealized view of marriage is not just an issue for those who marry. Some who are called by God to a life apart from marriage can sometimes fight resentment of their circumstances, or even envy of married couples, because they, too, have accommodated to the idea that finding "the One" is what will make life complete and endlessly happy.

A Christian vision of marriage, though, can neither denigrate marriage nor idealize it. If a marriage is what the Bible tells us it is, then marriage is not a vehicle for self-actualization. If we see it as such, we will be disillusioned and disappointed. Marriage is an embedded picture of the gospel, a gospel tract.

Marriage is important and can be joyful and life-affirming but only if seen in the context of the gospel, which means within the context of the cross. One of the biggest obstacles to marriage, and to marital happiness, is the search for the ideal—the ideal spouse, the ideal relationship, the ideal marriage. This is, in reality, a form of selfishness. One invests in one's marriage the ability to serve one's own needs. It is only, though, when one focuses away from self on the other that one can find happiness and contentment. Such comes, the gospel tells us, through uniting together, becoming one flesh. A cross-shaped marriage defines this unity in different ways than the world does. If we reflect on the gospel, we will see that a marriage that reflects this good news will look something like the gospel itself. Love will be defined both in terms of its objective fidelity and in terms of its subjective intimacy. A cross-shaped marriage, like a cross-shaped gospel, is defined by both covenant and connection.

To see why this is important, think of the gospel that saved us. On the one hand, the gospel is, to use Martin Luther's language, entirely outside of us. We stand before God not on the basis of our own works or worthiness but on the basis of God's faithfulness to his own promises. When God's people show themselves to be unworthy representatives of his character and mission, he does not toss them aside, but appeals to the promises he made, objectively in history. When Israel constructed the image of a golden calf to worship, Moses reminded God, "Remember Abraham, Isaac, and Israel, your servants, to whom you swore by your own self," and God relented of destroying the people (Exod. 32:13–14). In a similar pattern, we stand before God now because of the objective reality of God's covenant seen in the life, death, resurrection, and ongoing priesthood of Jesus Christ. The gospel, though, does not just come to us in terms of covenant fidelity but also in terms of a connectional intimacy. We are joined to Christ, as a body to a head, and he lives through us. We not only benefit from his love for us at the cross, but we, as his Spirit dwells within us, learn to love him and to love what he loves. We see something of the same reality in marriage. In both covenant and connection, we see a skirmish, fighting against our own selfishness to become one with another.

With marriage, covenant comes first. Wedding ceremonies differ throughout time and place, with different cultures signifying the union in different ways. In every culture, though, there is some sort of vow of fidelity between husband and wife. At first glance, this seems rather uncontroversial. After all, with all of our disputes over sex and marriage in contemporary Western culture, most people can agree on at least the idea of fidelity. Most people, even those who disparage monogamy, don't like the idea of one partner deceiving another or of breaking commitments to one another. And yet, the idea of love as covenant union is more disputed than we might think, and not just outside of the church.

Having mentioned earlier that one of my besetting sins is a sense of finding my identity in others' approval, in being liked by people, it is quite apparent that my high school guidance counselor should have warned me away from this vocation. Every day I deal with religion, culture, and politics—with some of the most incendiary questions of the day. And yet, the most controversial thing I ever say is usually not in a television debate about some "culture war" issue but instead is in my office when I talk to a couple about their wedding. Sometimes the controversy is because I won't officiate at a wedding I believe would cause me to violate my conscience (a believer to an unbeliever, for instance). Sometimes the blowback comes because I won't allow the wedding party to trivialize the occasion by, say, swinging at a piñata of the bride and groom during the ceremony or for the father of the bride to threaten publicly to shoot the groom should he ever cheat on his little girl (and, yes, that happened one time). Usually, though, the controversy arises when I tell the couple that they won't be writing their own vows. Sometimes this results in a huffing away of the couple. How dare I tell them they can't construct their own vows when this is their ceremony? And yet, that's the point. This is not, in fact, their ceremony.

A man and a woman do not innovate their own covenant vows because, apart from the rest of the community, they do not know what vows to make. Sure, they can speak of how much they love one another, how much they look forward to spending the rest of their lives together, but the primary purpose of covenant vows is not in reference to one's feelings in the moment but to one's commitment in the face of the unpredictable and the unimaginable. No one will step forward from a future time line to tell a couple that the husband will one day be asked to shepherd his wife through chemotherapy for her breast cancer or to announce that one day the couple will see their house foreclosed on and repossessed by the mortgage company or that one day the couple will spend their life savings not on their retirement or on a cruise around the world but on their son's drug rehabilitation programs. Those who have gone before testify of all the possibilities, both good and bad. In marriage, a man and a woman vow before witnesses, "no matter what happens, I'm with her; I'm with him." That is an objective vow that is completely independent of the particular circumstances of the couple. A friend of mine often tells newly engaged couples that the most important things about their wedding will not be what makes it different from everyone else's wedding but what makes it the same.

A ceremony—regardless of how big or how small—is not a party for the couple, celebrating their individualized love. The ceremony, of whatever sort, is a covenantal act. Those gathered are not an audience but witnesses. This is why in many wedding ceremonies we still have a feature that makes little sense given our cultural presuppositions. It is like the concept of a vestigial organ, serving no purpose but pointing back to a need in a previous stage in evolutionary history. I am referring of course to the time when, in many ceremonies, the officiating minister says, "If anyone can show just cause why this man and this woman should not be joined together, let him speak now or forever hold his peace." No one expects anyone to actually stand up and object (even if everyone in the room thinks the pairing is a bad idea). The closest we could come to imagining such a scenario would be in some clichéd film in which an old boyfriend stands up and asks the bride to run off and marry him instead. And yet this piece is crucial. The state issues a wedding license as a way of saying that there will be civil consequences for fraudulently making these vows (by, say, being already married to someone else or by being brother and sister) and civil consequences for breaking these vows (even if that is only the necessity to file the paperwork for a divorce). In a Christian marriage, the gathered witnesses are a sign that the church is here to hold the couple accountable to their vows before God. The marriage is not just about the couple but about the gospel. This means the marriage is the business of the whole church.

This accountability refers, first of all, to the covenant aspect of the one-flesh union: the vow to fidelity and to permanence. Covenant fidelity means that "what God has joined together, let no one put asunder." Just as Jesus has given to us signs of his covenant with the church in baptism and in the Lord's Supper, pointing us back to something he objectively did for us in joining us to himself in his atoning work, marriage is an ongoing commitment to be one flesh, regardless of what forces would seek to tear us apart from one another. That does not mean simply sexual fidelity (although it does of course mean that), but a fidelity to actively love each other, no matter the cost, "as Christ loved the church and gave himself up for her" (Eph. 5:25).

Several years ago, I happened upon a clip of a television evangelist answering questions written in from his audience. A desperate man sent along his dilemma: his wife had dementia, advanced to the point that she couldn't recognize him, but the man wanted to date other women. This seemed to be a simple answer for a confessional evangelical, as "You shall not commit adultery" is not a complicated matter of biblical interpretation. I was stunned when the Christian talk-show host told the man he should first divorce his wife, before dating the new woman. The wife, the preacher said, is "not there" anymore.

This was more than an embarrassment. This was more than cruelty. This was a repudiation of the gospel of Jesus Christ. Of course, his logic would seem to make sense. He is right that the sick woman won't know if her husband is at dinner with someone else. She wouldn't know she's divorced. In that sense, she's not there. That makes sense, and that's the problem. To step away from this wife, to whom this man had vowed his life before God, is to project a different mystery—that of a man who loves his own flesh but not his bride, of a Christ who will not carry a cross for his people. This is not just bad marriage advice, but a bad gospel. I do understand why a man would be tempted to walk away from his dementia-riddled wife. Someone with this sort of debilitating disease cannot do anything for her husband. There's no romance, no sex, no partnership, not even companionship. If marriage is just a sum of these parts, then why wouldn't you leave when they're gone?

Jesus had a bride who did not recognize him anymore. She forgot who she was—and denied who he was. The bride of Christ fled his side, and went back to her old way of life. Jesus did not divorce her. He did not leave her behind. When Jesus came to his church after his resurrection, the church was about the same things the members of it were doing when they met Jesus in the first place: out on the boats, nets in hand. Jesus didn't walk away. He stood by his words, stood by his bride. He walked out to the Place of the Skull, to the valley of Sheol, and indeed beyond it, all for his bride. Marriage is to reflect this, and as it does so, to point us all back to the Christ who is present in the vulnerable, in the marginalized, in the "least of these."

Sometimes, though, Christians will come to marriage with a kind of implied prenuptial agreement, of what to do if the marriage doesn't meet one's needs and wants. It may never be spoken, but many couples have a secret nuclear arsenal—the possibility of divorce—that they hope never to use except the way that most countries use their nuclear arsenal, as a deterrent against getting hurt by the other party. In other words, "I promise not to divorce you, as long as I can live with you." This contractual view of marriage is not, however, that of the Christian gospel. It makes as little sense as a contract between one's mouth and one's stomach stipulating how the stomach will retaliate should the mouth withhold nutrients. If in fact a couple are joined together as one flesh, a preordained exit strategy—even if unspoken—is little more than a pre-negotiated divorce. If divorce is a possibility for you, you will find a reason to pursue it. Your spouse will not meet all of your expectations, and you will not meet your spouse's expectations. You probably have not (I hope) planned out how you would take care of your financial assets should you murder your spouse. Why not? After all, sometimes murders happen in marriages. You don't plan out these contingencies because murdering your spouse should be unthinkable. Sadly, tearing asunder the one-flesh union is all too thinkable, even for many Christians. Such is not the case if we see ourselves as one flesh, joined together by covenant.

This covenant is renewed by memory. Notice how often in the Scripture we are told to "remember" what God has done objectively for us. The children of Israel are told, when it seems that God has abandoned them, to remember that he delivered them from Egypt. When walking through the valley of the shadow of death, David remembers the rod and staff of his good shepherd. When tempted to slide back into idolatry and a wasted life, Christians are told to remember that we are not our own but are bought with a price. That is true with the gospel, and it is true also with marriage. Every marriage will hit crises—someone will get sick, someone will be fired, someone will cheat, or any number of possibilities. The memory of the covenant, of the gospel mystery of marriage, is what it takes for us to fight when the world, the flesh, and the devil threaten to tear us apart.

* * * *

With covenant must come connection. Love—biblically defined—is both active and affectional. In Jesus' parable of what it means to love neighbor, the Samaritan is moved with compassion—he feels—when he sees the beaten man on the side of the road and, at the same time, he actively serves him. Christ loved his church, but loved in an active way, by giving himself up for her. A dry sense of objectivity in terms of our redemption would lead us to a cold, cerebral sort of faith that can easily become transactional. We stand by what God has done for us objectively in Christ, but we also live out a newness of life, a faith that works itself out in love as Christ himself dwells in us in love. We are in Christ, from the moment of our redemption, but we also grow up into Christ, over the long period of a lifetime of sanctification. Marriage pictures a one-flesh union that, like the gospel itself, is both legal and relational, both objective and subjective, both covenantal and connective. Our vows to one another mean that we are, objectively, a one-flesh union. Our intimacy in marriage, though, means that we grow into that one-flesh union by coming to live in harmony with one another. Intimacy, like fidelity, is harder than it seems.

Sometimes people are dismissive altogether of romantic love and companionship as a basis for marriage. Some who object to what they deem to be traditional notions of marriage will make the case that love-in-marriage the way most of us would define it is a modern innovation. Those who speak of a "biblical" definition of marriage, some would say, are speaking of an economic arrangement, designed to navigate relations between relatives or to provide financial security. Marriage, in this view, was an economic and political arrangement, not a matter of personal or romantic love, a matter more of acquiring in-laws than of acquiring a spouse.[16] In one sense, this is quite true. Many cultures around the world have, even now, marriages that are arranged by parents, sometimes with large dowries required, just as in the ancient world of the Bible. Certainly, sometimes these arranged marriages are loveless and transactional, but often they are instead filled with genuine affection and tenderness, and even romance. One simply cannot make the case that romantic love is entirely absent from the biblical witness to marriage. Even if one did not accept the authority of Genesis (which I do), one would nonetheless know that this is an ancient document that would have had to make sense, in some way, to its readers. In this account, the union of Adam and Eve is not simply economic but also tender and affectionate. Adam seems to exult when he sees the woman as "at long last, bone of my bones and flesh of my flesh" (Gen. 2:23). And note, for instance, Jacob's pursuit of Rachel, in which, upon meeting her, he "kissed Rachel and wept aloud" (Gen. 29:11). If all that Jacob was seeking were her father's goats, he could just as easily have received these through the marriage with Leah. Yet, he worked seven years in order to marry Rachel, "and he loved Rachel more than Leah" (Gen. 29:30). This sense of love as a feeling of personal affection is seen also in the erotic celebrations of the Song of Solomon. Marital love is not, biblically speaking, merely an economic arrangement, even when it is arranged by families.

Those who speak of the relative newness of love as defined by romance and companionship are quite right, though, when they speak of the value romantic love has in our culture, not just for marriage but for one's sense of oneself as fulfilled and even whole. This deification of romance can be deadly to both fidelity and to intimacy, to covenant and to connection. Here is why: The power of sin and destruction is never in the creation of something entirely new, but in the misuse or twisting of something God created to be good. The passionate and affectionate longing of love is no exception. The critics of "marriage for love" are quite right that the project seems to have failed, given skyrocketing divorce rates and infidelity and cohabitation, but I would argue that what has changed is not a move from arranged marriage to marriage for love but rather our very definition of love, which we have indeed, as one observer notes, idealized and thus over-burdened the institution of marriage beyond what it can bear.[17]

God designed us to "leave" mother and father and to "cleave" to one another in order to become "one flesh" (Gen. 2:24 KJV). In some ways, this transition is as traumatic as birth. We leave behind the familiar and step into a new world, one in which we are responsible for one another. In God's plan, part of the reason we do so is because of the overwhelming drive toward one another, manifesting itself in the hormonal haze of early love. In this stage, the couple wants to be together, just the two of them, for endless amounts of time. They could talk on the telephone with each other for twelve hours, if they could find the time. They can stand on a pier and kiss until the sun comes up. They baby-talk with each other about how they feel about each other. This surge of romantic affection feels really good. The problem comes not with any of that, but only when we assume that this is, in fact, what "love" is. This is easy to do in a society where popular culture reinforces this notion.

Popular culture is, after all, driven by advertising, and advertising is driven by youth. Commercial markets don't want to sell toothpaste to a fifty-year-old man. A fifty-year-old man already has his toothpaste brand and, apart from some major life disrupter, will probably keep using the familiar for the rest of his life. The corporations want to sell toothpaste instead to future fifty-year-olds, to lock down the preference in the years before those preferences have concretized. This is the opposite of what typically happens with, say, political advertising, which tends (with some exceptions) to target older tastes and inclinations. The reason for this is obvious: old people vote and younger people don't tend to do so in large numbers. Popular culture, though, seeks to mirror their experiences back to the target demographic. The most seemingly transcendent of those experiences is the feeling of love. When, though, this is presented only in adolescent terms, one is less likely to recognize love when it deepens and matures. Often when I find young men who express frustration in finding a mate, I can trace their struggles back to this phenomenon. They are seeking someone to "complete" them in every way, someone who can meet every physical, emotional, and mental need for them. In the pursuit of this, some young people find those who can excite them with novelty and unpredictability but not in ways that are sustainable over the long term of a marriage that will be filled, in every case somewhere, with difficulty and pain, not to mention the everydayness of establishing a household.

I once knew a young man who wanted to be married and actually had many enviable options, but consistently found himself pursuing women who would end up hurting him. I told him one day that I thought the problem was that he was looking for a twenty-five-year-old woman when he should be looking for a seventy-five-year-old woman. I should have worded this better, it became clear to me, because he thought I was recommending some bizarre elder fetish. I did not, of course, mean that he should marry a woman who was literally fifty years older than he. I meant that he was evaluating potential mates only with the present in mind—how "hot" is she; how "fun" does she seem; how "accomplished" is she at her job. Preparing for marriage, however, means preparing to seek someone who can love and be loved throughout the long haul of a life together. The wise path would be to choose a mate that one can imagine not only lying in bed on a honeymoon, but kneeling by a bedside at hospice. Such a covenantal view of the whole sweep of life, of belonging to one another through everything, is the only way to bring real joy. You will put on weight. You will see your hair turn grey or fall out. You will sin and fall short of the glory of God. A covenantal view of marriage would show that you are not partners keeping score on your contract agreements, but you are one flesh, committed to love and serve each other not because of what you can get out of it, but because you simply belong to each other.

* * * *

It is simply not the case that people remain in a state of sweaty palms, pounding hearts, and butterflies in the stomach around each other perpetually for the rest of their lives. This is bound up with novelty, with driving the couple out of the shire and toward each other. Often, though, someone will note the loss of these signs of novelty without cultivating the signs of a maturing, deepening affection. They will assume, then, that they have "fallen out of love." When then they find someone who makes them flush like they experienced in adolescence, they can easily conclude that they have found their true "soul mate." And then the cycle begins again. Even when this does not end in physical infidelity or divorce, some couples seethe in resentment of each other, comparing their lives to the imaginary lives of others—perhaps in movies or in romance novels—who immediately start panting when they see each other walk in the door. Marriage is to include genuine affection and passion toward each other, an affection and a passion that should be cultivated. But the sense of this changes as you change. Familiarity is not a drudgery but can instead be the tangible result of a couple growing increasingly into one flesh. This should be received with gratitude. That can only happen, though, if a couple is committed to a real marriage, with real joys and real sorrows, and to vows that are permanent, no matter what.

Now, again, I am not for arranged marriages. Nonetheless, I am drawn consistently to something I learned from a man from an Eastern country, who met his wife for the first time on his wedding day. "We did not know one another when we married," he said. "But the same is true for you and your wife, for every married couple. Who can really say that they know one another fully at the beginning of a marriage?" He has a point. Even when we choose our own mates, and even when we do so carefully, we still grow to know each other over time, to cleave to each other mentally, emotionally, spiritually, physically, as one flesh.

This was a hard lesson for me to learn. For a couple of years, I was tyrannized by the thought that I needed to be "ready" before I could marry. Now, of course, in one sense that is obviously true. No one should marry who lacks the maturity to carry out one's responsibilities to one another, or who is not sure about what he or she should look for in a mate or in a marriage. That's not though the sort of "ready" that I mean. I knew on our first date that I loved her and wanted to spend my life with her. But many told us, "Wait until you can afford it before you get married." It's true. We had nothing. I was a twenty-two-year-old first-year seminary student; she not much out of high school. I worked and reworked budget scenarios, and never could find one that would suggest that we could pay our bills. That's why I kept delaying asking her to marry me, even after I knew she was "the one." I thought I needed stability and a put-together life before I could ask her into it.

My grandmother wisely asked one night when I was finally going to ask "that girl from Ocean Springs" to marry me. I answered, "When I can afford it." She laughed. "Honey, I married your grandpa in the middle of the Great Depression," she said. "We made it work. Nobody can afford to get married. You just marry, and make it work."

Apart from the gospel, those were, and remain, the most liberating words I ever heard. I bought a ring that wouldn't impress anyone, then or now, but we were headed for the altar.

My grandmother's wisdom was akin to what sociologist Charles Murray called the difference between a "startup" marriage and a "merger" marriage. A "merger" marriage is the sort one sees in the *New York Times* wedding pages—a groom and a bride who have "made it" financially, educationally, and emotionally and who now join those completed worlds together. A "startup" marriage is not a capstone but a starting point, in which, as much as possible, a husband and wife start their grown-up lives together, often with nothing but each other.[18] It goes without saying that not every person can start out adulthood with that sort of solid foundation. The problem is that contemporary culture would say even to aspire to marriage without this kind of stability is wrongheaded. Some studies indicate that weddings themselves, as we now know them, are one driver of cohabitation. With a wedding not about a churchly covenant and more about the achievements of the bride and groom, many delay a wedding until they've saved up enough money for a "proper" event.[19]

We weren't ready to get married. That's true. But our finances were the least of our worries. I wasn't ready, at twenty-two, to know how to console a sobbing wife when she learned that her parents were divorcing. I wasn't ready to collapse into her arms when I heard that my grandfather had died. I wasn't ready to see an ultrasound nurse grow quiet when no fetal heartbeat could be found on the screen. I wasn't ready to hear that we'd never have children. And then I wasn't ready for the doctors to be proven wrong, and to find ourselves, in what seemed to be really quick order, the parents of five sons. I wasn't ready to be celebrating our twentieth anniversary with a two-year-old toddler in the house. And I could go on and on. Of course, I wasn't ready for all those things. In a very real sense, "I" didn't even exist. The life that I have now is defined by our lives together. That's why the Scriptures speak of marriage as a "one-flesh" union, of a head and a body together. These aren't two separate lives, bringing their agendas together. This is two people joining together for one life: life together. One can prepare oneself to be a husband or to be a wife. But one can never be really "ready."

As I look back, I can see the intense joy in our lives that would never have made it into our daydreams about the future. We loved those nights eating only cheese sandwiches because that's all we could afford. We loved doing youth ministry together, and figuring out what to do when a teenager showed up on a mission trip with marijuana in tow. We loved sitting up together while I wrote a dissertation, taking breaks to watch reruns of a television show we knew so well we could mouth the lines right along with the actors. Truth is, there's no way we could have made that budget work. And there's no way we could have grown up enough to be "ready" for what providence had for us. We needed each other. We needed to grow up, together, and to know that our love for each other doesn't consist in our having it all together. It didn't start that way, and we still had us. We had passion right at the start, to be sure, but we didn't have intimacy of that kind. That sort of intimacy takes a long, slow merging of lives together, and it requires vulnerability and risk. The Scripture says that the ancestral parents were "naked . . . and were not ashamed" (Gen. 2:25). Generally, we tend not to give much attention to this, apart from ensuring that children's picture Bibles feature branches or giraffe's necks strategically placed to cover private parts. This reality, though, is essential to what God meant for marriage.

In a church I once served, I stood in the foyer after the service talking with a group of elderly couples, one of which had just returned from a Caribbean vacation aboard a cruise ship. Expecting to hear of their enjoyment of this time of recreation, someone asked about the trip, only to see both the woman and her husband turn crimson-faced. "Oh, it was awful," the wife said. "We chose this cruise because it was the cheapest we could find, but when we boarded we discovered, as soon as walked out to the pool, that it was a topless cruise."

This staid evangelical couple were not expecting the sort of environment where, like a European beach, women walked about as shirtless as the men. "A topless cruise," the wife repeated. "Can you imagine?" An awkward silence ensued for a few minutes before an even more elderly woman, a faithful pillar of the church, said, "That sounds wonderful. I've always wanted to go on a topless cruise." We all looked at one another, wide-eyed, until she said, "I think it would be so pretty, at night, to see the stars like that." Exhaling, we realized that this sweet old saint thought "topless" referred to the lack of a ceiling covering the upper decks of the boat. No one volunteered to explain to our aged sister what "topless" means, most of us deciding she could safely go to her grave naïve about that, and, if not, none of us wished to be the one to enlighten her. She no doubt would have wondered how any decent Christian would even know about such things, and I suppose I would have to grant her that point.

Not everyone would be offended by a display of partial nudity like this (obviously, or they wouldn't, for one thing, be able to fill cruises like that one). But there's a reason why such displays attract people, and a reason why there must be warnings to keep away minors and those who would be offended. Even among those who don't see nudity as a matter of morality can see it as a matter of vulnerability. Everyone has some sense of the sort of embarrassment or feeling of shame that can come with nakedness. Those who dream that they look down at school or at work to realize they forgot to dress usually do so at a time of great personal vulnerability or insecurity. The sense of nakedness is, at once, a kind of intimacy when rightly contextualized, but a kind of exposure when not. Many of these points of awkwardness would come between the sexes, between those whose bodies display their differences from one another. This goes, though, far beyond the merely physical. The nakedness and shame of the primal humanity was about their grasping to be, in the Serpent's words, "as gods" (Gen. 3:5 KJV).

And yet, as philosopher Leon Kass rightly observes, the sight of their own naked bodies shows them otherwise. "In looking, as it were, for the first time upon our bodies as sexual beings, we discover how far we are from anything divine," Kass writes. "More concretely, we discover, first, our own permanent incompleteness and lack of wholeness, both within and without. We have need for, and are dependent upon, a complementary yet different other, even to realize or satisfy our bodily nature. We learn that sex means that we are halves, not wholes, and, worse, that we do not command the missing complementary half."[20] Marriage is intended to merge two complementary realities into a union just as real as the unity of the organs of the body itself.

In one sense, this is, of course, about sexual union (to which we will turn in the next chapter), but about much more than that too. After all, your sexual organs and your XX and XY chromosomes are not the only things complementary about you. Everyone comes into a marriage with certain points of strength and vulnerability. Part of what it means to actively love each other is to know what these things are, and to work to shore them up. Intimacy means that you love these realities and that, as you grow to love the other spouse, the more you grow even to love these dynamics without either taking the other's strengths for granted or resenting him or her for not having other strengths. Often, the "other woman" or "other man" in a marriage is not a real person with which a spouse is having an affair, but instead is an imagined, idealized husband or wife to which the spouse is constantly compared. Our marriage would be miserable if my wife expected me to be the sort of husband who is repairing items, pouring himself into yard work, and taking care of tasks such as patching the roof or killing moles in the backyard. She is instead married to someone who can preach sermons and write books, but that's about it. I can map out the kings of Israel and Judah for you, if you want, but I genuinely would not know how to boil an egg. I can go on television and debate the causes of global poverty, should you ask, but I couldn't, with a court order, tell you where we keep the lightbulbs.

By contrast, I know people in the sorts of public ministry positions that I hold with spouses who are just as public-facing, constantly weighing in on the ministry's mission, raising funds, and what have you. My wife would rather endure an invasive medical procedure than give a speech or participate on a panel at some conference. This turns out to be a great blessing for me. Unlike some people in the world in which I operate, I can actually leave my work behind. There are many people with ambitions for me and for my ministry, and sometimes this can lead to all sorts of pressures from people who all know what I should be doing (at least in their minds). Maria is not one of those people. I could genuinely come home today and tell her that I have decided to return to our hometown and work in anonymity on a shrimp boat for the rest of our lives, and she would be game. That's not because she is disengaged, but just the opposite. She does not love my "ministry platform" or my "brand"; she loves me. She knew and loved me before anyone outside my zip code had ever heard my name, and, in relationship to her, nothing has changed at all. If I longed to be part of some sort of "power couple" (I don't), I might have the temptation to conform her into that sort of person. If she expected me to live a more "normal" life, she might resent the amount of time I have to give to study or to travel. Intimacy means we know who the other actually is, for good and for ill, and we do our best to compensate with strength where the other is weak.

Intimacy means, further, knowing what brings joy and what brings pain to the other. Again, back to the head and body analogy, one can only "love his own flesh" if one knows where one has been hurt. Arm wrestling with a friend at the kitchen table might be perfectly appropriate for you, but not if you have a broken arm in a cast. Eating seafood is a very good thing, but can be deadly for someone with a shellfish allergy. There's a great deal of ridicule toward so-called "trigger warnings" in colleges and universities—warnings given about certain ideas or concepts in a piece of literature or film or music or speech. To a large degree, this ridicule is warranted, as many students are "triggered" by ideas with which they disagree and so, rather than engage these ideas with arguments, prefer to shut them out. The idea of "trigger warnings," though, started with a legitimate concern for those who had experienced genuine trauma. If one is recuperating from the recent stabbing murder of a parent, one probably wouldn't want to watch a crime procedural on a knife-bearing serial killer that same week. A typical viewer, though, might watch the program without any hesitation. The same is true in a marriage. There are certain actions or words we should never use with each other, regardless of one's context. "You're turning into your mother" might well be a compliment for someone born in a stable with a star overhead, but for many people it's not meant—or received—that way.

Intimacy means that we are not just marrying one another, but marrying also one another's memories and experiences. If you grew up in a family that loves to debate with raised voices, this sort of banter might seem like family bonding to you. Your spouse, who perhaps grew up in a home where raised voices meant discord and hatred, might find it anything but that.

A friend of mine, one of the most sincere and straightforward people I know, once told me how difficult it was to visit her husband's family because of the sarcastic barbs they constantly traded back and forth. In his family, sarcasm meant belonging. One was teased as a way of signaling that one was an "insider," and expected to strike back just as hard. For her, this was stressful. In a marriage, one must know not only how to act with love toward each other, but specifically how certain words or actions may be perceived. I know a couple in which the wife's father had been a serial adulterer. For her, the biggest difficulty she had was learning to trust her husband. When he would come home a bit later than she expected, she would subject him to an inquisition, demanding he account for every spare minute. For him to love her, he must know this, and work to instill trust. That may mean ensuring that he calls in constantly when his whereabouts aren't known. He could easily point to his coworker's spouse who doesn't get alarmed by such things, but to do such would be to love some shadow wife, not his real one.

* * * *

Connection is filled with luminous joy. That's precisely why it is difficult. For some people, this difficulty comes at the sexual level. For others, it comes at the emotional level, of disclosing when, for example, one is scared or depressed or angry. For others, it is spiritual intimacy that seems difficult. For me, it is very easy to initiate sex, and very easy usually to disclose to my wife my emotional state, but it is very difficult for me to initiate prayer with her. This might be surprising, since I will pray with ease with a stranger on a plane or lead a prayer in a crowd of people. I even find it easy to pray with my wife and children together. But praying, just her and me alone, feels awkward and almost painfully intimate, like looking at oneself in a close-up, lit-up mirror. I think this is because no one knows me better than she does. She knows all my hypocrisies, and how far I fall short of my ideals. Now, this is, at the rational level, not a sensible objection. After all, I am an evangelical Christian who believes that every prayer is offered and heard by grace, and that I come before God, every time, as a sinner through Christ. I have to know, though, that at the subconscious level this is an obstacle for me in order to combat it. For you, the tripwires for intimacy might be different, but finding them and seeking to fight them, together, is necessary in the growth toward one flesh. To be "naked and not ashamed" is an act of war.

A few years ago, ambulance lights bounced off the walls of my house, as emergency medical workers yelled codes to one another as they strapped my wife onto a stretcher. She had suffered a miscarriage—our fourth miscarriage—in recent days and since then something had gone seriously awry. She started hemorrhaging blood and passed out on our living room floor, prompting me to call the emergency line for help. All of our sons, ranging from ages two to eight-years-old, were huddled on the floor of one of their bedrooms. I tried to project calm. "Everything is going to be okay," I said. "Your mom's just feeling bad, but she's going to be fine." My then-four-year-old Samuel has never been easily manipulated by propaganda.

He knew I was lying. He knew I had seen the terror in the eyes of our neighbor, a nurse, who was trying to pretend calm for me just as I was for the children. "She's not going to be okay, Daddy," Samuel said through tears. "I know what an ambulance is for. I know what all that blood is about. My mama's going to die and we will all be orphans." I wrestled back nausea because I feared he was right.

Back at my wife's side, walking beside her as they carried her out the door, I cringed as I looked at her pale bloodless face before I noticed something. I could see an image reflecting up from the metal bars of her stretcher, the reflection of a picture on our wall of the two of us on our wedding day. I couldn't help but look back into those faces and realize that those two happy faces framed in that photograph were worried only about the possibility of a ruined honeymoon. The joy of that day back in the past made the terror of this day in the present all the worse. I loved her more now than I had back then. I knew what I would be losing. After a rough night in the hospital, where it looked at several points as though she would die from loss of blood, Maria's vital signs all stabilized. After a couple of transfusions, she was back. My children were not orphans after all. When I went home to get her a fresh change of clothes, I stopped and looked at that wedding photo. I paused to wonder what I would say if I could send a message back through time to my skinny twenty-two-year-old self. What would I say to him about love and marriage?

I realized I would tell him to thank God for his ruined honeymoon. I would tell him he doesn't know a thing, yet, about love or marriage. I would tell him that nobody's wedding goes perfectly, and that every honeymoon has some hitches. And I'd tell him that's a good thing because life isn't lived in the abstract ideals of one's own script but is lived instead in the sort of unity that comes through trials and struggles and cross-bearing, together. I would tell him the little turbulences he was facing then would pale in comparison to the trials they would face later on. I would tell him to stop being so ridiculously uptight and entitled and thank God for showing such goodness to him, with a wife like this, with a life like this. My twenty-something self was a fiery stubborn little fellow so he would probably argue with me. I would just laugh and say, "Shouldn't you save your voice for your vows?" I would tell my younger self what my real problem was. I had confused happiness with tranquility. I had assumed that what it meant for a ceremony or for a honeymoon to be "good" in one's memory would be for it to go according to my own plan. I was deeply and profoundly stupid. And I wish I could say that I have outgrown all of that. But I expect that my self of twenty years from now would probably have similar words for me right now.

* * * *

Often at weddings, we hear that our Lord Jesus blessed marriage with his attendance at a wedding in the village of Cana, where he turned water into wine. This is true. What we often miss, though, is that overshadowing that wedding party was a cross. The wedding celebration ran out of wine, which could have ended in the social humiliation of the family before their kin and neighbors. Jesus' mother asked him to intervene. What astounds me is not that he could make this happen, what John calls the first of his signs, but rather that he did so with crucifixion on his mind. In Jesus' gentle rebuke of his mother, he said, "My hour has not yet come" (John 2:4). All of the Gospels are oriented around this "hour." He had set his face toward Jerusalem, where he would die. There at the wedding, John recounts, Jesus "manifested his glory" in the provision of wine (John 2:11). Later, John will tell us, Jesus stepped into Jerusalem and announced, "The hour has come for the Son of Man to be glorified" (John 12:23). The hour was the cross. The glory was the cross. The mission was the cross. The glory of Christ is a crucified glory. Jesus first showed this at a wedding. He still does.

There's a lot of marriage advice out there, especially for Christians. Some of it is deeply therapeutic—drawing from scientific insights on how to communicate better with each other. Some of it is almost clinically gynecological—how to deepen intimacy through sexual techniques and positions and so on. Much of this counsel is wise, while some of it is hollow or carnal. But regardless, the primary trouble going on in most Christian marriages is not that we don't grasp how to live together (although that's certainly part of it). Our primary trouble instead is that we don't grasp fully enough the gospel by which we've been saved, the gospel we've been called to carry to the world.

Whether married or not, you bear a calling to support and uphold the marriages within the family of God, to hold one another accountable to stand by our words. And, whether married or not, we should pay attention to what we can see in the marriages around us, even as sin-riddled and foible-filled as even the best of them are. In them, we can see a picture of a Christ who is one flesh with his bride, a Christ who is present both by covenant and through connection, by fidelity and through intimacy—a Christ who is joined to his church, for better or for worse, by a cross. That means we will find joy and peace and wholeness in our marriages when we stop expecting marriage to meet all our needs, and start seeing marriage as a war to find contentment in the gospel. That's a struggle that takes us right to the brink of death, still holding on to each other, knowing that someone is holding on to us. Make love. Make war. And make war by making love. Crucify your honeymoon.

CHAPTER EIGHT
Reclaiming Sexuality

SHE WANTED JESUS, BUT SHE wanted sex first. As I listened to his girl in the church van, I was simultaneously appalled at her kind-of-blasphemy, and secretly enthralled she would tell the truth about something that, if I had been forced to admit it, I believed as well. And I suspected every other fourteen-year-old on this youth trip felt as I did.

In order to understand the context for this late-night conversation of teenagers headed down the highway somewhere in the South, one must know something about the complicated history of the Christian future. For two thousand years, Christians have looked for the return of Jesus Christ. In some time periods this expectation is more heightened than at others. I came of age during a fever pitch of apocalyptic fervor in the 1980s. My church at the time went through often elaborate renderings of prophecy charts relating current events to the end times. Pastors and evangelists told us the signs were clear: we were the "terminal generation," and the skies would explode any day now with the promised advent of Christ. That was all right by us, especially since we really didn't want to complete the semester of algebra in front of us. But this girl sighed and said, "I really want to be ready for heaven, but I sure hope Jesus waits until I've had the chance to . . . you know, have sex . . . at least once."

What this adolescent woman wanted was actually not anything immoral. She agreed with our church's commitment to sexual abstinence before marriage, and planned to keep those commitments. She meant that she wanted to experience a perfectly moral, marital, conjugal union. She wanted, I think, more than sex. She wanted the experience of falling and being in love, of romance and union with another. On that church van, I'm quite sure, there were several teenage boys who would've gladly volunteered to help her through the apocalypse. Since I vividly remember this conversation, and since I ended up doing my doctoral work and basing my entire ministry around eschatology, I don't want to psychoanalyze this much further.

This desire for orgasm-before-Armageddon is no sign that this teenager is an idolater or a nymphomaniac. She was normal. Sexuality is a powerful, driving force, and is so for all of our lives. Years later, when I had adolescent children of my own, I remember the horror one of them expressed when I explained the sorts of hormonal surges and inconvenient desires that would emerge with puberty. He seemed ready to withstand all of this, but asked, "And how long does this last?" I said, "Well, pretty much all of your life." He looked at me as though I had told him that he would be symbiotically joined to a werewolf spirit for the rest of his mortal existence. Sometimes it seems like that. Sex can be a pull so strong that we would want to postpone eternity to get to it. And sex can be so scary that we wonder if it will break us apart. That's because sex is not just about sex.

* * * * * * * *

If love and marriage were merely about affection and companionship and economy, we might be led to conclude, even more than we already do, that the universe is a disenchanted blank slate ready for human will and technology to master it as we will. Sexuality is a perpetual reminder that there's something within us that is quite beyond our control. Yes, we can control the expression of our sexual desires, and we can practice the disciplines that will help us to do so. But the desire itself seems to come out of nowhere. That is by design.

Frederica Mathewes-Green writes about the incomprehensible ingenuity of the sexual act as a sign of grace. "How could we understand what it's like for two to become one, union without annihilation? God came up with a human experience that would be universal, common and enjoyable, and said, 'Here, this is what it's like. This is where you're going.'"[21] She's exactly right. The sexual union is a vivid signpost of the gospel reality of two persons who remain personally distinct and yet join together in one unified, ecstatic mystery. For that reason, because sexuality is charged with joyous mystery, sexuality is an ongoing arena of spiritual conflict.

Since the Fall, humanity runs aground perpetually toward either trivializing or deifying sexuality. See, for instance, the incoherence abounding in our own era. On the one hand, sex is seen as not meaning all that much. Persons are expected to have multiple sexual partners throughout their lives. A casual "hookup" is not seen as having necessarily any permanent lingering effect after the wave of orgasm is gone. And yet, at the same time, sex is seen as crucially important. Endless books and videos are produced on sexual technique, and those who feel as though they are missing sexual fulfillment often believe themselves to be missing out on life itself. A Christian vision of sexuality is neither of these things. But in a universe under the occupation of unseen rulers, we should not be surprised to see sexuality unhinged from the gospel, and indeed in many cases becoming a counter-gospel of its own.

In our day, many outside the church will accuse Christians of being "obsessed with sex," usually noting a Christian "sexual repression" that they tell us goes back at least to Augustine. Some will point to, for instance, the Law of Moses, which pronounces a certain amount of days in which a person is ceremonially unclean after a menstrual period or a seminal emission or a sexual act as a sign of the biblical rejection of human sexuality. This code, though, does not pronounce such things as sinful or as "disgusting." Instead, these laws carefully disentangle the worship of God from the sort of sexual idolatry claimed by the pagan nations around Israel. In a world of fertility gods and temple prostitutes, the Word of God must emphatically reassert that God is outside of his creation and is not to be identified with the rhythms of reproduction, powerful as they are.

Are there Christians who are obsessed with sex? Of course. Are there Christians who hold to sub-biblical views of the body in ways that see sex as almost inherently shameful? Undoubtedly. There have always been Christians who hold to false teachings. On the whole, though, such is hardly the case. The Bible speaks often of sexual immorality not because the Bible disregards the goodness of sexuality but because it affirms it. The Christian vision of sexuality is so high and positive that those forces that would twist it apart do great harm, both to human flourishing and to the grasp of the good news of the gospel. Moreover, in an era obsessed with sexuality (as most eras are, in differing ways), the Christian message must inevitably speak of how it differs from the spirit of the age. A word of repentance must tell us of what we must repent. A word of forgiveness must tell us from what we have been forgiven. A word of spiritual warfare must tell us what it is we should fight, and for what we should fight.

The concept of sexuality as spiritual warfare is easy enough for most faithful Christians to see in the case of fighting against sexual temptation. That is, as we shall see, certainly part of it. But, there's more involved than just avoiding the negative. In his letter to the church at Corinth, the apostle Paul commanded married couples not to abstain for long periods of time from sexual relations. Even if the couple abstains for a time for prayer and fasting, that time should be limited. The couple should come back together quickly, he wrote, "so that Satan may not tempt you because of your lack of self-control" (1 Cor. 7:5). These instructions from the apostle are not simply about sexual abstinence leading one to look for sexual fulfillment elsewhere, although that is clearly part of it. Taking such a limited view adopts the modern assumption that sex is transactional—one "partner" exchanging physical pleasure in return for pleasuring the other. Paul, though, assumed a covenantal, organic bond between husband and wife. The husband's body belongs to his wife, and vice versa (1 Cor. 7:4). The one-flesh union, as we have seen, is about more than sexual intercourse, but it is certainly not less than that. In the creation account, the one-flesh union included the man's "holding fast" to his wife, of "knowing" her. In the beginning, Satan sought to divide the male and female poles of humanity by driving them away from each other through shame and conflict. The old serpent still does this. Sexual intercourse, in a Christian rendering, is a reiteration of the union, a kind of renewing of vows. As a couple cling to each other in this way, they signal once again that they belong to each other. This is a sign of the gospel. And this includes even the pleasure that goes with sexual union. Instead of shame and conflict, marital sex demonstrates the beauty of consummated love.

Some will suggest that the primary purpose of sexuality in Scripture is procreation, contrasting such with the allegedly "liberated" modern view of sexuality as primarily about pleasure. I don't argue with the fact that the biblical account of sexuality keeps procreation central such is true in the Genesis account and runs through the Bible. Sexual love points, even when not resulting in children, to the connectedness of the generations, to the incarnating fruitfulness of love. But sexual union in Scripture is never a utilitarian chore one merely performs in order to reproduce. The Bible repeatedly speaks of the joy that accompanies the sexual union, a joy that is meant to drive us toward one another (Gen. 2:22-24; Eph. 5:25-31). The Bible uses the language of "knowing" each other in reference to sexual union (Gen. 4:1, 17; 1 Sam. 1:19). This is not a prudish euphemism, but a subtle revelation of what the union is all about.

In some marriages, a husband responds immediately to his wife's showing initiative toward sex, or she to him. In other marriages, more subtlety is appreciated. He learns if she hates sex before she's had her coffee in the morning, or to avoid initiating sex when he's fighting a sinus infection. He learns if she likes him to speak to her during sex, or if she finds that awkward and off-putting. The list goes on and on, but this is a knowledge that isn't present, *ex nihilo*, from the first time in the bedroom together. It grows as their knowledge of each other grows over time.

Monogamy and fidelity don't restrict sexual freedom; they fuel it. There is something I often tell Christian couples in counseling before their marriages: "If all goes well, your honeymoon should be the worst sex of your life." What I mean is that, by God's design, intimacy grows with knowledge of one another. Aging will tame the wildness of one's sexual urges somewhat, to be sure, but time together does not, in and of itself, rob the union of pleasure. It should instead enhance it. This should be especially clear in a culture of so-called sexual freedom and spontaneity in which sexual experiences are often negotiated like contracts, of what each partner likes and needs.

Part of what kills sexual joy is the need to be "sexy" in ways that are unrealistic. Many who feel sexually "free," and who see sexual experience as almost akin to a hunting or shopping trip, find that as time goes by they lose the youthful "look" needed to maintain their attractiveness to relative strangers or their own self-confidence. In a marriage though, as defined by Christ, we do not love each other because we find each other sexually attractive, but the other way around. We grow in our sexual attraction to our spouse because we have love and affection for that person. When I don't fear that my spouse will leave me, I lose many inhibitions I would otherwise have. How many men feel sexually inhibited because they are growing bald or gaining a paunch in their mid-section? How many women feel "unsexy" because they have (as is normal for any aging person) some grey hair or some extra pounds? And yet, if a husband does not feel as though he is competing with athletes or his wife with models, but knows they are secure in a lifelong union, where they will love and cleave to each other, regardless, that gives them freedom to leave the light on, should they desire to do so. This doesn't mean "letting oneself go" physically. A vow-keeping couple will want to know what they both find attractive and play to that as much as possible. It does mean, though, that a man finds his wife beautiful because he loves her; he does not love her because she is beautiful. A woman wants to have sex with her husband because he is her husband; she does not keep him as her husband because she wants to have sex with him. In the freedom of fidelity, pleasure awakens.

* * * *

God said of his bride Israel: "For as a young man marries a young woman, so shall your sons marry you, and as the bridegroom rejoices over the bride, so shall your God rejoice over you" (Isa. 62:5). As one scholar puts it, sexual intimacy in Scripture with its ecstasy and bliss pointed to hope for the future, while its absence was often a vision of doom.[22] A joyless sexuality does not picture what marriage is intended to picture: the sort of exuberant, self-giving love that God has for his people, that Christ has for his church. When the apostle Paul demanded that the "conjugal rights" of both spouses be maintained, he is not speaking of the equivalent of a contract for a stud servicing a mare, but of the attention that one lover gives to another. The pleasure that results from marital sex is not primarily the manipulation of nerve endings, as though one were a sex toy made of meat. When a husband learns what is pleasurable to his wife, or vice versa, the couple is learning to know each other in the most intimate of ways—in a way that reminds both husband and wife that they should live to please not the self but the other.

The Scriptures and the Christian tradition are clear that sexual expression is only allowed within the covenant of marriage. That does not mean that only married people are endowed with sexuality. If this were so, sexual feelings and desire would awaken only with marriage and subside in old age. Such is hardly the case. Middle schools and high schools are buzzing with sexual tension, and so are senior citizen centers (sometimes the latter even more than the former). Those who are not married should not expect themselves to be free from sexual feelings and pulls. Those who are called to be married one day should see these feelings as pointing them toward their future husbands or wives. Those who are called to a life of singleness will also experience sexual feelings and desires. This does not mean, contrary to the counsel of some, that any sexual tension means that one must marry. Instead, the near-universal experience of sexual longing should remind all of us, including those not married, of one of the fundamental truths that God shows us in marriage: we do not belong to ourselves but must pour ourselves out in service to others. The call to celibacy is not just about having the freedom of time—from responsibilities to spouses or children—to serve, but also about channeling the other-directed energy of sexuality toward something else: serving God and neighbor through the mission of Christ. This is difficult in any era, but especially difficult in a culture that views sexual satisfaction as a preeminent vehicle of meaning and purpose.

Sexuality is powerful precisely because it is intended to be a transcending of the self. The word *ecstasy* is rooted in the idea of standing outside of oneself. Turned away from God's design—as the fallen order always seeks to do—sex can easily become an attempt not to transcend the self but to escape the self. As all distance between lover and loved is erased—through pornography or casual sex—we substitute crowding for closeness and abandon the tension necessary for mystery. Love, then, in becoming a method of driving positive feelings, "no longer represents plot, narration, or drama—only inconsequential emotion or arousal."[23] Sex becomes just one more consumer aspiration in an achievement society. All of this is to say, when sex is reduced to physical contact in pursuit of orgasm, it loses the very qualities that make it powerful and alluring.

God warns us against sexual immorality and distortion, not because God wishes to restrict us from pleasure (this is the satanic suggestion of Genesis 3), but because God knows how sex flourishes and how sex can destroy. The various sexual revolutions—and history is littered with countless of them—always promise sex as simultaneously a momentary escape from the self (by distracting you from the pain of life) and as a means of actualizing the self (by offering you purpose in life). These attempts never achieve their goal. True and lasting union cannot be achieved through the superficiality of isolated sexual encounters. This is akin to mimicking the adrenal rush of courage in warfare by riding a roller coaster with animated images of cannon fire all around. The feeling is there, for the moment, but cannot be sustained. Once one knows it is an illusion, it cannot replicate the reality. Neither can a sexual tryst ever substitute for the one-flesh union. A Christian vision of life is one of genuine living sacrifice, not a series of self-absorbed transactions. In order to gain one's life, one must really lay it down. That is the word of the cross, and the cross is to shape our sex lives as much as anything else.

Nonetheless, the biblical pattern of sexuality is not simply a matter of God knowing what will be genuinely fulfilling. Those who think so are tempted to replicate the hoary old joke of the boy who is told (erroneously) by the nuns of his parish school that masturbation will cause him to go blind, to which he responds, "Well, can I do it until I need glasses?" Many can conclude that sexual joy in marriage is God's perfect ideal, but, short of that, they can live with a substitute. The Bible speaks of sexual immorality not merely in terms of relational or social consequences—although those are certainly present, especially in the wisdom literature of the Proverbs—but, beyond that, in terms of sexual immorality as a kind of occultism. The prophets repeatedly tied idolatry together with imagery of sexual immorality.[24] This is precisely because sexuality is about more than the firing of neurons for pleasure. Just as the prophets could speak simultaneously of idols both as "nothing," those with "no breath in them," and as "other gods" but also as demons with real existence, so the prophets could speak of noncovenantal sex as both meaningless nihilism and as fraught with dark meaning. Sexuality is intended to merge together two promise-making persons into a life-giving, covenantal union before God. The prophet Malachi wrote of marriage,

"Did he (God) not make them one, with a portion of the Spirit in their union?" (Mal. 2:15). Likewise, the apostle Paul warns that the one who joins himself to a prostitute joins Christ to that prostitute, since the one-flesh union means a joining of spirits (1 Cor. 6:15-17).

The blurring of sexual lines is a sin "against [one's] own body" (1 Cor. 6:18–20). This does not mean, though, that, like eating too much sugar or smoking cigarettes one is "only hurting himself." The body, for the one who belongs to Christ, is not his own but is a temple of the Holy Spirit. Sexual immorality is the desecration of this temple. Imagine how horrified you would be (rightly) to see a pagan religion sacrificing a goat on your church's communion table. Even those of us in lower-church traditions would be outraged. Something set apart for God's service, something holy, would be used for something unholy, something contrary to the gospel itself. That's what sexual immorality—of whatever kind—is. That's why Scripture warns against such immorality from the opening chapters all the way through to the closing revelations of the coming judgment. That's why the people of Israel were commanded to flee from sexual immorality, and the Jerusalem Council—which did not obligate Gentile Christians to submit to circumcision or other aspects of the Mosaic covenant—put forward the same prohibition for all of those who are in Christ (Acts 15:20).

Some would wave away too much talk of sexual immorality by dismissing it as the priorities of the Old Testament or of Paul, not of Jesus. Jesus, in this view, is presented as a smiling, sexually permissive anti-Paul. Such is hardly the case, though. Jesus, first of all, does not speak merely in the words he spoke during his pre-resurrection ministry. The Bible is breathed out by the Spirit of Christ (1 Pet. 1:11; 2 Pet. 1:19–21), so Jesus not only affirmed the Word of God in its totality in the Old Testament Scriptures (Matt. 5:17–18), but also committed himself to speak further truth (John 16:12–13), which he did through the inspired writings of apostles and prophets (Eph. 2:20). After his resurrection, Jesus himself directly warned an early congregation that their toleration of sexual immorality would bring his judgment (Rev. 2:20–23), even calling such permissiveness part of the "deep things of Satan" (Rev. 2:24). But even so, during his earthly ministry, Jesus was, if anything, stronger on sexual immorality than the Old Testament or the New Testament Epistles. He said that the one who has lust in his heart has already committed adultery (Matt. 5:27–30). This does not mean, contrary to the interpretation I once heard from a severely under-discipled evangelical college student, that if a man has lustful desire for a woman "he might as well go ahead and sleep with her." Nor does this mean Jesus' similar teaching about anger in one's heart making one guilty of murder (Matt. 5:21–22) justifies the one with inner hostility toward his neighbor stabbing him to death. In both cases, Jesus identified sin as beginning not in acts external to us, able to be manipulated merely by changed habits or rules, but in our own psyches. And, in both cases, Jesus warns us that these inner realities, unless recognized, repented of, and covered in atoning blood, will lead to separation from God in hell (Matt. 5:22, 30). That's stout stuff.

The Jesus who warned us not to judge others (Matt. 7:1–6) also spoke to us through his apostle that the church should discipline one who is unrepentantly sexually immoral (1 Cor. 5:1–5). This does not mean, the Bible says, that we should separate ourselves from sexually immoral people; Jesus did not do that and bore the criticism for it. We should instead, the Bible continues, maintain accountability for the one who "bears the name of brother," that is, one who is part of the church (1 Cor. 5:11). Why? Salvation is only for sinners. The one who refuses to repent of a sin is refusing to trust Christ to mediate on his or her behalf. This person, if his or her refusal to repent persists, is demonstrating that he or she has not been to the cross (1 Cor. 6:9–10). This is not at all in reference to those who wrestle against temptation and fall—even sometimes over and over again. We are sheep who are shepherded with a rod and staff, and we must be redirected away from the cliffs and rescued out of the thickets over and over. This is rather directed toward the one who justifies himself, saying that what God calls wrong is in fact right, and thus says that, at least at that point, he is without sin or that he loves his sin and is not willing to, by God's grace and the church's help, walk away from it.

Some might think that their church or their family is secure because they define sin the way that God does and heartily denounce it. Such is not at all the case. "For what have I to do with judging outsiders?," the apostle Paul wrote. "Is it not those inside the church whom you are to judge? God judges those outside" (1 Cor. 5:12–13). We tend, though, to want to do the precise reverse: to speak with outrage about the sins on the outside of our congregation and speak in muted tones about the sins on the inside. The world outside is our mission, not our mirror. Too often, though, we act as if things such as the sexual revolution could be countered with culture wars instead of spiritual warfare.

* * * *

It turns out we are often only as counter-cultural as we want to be. Far from the guardians of biblical orthodoxy, we are often slow-motion sexual revolutionaries, accommodating to what we once called immorality a decade or two after the culture around us. A biblical call to sexual morality was never meant to be marketable. Even Jesus' own disciples wondered how anyone could follow this path, once they understood just how radically Jesus meant his call to holiness. The biblical witness to the spiritual warfare of sexual integrity is to point not to our moral superiority but to gospel proclamation. The twentieth-century monk Thomas Merton put it this way: "It is Satan's theology to make Christ the most perfect of all the Pharisees, so that the publicans will despair while the Pharisees will come to him and be confirmed in their self-righteousness."[25] We tell the truth about the Bible's high standards for our sexual lives—and for every aspect of our lives—not to distinguish ourselves from others but to announce the good news of God's mercy for sinners like us. This shows up in a word not of worldly power but of the cross. The end result is not family values, but families—families shaped by the cross.

And, as they relate to sexuality, our families—and by "our" I mean "the church," not "America" or "Western culture"—are in crisis. Consider, first of all, fornication. I don't mean to consider the act of fornication or the idea of fornication, but the literal word *fornication*. Former President Richard Nixon infamously asked a journalist right before an interview, "So David, did you do any fornicating this weekend?" The question is memorable because it carries all the same connotations many associated with Nixon himself. It seems awkward, out-of-date, censorious, and kind of inquisitorial, trying and failing to be one of the boys. If the word is ever used these days, it is most likely used as part of a joke making fun of how conservative Christians are likely to talk. The joke doesn't work, though, because conservative Christians don't use that word either, and haven't for a long time. "Fornication" seems as creepy and out-of-place to a Christian's ears as it does to anyone else's. Sure, we talk about sexual purity and warn against sexual immorality, but more often we teach our children and unmarried church members to "practice abstinence" or to avoid "premarital sex."

To some degree this is inevitable. In order to communicate with people around us, we must, to some degree, use language and concepts they understand. But "premarital sex" and "fornication" (the word the Bible uses) are not identical in meaning. To be sure, fornication is "premarital," but in the language of "premarital sex" the emphasis is on timing. The act itself is assumed to be the same. What changes "marital sex" to "premarital sex" is simply when one chooses to engage in it. Premarital sex is presented as merely a premature ejaculation. This assumption, though, is right at the root of the American Christian crisis of sexual ethics.

The Bible is clear, as is the two-thousand-year consensus of the church—whether in its Orthodox, Catholic, or Protestant wings— that sexual activity is to be limited to the marital union of man and woman. The sexual union does not, in and of itself, constitute a marriage. Jesus recognized the woman at Jacob's well as having "no husband" despite the fact that she was with (presumably in a sexual context) someone at the time (John 4:16–18). Moreover, Joseph of Nazareth and the Virgin Mary were genuinely married, even without an accompanying sexual union (Matt. 1:24–25). Nevertheless, the Bible speaks of sexual consummation of a vowed union as the normal course of events, and it speaks of sexual contacts outside of that union as establishing real, though mysteriously spiritual, attachments—attachments that point to something quite different than the head-body, one-flesh union of Christ and the church.

Many churches and denominations attempted in the last generation to shore up this consensus with programs encouraging adolescents and young adults to pledge themselves to uphold these standards until marriage.[26] These programs had some success in at least delaying sexual intercourse, though it is not at all clear they achieved anything resembling a sexual counterculture. One study demonstrated that evangelical Protestant teenagers were *more* likely to engage in sex while unmarried than their Jewish, Mormon, or even mainline liberal Protestant peers. The answer, in this study, has to do not with religious conviction but with upward economic mobility. Evangelical teenagers are more likely to come from lower socioeconomic ranks while those in other, more latitudinarian, religious communions tend to come from higher classes. The pressure on children in the upper quadrant to succeed rules out certain forms of risk-taking. They avoid sexual intercourse not because they don't want to go to hell, but because they do want to go to college. As conservative evangelicals grow more socially and economically ascendant, this study predicts, they will be more likely to adopt the same forms of sexual risk management focused on economic viability.[27] The study further demonstrated that much of the "abstinence" taking place among Christian adolescents and young adults is not, in fact, abstinence at all, but the maintenance of a "technical virginity" in which oral sex or other practices substitute for intercourse and are thus ruled out as "sex."[28] As long as this reality persists, our triumphalist boasting about surveys showing a decline in adolescent sexual rates and teenage pregnancies will not be the celebration we convince ourselves it is.

Much of this is contributed to by our own preaching and teaching. One does not need to be a wild-eyed "hellfire-and-brimstone" preacher to see that the apostles warned us that the unrepentantly sexually immoral "will not inherit the kingdom of God" (1 Cor. 6:9–10). But we often cement the idea of sexual morality as "risk management" by presenting these warnings in terms of earthly "values" rather than the Judgment Seat of Christ. We speak mutedly of "struggling" and "accountability" in generic terms but hardly with prophetic force. The truth is that too many Christian parents unwittingly pressure their children toward sexual immorality by assuming that the main problem to avoid is marrying too early. While it is true that one should be old enough and mature enough to carry out one's marital vows, this is not the only danger. The apostle Paul counseled, "If anyone thinks that he is not behaving properly towards his betrothed, if his passions are strong, and it has to be, let him do as he wishes: let them marry—it is no sin" (1 Cor. 7:36) since it is "better to marry than to burn with passion" (1 Cor. 7:9). Depending on the economic rank of the household, often the assumption is that grown children must finish several levels of graduate education, pay off their student loans, gain a secure position on the career ladder, and pull together a home and a savings account, before ever marrying. The unspoken assumption is that it would be worse for a child not to succeed in America than it would be for the child to sin against God.

Another study has shown that, just as with adultery for the generation up from them, professing Christian adolescents and young adults do not start by rejecting, as ideas, the Christian teaching on sexual morality. As one study found, interviewed churchgoers who practiced oral sex often were not, at least at first, morally permissive but "selectively permissive." They don't feel that they are rejecting moral claims but instead navigating two competing moral claims: "the script about what boyfriends and girlfriends in love want or are supposed to do for and to each other, and the script about what unmarried Christian behavior should look like. They want to satisfy both, but find themselves rationalizing."[29] That cultural expectations (made more powerful, of course, by biological dynamics) are seen as virtual moral claims is telling, and is precisely the point. The struggle here is not so much about morality as about identity, not so much "What is right and what is wrong?" as "Who am I?" If I see myself both as part of the body of Christ and as enmeshed with my peer group, to the same degree, one must give way to the other.

This is furthered by even the "life cycle" of childhood development and evangelism in many of our churches, which almost presupposes sexual activity prior to marriage. The American Amish population, sheltered as it is from the rest of American culture, carries out a little-known practice called *rumspringa* or "running around." In this culture, children raised in the isolated community are given the "space" upon achieving late adolescence to go out into the world and "roam," to experience the outside culture in ways ranging from automobiles, contemporary fashion, and cigarettes on one end of the spectrum to sexual experimentation, alcohol abuse, and narcotic drugs on the other. This "running around ends when the adolescent returns home to the Amish, agrees to be baptized, and assumes his responsibilities as a mature member of the community."[30] We should ask whether we have adopted an American evangelical version of *rumspringa* in which sectors of church life often expect their children to make early professions of faith, wander away somewhat in high school, depart from the faith at college-age, and then, after marrying and having children, return to the church to serve, within a couple of years, as a deacon or small-group leader. Do prodigals return home? Yes. Do Christians experience times of drifting from the Lord? Yes. But when this is an implicit assumption, something has gone awry from the biblical expectation. This "works" in a context of nominal, cultural Christianity in which, first of all, people see the church as part of what it means to "settle down," and, secondly, in which people actually marry and have children at an early enough age before they are "set" in their habits and preferences. Even on these terms, the project is faltering, as secularization evaporates the concept of church as necessary for social formation and as people are waiting later and later to marry.

Beyond the obvious erosions of the family here, the most important is an eclipsing of the message of the gospel. Our culture still has not lost a sense of the wrongness of adultery—except perhaps in the abstract. One might justify one's own affair, but few people see being cheated on as morally neutral. And it is not difficult to see the ongoing consequences of infidelity—even in marriages that stay together. The language of "premarital sex," though, presupposes that the problem is resolved once the timing is brought in line with the activity. A couple who have sex outside of marriage often assume that all will be well after the wedding ceremony, without any awareness of the enduring consequences of their sinful behavior, and more importantly without seeing that their fornication pointed, wrongly, to an icon of a Christ who is not bonded in covenant to his church.

Adultery, in some ways, is easier to repent of, because it's easier to know what repentance looks like. A person who breaks his marriage vows can see that he has hurt his marriage and must work to repair it. With "premarital sex," on the other hand, marriage seems to have fixed the problem. Often a husband finds it then difficult to lead his wife spiritually, or to fully gain her trust. Sometimes this shows up immediately, sometimes years later. At root is the issue one writer noted in the Genesis account of the divided primeval couple: "Nothing drives a couple further apart than sinning together." Moreover, she knows, especially if he professed Christianity before the marriage, that his libido is stronger than his conscience. If he could justify sexual sin with her, how can she be sure he will not do the same with someone else? This is not irreparable—nothing this side of the grave is irreparable, given the reality of the cross. But the repair comes not with time healing sin but instead with confession of sin, to God and to one another.

* * * *

The spiritual warfare of sexual disorder before marriage comes with the illusion that such sin is expected and natural. The spiritual warfare of sexual disorder after marriage is just the reverse: the idea that infidelity is something that love itself can prevent. When doing premarital counseling, with an engaged couple, I throw out an exercise that almost always throws both of them into visible turmoil. I ask the couple to do a homework assignment, apart from each other. Each one of them is to think through and write out a letter to the other explaining these scenarios: "If I were going to cheat on you, here's how I would do it" and "Here are the ways you could tell that I am lying to you about an affair." To even bring up such a question seems jarring, maybe even insulting, to most couples. After all, they cannot imagine being unfaithful to one another. They are in love, and all they want is to be together, gazing into one another's eyes, in the eternal now of forever. That's why I ask them to do it.

I know, of course, that this exercise will not prevent infidelity. Often, we do not know ourselves well enough to predict with great accuracy how we would carry out a sin we haven't committed yet. And I've counseled enough marriages in crisis to know that often denial runs too deep for a couple in that situation to recognize what's happening within the other spouse, within the marriage, or even within his or her own heart. That's all beside the point, though. The document isn't meant to be a blueprint for the future. It is meant to rattle the couple, if only for a few minutes, to contemplate that they are not, in fact, immune from sexual sin. Moreover, it is an attempt to get a couple to start off with at least one example of talking to one another about their sexual vulnerabilities and temptations, in order to show them that this need not be fatally awkward or incendiary. Most of all, I do it to get the couple thinking about how best to fight spiritual warfare in their marriage bed.

As I referenced earlier, the apostle Paul warned, universally, all married couples of the possibility of adultery, as not simply the pull of biology but as the temptation of the devil, and he spoke of ongoing marital sexuality as a key way of fighting against this. This is not, though, for the reasons we sometimes think—that keeping a spouse sexually satisfied is the way to keep him or her happy and not likely to stray. Instead, it is because the cultivation of sexual union is a means of "cleaving" to one another, to use the Genesis language, of "knowing" one another. The haze of hormonal love might well draw us together in the first place, but will not keep us together. In order to do that, one must keep in mind the words of songwriter Johnny Cash: "I keep a close watch on this heart of mine; I keep my eyes wide open all the time." To walk this line, though, we cannot fight alone. The husband's sexuality belongs to his wife. The wife's sexuality belongs to her husband. As we grow to know each other, we are to learn how the other responds sexually. But this knowledge continues into the fighting for each other in the arena of sexual brokenness and temptation.

I have counseled hundreds of couples in the wreckage of marital infidelity over the course of my ministry. So far, I have not met one person who cheated because his or her spouse was not sexually attractive enough. In fact, honestly, I rarely find a situation where the secret lover is, in most people's assessment, as attractive as the cheated-on spouse. And, in all of that time, I've also rarely seen "happiness" within a marriage prevent an affair. It is simply rare to find someone who commits adultery out of a desire to flee a bad relationship. Affairs are usually not about a lack of happiness or a lack of sex. That's because adultery is not a means of getting to the same sort of sexual union as in marriage through a slightly different channel. There's more afoot here. One therapist notes that often the "other partners" chosen by adulterous mates are not at all the sort of people the cheating spouse would ever want in a life companion. What's at work is not a quest for a better lover or a better spouse but for "the unexplored self." An affair is not about orgasm but nostalgia.[31] The person who cheats, this counselor, argues, is usually looking to reconnect with the person he or she once was, before the daily responsibility of working a job or maintaining a household. When, for instance, a person looks up someone from high school or college or a previous workplace, the issue is not so much that the potential adulterer is pining for this old connection as much as he or she is pining to be, once again, the person that old connection once knew. The question is: "Am I still the person I was back then?"

A common theme I have observed in adulterous affairs is that the one cheating is almost never looking for a new spouse to replace the deficiencies of the old one. He or she is seeking to recapture the feeling of adolescence or young adulthood. They are not so much looking for sexual sensation as for drama. For a short period of time, the person can be swept up into the drama of "I love you; do you love me?" romance, without all the burdens of who is picking up Chloe from school or what day to put the recycling bin out at the curb. The secret lover seems to make the married person feel young or "alive" again—until everything comes crashing down. The person cheating is looking for an alternative universe, to see what would happen if he or she made different choices.

In fact, our ideas and expectations of what make a marriage "happy" can actually contribute to adultery. We are told to expect "the One," the "soul mate" who can meet our every need. As this therapist puts it, "We have conjured up a new Olympus where love will remain unconditional, intimacy enthralling, and sex oh so exciting, with one person for the long haul. And the haul keeps getting longer."[32] The best, most secure and stable marriages I know are not typically those that seem "happy" in the sense of self-actualization. They are instead those marriages in which, often through deep suffering, the husband and wife model self-sacrifice and care for each other. Like Christ and the church, their one-flesh union is forged not through demands for one to meet the other's needs but through a sense of common purpose, of common mission. In those healthy marriages, one spouse does not look to the other to provide one's identity. Both spouses find identity in Christ. My life, then, is not imperiled by comparisons with other—seemingly happier—marriages or with my idealized, younger life because my life is hidden in Christ. This gives us the freedom to love and to, as the Bible puts it, rejoice in the wife (or husband) of one's youth (Prov. 5:18). A couple, even a strong Christian couple, should not assume they are immune to infidelity because they love each other, because they are happy, or because their sexual acrobatics are frenzied. The devil knows the way to take one down is not through a deficient spouse but through a deficient self.

The sexual union can help preserve the marriage, not by being "better" than any potential competitor, but by drawing the couple toward the sort of intimacy that goes beyond only genital intimacy. The power of adultery is in the mystery of it all, the hiddenness. A spouse should learn the sort of vulnerability to confess to the other, at the very beginning of the temptation, when he or she is starting to mentally drift or take notice of someone else. This does not mean, of course, that a spouse should share with her husband every time she has a sexual fantasy about someone else, or every time he finds himself staring at another woman's neckline. It does mean, though, that a spouse should not be shocked when his or her partner is tempted toward adultery. Every marriage will be. Openness to one another, seeing my body and my sexual script as belonging to the other, can break the power of secretive drama in which adultery thrives. The sort of offense we take at our partner's temptations is a sign of pride. The same is true of our denial that we experience any temptation. Why would we expect to be exempt from spiritual attack on our marriage, if our marriage is not about our skill but about the icon of the gospel? Why would we believe that any one of us is strong enough, on our own, to stand against the pull to sever a union the spiritual powers-that-be despise?

Early in our marriage, I served as an associate pastor in a church. Though I was in charge of youth ministry, I frequently preached before the whole congregation. Often, after one of my sermons, a woman would come up to tell me how brilliant my sermon was, or to ask questions about the text. When I wasn't preaching, she would come sit beside me before church and ask even more questions or walk alongside me as I left, always discussing exegesis or theology. My wife said, "You know she's into you, right?" I knew no such thing, and I protested vehemently. "First of all," I said, "I look like a cricket; she would never be interested in me."

Let me pause to say to young husbands that, from experience, I've learned that "Do you really think I would have a chance with her?" is not the most reassuring rhetorical move with a skeptical wife.

I went on to opine that my wife was being judgmental of this sweet, godly sister who just wanted to know more about inaugurated eschatology themes in the book of Amos. My wife, though, did not take any of this personally. She said, "Well, I may be wrong, but I know how a woman acts when she likes a man, and I just want you to be aware of it." She didn't seethe with anger. She didn't withhold sex (my wife, I mean, not the woman at the church). She just saw to it that every time this woman approached me, my wife was right there, holding my hand. Now, I don't know whether my wife was right about this woman or not. There is a very real overreaction to marital security that tends to see women in general as "temptresses," but that's never been an issue for my wife, who is very comfortable with my having women friends and colleagues. But, regardless of whether she or I saw the situation rightly, I learned a lesson about her that may well have saved our marriage from who knows what sort of potential temptation in the future.

One thing I've learned in watching endless marriages split up over sexual infidelity is that one cannot expect people, in the throes of such sin, to act rationally. One can say, over and over again, "Why would you put your marriage or your children at risk over this? Haven't you seen how this ends in misery for them and for you?" And yet, such appeals rarely work, because the fires of passion tend to make one feel and act almost crazy. The cheating spouse will often say that the innocent party is "crazy" and sometimes will make him or her feel as though that's true, but it is the adulterer's actions that are, in fact, out of touch with reality.[33]

My wife and I have, thankfully, to this point not had to deal with any challenge to our fidelity (though I do not assume therefore that we won't ever face that), but we have many times had to learn how, in other situations, not to go crazy at the same time. Often bearing one another's burdens means knowing when the other spouse needs stability and rationality and patient understanding. I think I learned that from that situation. More than that, I learned that she would not be shocked and offended if I were to face a potential pitfall, that she would not fume or blame but that she would fight, right alongside me, against the principalities and powers, even if I did not know what was going on around me. That is wisdom and maturity. In order to do that, she needed to see that we were, in fact, vulnerable. We needed each other, and we needed the power of the cross. We still do.

* * * *

Marital sexuality is to show us our vulnerability, our dependence on one another. That's why the Scripture tells us to delight in sexual union with each other. It's not because sex is an appetite that must be filled, but because sex is to connect us to one another, reminding us who it is that we are called to love and serve. Seeing this, learning this, is what we need to be the sort of people who can stand by our promises, stand by one another. That means seeing love not as a means of making oneself great but as a means of pouring oneself out for another. Love means seeing that the arena of marriage is not a mirror but a cross.

Often, though, spiritual warfare is not about adding illicit physicality of relationship to one's life but instead requires stripping one's relationships of physicality. I am unnerved by how often I am approached by young couples—whether Christian or not—asking what to do about a lack of sex in their marriages. This is relatively common among those who are elderly, and battling the physical changes that come with age, or those in the middle of life who are often overstressed with schedules and children and feel too exhausted for regular intimacy. Increasingly, though, I find this happening among very young couples in their twenties or thirties, who struggle for intimacy.

Behind this, there are a variety of factors. Sometimes one of the partners is grappling with guilt or shame, often due to no fault of his or her own but due to some trauma from the past. That's an opportunity for a spouse to love and to understand, and, working together, to cultivate an actually deeper intimacy. Couples who have "settled" into sexless marriages, of living as roommates, are not the equivalent of, say, vegetarians who have decided to forego eating meat. They are instead, apart from those with medical issues, giving up on a biblical means of cultivating their union. Your sex life is, of course, in many senses, your business. But your sex life is for the purpose of shoring up your union. That means your children are dependent on your sex life (though they don't want to hear about it). The church is dependent on your sex life (though we don't really want to hear about it either). The routinized de-eroticizing of a marriage should be viewed not with a yawn but as a surprise attack from an enemy power. In the spiritual warfare against the gospel, Satan wills disintegration. In Christ, God integrates—sums up together—what was divided, together in Christ (Eph. 1:10). The powers seek, though, to keep apart what should be together, and sexuality is not exempt from that. Sometimes the most immediate way to fight the devil is to go to bed, together.

So how does the church help sustain the marriage covenant? Like medieval allegorists finding the Trinity everywhere in the book of Nehemiah, some popular evangelical preachers wow audiences by locating exotic sexual techniques in the pages of the Song of Solomon. But this notwithstanding, the church can cultivate such healthy sex lives not so much by offering tips for a more sizzling sex life from the pulpit (although we should admonish one another to maintain a healthy sexuality in our preaching and teaching), but rather by demonstrating within the church how to renew our own covenant vows.

In my church tradition, it is of endless frustration to me how many of our churches, despite the clear New Testament practice of weekly communion, come to the Lord's Supper once a quarter, or even less often. In justifying this, some churches will say they don't have adequate time to prepare the elements or time in the service to explain the Supper. Others will say that the Supper is too "internally-focused" when they want their services to be more about reaching unbelievers. Still others, the majority of these, will say that they put long spaces between times of communion so that it doesn't become routine or ritualized or boring. This is precisely the logic sexless marriages have. Why go through the work and effort to maintain a physical renewing of our covenant vows? And yet, having sex once a quarter does not make it more special, but just the reverse. In communion, Jesus feeds his church, transports us to the Wedding Feast that it is to come, proclaims to us the cross through which we were purchased. How could that ever happen "too often" for us? Is it any wonder then, when we downplay the physicality by which Jesus nourishes his church, that we would then see some among us downplay the physicality by which they are to nourish their marriages?

Often, though, I find that the issue is not a lack of sexual desire, or a sexual desire redirected into another relationship, but a sexual desire directed toward images on a screen or characters in a book. In one sense, pornography is not new. Jesus told us that human lust for covenant-breaking sexuality is not in anything external to us but in our fallen passions (Matt. 5:27–28). Every generation of Christians has faced the pornography question, whether with Dionysian pagan art or with Jazz Age fan-dancers or with airbrushed centerfolds. The difference now is a technology that can promise near universal reach along with an illusory guarantee of anonymity. Pornography has been weaponized. We are arousing ourselves to death.

Pornography, by its very nature, leads to insatiability. One picture, stored in the mind, will never be enough to continue arousing a person. God, after all, designed the man and the woman not to be satisfied with a single sex act but with an ongoing appetite for each other, for the unitive and procreative union of flesh to flesh and soul to soul. One seeking this mystery outside of the marriage union, in a harem of digital prostitutes, will never find what he is looking for. He will never find an image naked enough to satisfy him. Pornography enables a person to use images of another, whether visual or literary, and to then use another person as a substitute, a physical object with which to masturbate. This leaves the user numb and empty because human sexuality is about much more than mere body parts rubbing against one another. Moreover, pornography brings with it a kind of sham repentance. After viewing pornography, the person feels a kind of revulsion or self-loathing or, even more typically, a sated appetite. He or she will commit to "never do this again." This is not repentance. Even Esau, belly full of red stew, wept for his lost birthright, but "found no chance to repent, though he sought it with tears" (Heb. 12:17).

Without genuine repentance, the cycle will grind on. The answer to this is confession of sin. One tempted by substitute sexualities should habituate himself to, in the moment of temptation, cry out, perhaps even audibly, "Jesus, I am tempted to this sin; deliver me." Moreover, he or she should submit himself or herself to the direction of the church, to find adequate means of escape from this temptation. Ingeniously, the satanic powers have found a means to direct human erotic energy in a direction that ultimately saps one of erotic energy, and, in due time, of the very possibility of human intimacy. The powers of the age will collaborate with the biological impulses to make this seem irresistible and will supply such pseudo-repentance. This is devil-work, and is among those things our Lord Jesus came to destroy (1 John 3:8).

What substitute sexuality seeks is not intimacy but sameness. In whatever form, it is based on an illusion, whether of an always-aroused woman or an always-empathetic man. Men too often want the illusion of women with female body parts but who are, in terms of sexual response, just like men. Women want the illusion of men who are "real men," but, in terms of a concept of romance, are just like women. In both artificial Eros and in artificial romance, there is the love of self, not the mystery of the other. In these cases, contentment is the object of destruction, whether contentment with a real spouse, with all the foibles and deficiencies that come with a real person in relationship, or contentment with a life of faithful chastity before God. We must then constantly ask, "Is what I'm consuming leading me toward my spouse (or future spouse) or away? Is it pointing me to the other in one-flesh union or to an eroticized embodiment of my own desires? Is this the mystery or a mirage?

* * * *

Sexuality within marriage, whether keeping it in bounds or keeping it kindled, is difficult. That's because we don't shape our sexuality within marriages, but we bring our sexual scripts to marriage— often formed as they are by a trillion different influences and experiences over which we have no control. In marriage, we then join not just our bodies, but also these backgrounds to one another. This can be far scarier than the thought of a casual, transitory fling with another person, to whom one does not pledge one's life. The linguist Noam Chomsky once proffered a theory as to why there are more slang words for death and for genitals than any other words. "Death and genitals are things that frighten people, and when people are frightened, they develop means of concealment and aggression."[34] I would add to that list one more: God. Think of how much profanity in our culture is rooted in sexuality, scatology (our sense of our animal mortality, of a bodily existence in which death and decay loom), or in the names or potential actions of God. All these realities frighten us because they are bigger than we are. We feel vulnerable before them.

The cross, though, finds glory in vulnerability—in death and in sex. The Scripture tells us to combat sexual sin and brokenness not with guilt and shame but with joy and rest. That comes only through the grace we find in Jesus Christ. There's a peril in the biblical tension from which a thousand heresies have sprung. The gospel tells us how through the cross God is both "just and the justifier of the one who has faith in Jesus" (Rom. 3:26). There are always "almost gospels" that seek to circumvent one or the other aspect of this good news. On the one hand, there is airy antinomianism that assumes that God's free mercy means we should "continue in sin that grace may abound" (Rom. 6:1). The Spirit's response to this could not be much stronger: "God forbid!" On the other hand, there is the equally perilous temptation to emphasize the righteousness of God's law without the mercy of the cross. Such an error evidences not only a low view of the gospel but a low view of the law.

Whoever has broken the law at one point, the Bible tells us, is a lawbreaker. Jesus has shown us that, even in the area of sexual sin, we have all broken this law, whether in heart or in deed. I see those who miss this truth in the self-condemnation of those who have repented of sexual immorality but still believe themselves to be mired in shame or guilt, as though God still sees them in those terms. Look to the cross! I also see this in those who see themselves as sexually moral as opposed to the immoral, instead of seeing ourselves as we are—as those forgiven of sin and who are vulnerable even now to any sin short of blasphemy against the Holy Spirit. Sometimes this will even show up in those who have (by God's grace) fought sexual sin and who then believe that a potential spouse is automatically disqualified because he or she has not done the same (though repentant). Again, the answer is the cross. I suppose if there were "pure" people and "impure" people, then we could divide the world up into the two groups and marry accordingly. But purity is relative when judged against the tribunal of God's righteousness.

The Christian is one who stands by mercy. Hearing ourselves pray, "Thank you, Lord, that I am not like that fornicator over there" is not success. One can easily go to hell with one's virginity intact. The issue isn't whether sexual immorality is damnable—it is. The question is whether damnation can be turned back, and the cross says it can, by Skull-Hill crucifixion and Garden-Tomb resurrection. The first marriage was between two virgins; that is true. But the primeval one-flesh union reflected something else, something unveiled only ages later in the preaching of Christ. Jesus was a virgin; his bride wasn't. He loved us anyway.

The liberating power of the cross also comes through seeing that sex is not the ultimate human experience. The unmarried person sometimes feels as though he or she is missing out on life by not experiencing sexual expression. The married person sometimes feels as though he or she is missing out on life by not having, as the grocery-line magazines would put it, "mind-blowing sex." The established sexual rhythms and habits of a married couple, growing in contentment with each other, can seem boring by contrast. And yet, sexual revolutions are what actually give us boring sex. Ultimately, what makes sex exciting for the human race is not firing neurons or the thrill of the forbidden. That is gone as soon as one walls over his calloused conscience—as any experienced adulterer knows. What makes sex exciting is the mysteriousness of the sexual union—the sense in which this act of union transcends everyday life, the sense in which this act can reach to the very core of who we are. The apostolic faith tells us why this is. That's why sexual revolutions start with such fervor but end with such dullness. The search for sexual excitement is not really men and women looking for biochemical sensations. We are not, ultimately, even looking for each other. We are looking for that to which sex points—something we know exists but just can't identify. We are looking to be part of a love that is as strong as death (Song of Sol. 8:6), stronger in fact. We are looking, whether we know it or not, for a Christ and for a church.

* * * *

A Christian vision of sexuality can actually make sex more satisfying, not less, by dethroning sexuality from its place of ultimacy. This, and this alone can restore the only thing that can make marital sexuality truly good—a sense of playfulness and affection that can come only when one does not feel the pressure to perform. If sex is not the best thing in life, one is free to have good sex. The Bible speaks often of sexual joy but does not, unlike some Christian sex manuals, give us detailed viewpoints, except to tell us to delight in one another, to do so often, and to keep the marriage bed undefiled (Heb. 13:4).

Often, our evangelical Christian culture works against that. I hear repeatedly that evangelical Christianity, or a "purity culture" within evangelical Christianity, leaves people sexually stunted and repressed with a sense of sex as dirty. I suppose that could happen, but I rarely see it. Instead, I see the reverse quite often. The Bible though—all of it—points to something better: Christ and him crucified. With that truth in mind, those who are married need not live up to the imagined comparison of their neighbors' frenzied sex. And those who are called to singleness, whether for a moment or for life, need not live up to the imagined comparison of their sexually "free" generational cohorts.

Several years ago, while serving as a youth pastor, I took a vanload of students to an evangelism conference for teenagers. The speaker, chosen probably for his youth and "edginess," told the assembled crowd his conversion story: he had come to Christ after years of "wildness," including sexual promiscuity. He had now found Christ and was serving in ministry. He pointed to his wife in the crowd, and told of her "hotness," as well as their storybook-beautiful children. "God gave me the testimony I needed," he said. "He knew I would need to know that I was not missing anything, so he let me experience all of that, and then saved me and gave me this great marriage." I boiled internally with rage because I could see, as a former eighth-grade boy, the thought balloons forming over all of the eighth-grade boys in our group: "That's the testimony I want. All the sex I can have, followed by heaven and a hot wife." It's the same mentality the young woman on the church van in my own middle-school days had expressed in her reluctance to meet Christ in the air just yet. Such fits perfectly with the spirit of the age, a spirit that leads many single Christians into despair or immorality and many married Christians into discontentment or immorality. That spirit is not telling us the truth. If the cross has given us what Jesus tells us it has, then our culture's view of a person's life consisting in the multitude of his orgasms is false. Whether we are sexually abased or sexually abounding, we are missing nothing. We can do all things through Christ who strengthens us, even if what we are called to do is nothing at all.

Sex is good, but it's not the best thing in your life. Knowing this can enable you—if married—to please your spouse sexually and be content in that union. Knowing this can enable you—if single—to channel your sexual desires toward service to others. In either case, a cross-shaped sexuality can give us the power to fight temptation and the power to find joy in the moment, without clamoring for some sensation we fear we might miss. Jesus can return whenever he wants.

CHAPTER NINE
The Road to and from Divorce

WOMEN THESE DAYS ARE AS "carnal as hell," he said, and that's why he wanted dating advice from me. He was a stranger to me, but he came to my office wanting to make sure that as he dated in this cultural environment that he would know how to find a godly Christian mate. He wanted, he said, to find a "Proverbs 31 woman." She needed, he said, to agree with him doctrinally, especially on matters related to the doctrines of election and predestination. We were five or six minutes in before I made some comment about a passage of Scripture to which he replied, "Yes, that's what my wife says." It took me several seconds to orient myself. "Your wife?" I asked. "You're married?" He said he was. "How on earth are we then talking about your dating?" He laughed, seeing my confusion, and said, "Oh, don't worry. I'm not cheating on her. I'm going to divorce her."

Didn't I agree, he asked, that one could divorce if one is "unequally yoked" with another? Before I could even answer "no," he further explained that his wife was not an unbeliever, but rather, he believed them to be unequally yoked because he was spiritually mature while she was, in his words, "carnal as hell." His major issue with her was that she had a hyphenated name—her maiden name joined with his—which was apparently all the evidence he needed that she was not submitting to him as "the head of my house." But, even beyond that, he said, her biblical ignorance sparked constant theological debates that would frequently confuse the children. So, he surmised, he could when freed from her, find a good, properly submissive, theologically-educated woman.

Intrigued, I asked about the theological disagreements, which he then told me were about the moderate use of alcohol. As I've mentioned, I am part of a church communion that sees wisdom in abstinence from alcohol, but I know that this is a minority report in the history of the church and that many Christians do otherwise. I couldn't imagine this being a doctrinal fight that would disrupt a friendship much less a marriage. I asked, how do the arguments manifest themselves? "Usually it's when she sees me moderately using alcohol," he said. I pressed a little further, asking him to describe his moderate use of alcohol. "Well," he said. "Every night I'll start drinking a bottle of bourbon and a twelve pack of beer until I go to sleep." Now I had some clarity. I started to reference biblical passages on drunkenness, and ministries various churches had for those who grapple with chemical dependence issues. He looked at me, confused, as though I had suggested swapping recipes for seven-layer salad or some other matter irrelevant to the issue of concern. He reached out his hand and said, "Oh no. I've never been drunk in my life."

Now, I don't know much about drinking, but I've dealt with many people who do, and I've listened to country music since I was three years old, so I feel confident in saying that consuming a bottle of whiskey and a twelve-pack of beer until you pass out is drunk. "You're starting to sound like my wife," the man snapped. "By the way, did you know that she has a hyphenated name?"

Carnal as hell, indeed. The problem wasn't his wife, or at least it wasn't only with her. This man sought to use biblical directives on marriage in order to prop up his appetites and to "free" him to violate his marriage vows. He wanted to win an argument, not to carry a cross. I am surprised that his wife agreed to take any part of his name—hyphenated or not. I also thought long and hard after this man left my office: where is his church? I don't know what happened to this marriage, but, unless he pivoted toward repentance quickly, there's a wife and children out there somewhere who had their entire lives pulled apart, all the while being told that this was Jesus' will. And God help that Proverbs 31 woman who is next in line. His situation is extreme, of course, but it was easier for me to see from the outside than it would be from the inside.

How many times in my own marriage, I wondered after he left, have I also selfishly sought to think first of myself and my appetites? And how often have I done so, all the while believing myself to be secure in my biblical maturity? Marriage can reveal, sometimes as nothing else can, just how oriented we are to the self. Granted, again, his is an extreme case. Most people are not this brazen in their willfulness, but the brokenness he leaves behind is all too common. It's easy for me to see this man as a villain or a buffoon, but I wonder what had happened in his life that led him to this view of marriage, and of what it would mean to have a meaningful life? Maybe back there, behind all of that, was some hurt that I couldn't even fathom. Indeed, even with this man's rather obvious (to me) self-deception, he really wasn't that unusual except in his brazenness. In reality, much of the church has gone right down the path this man had trod: loud denunciations of other people's sins, while convincing ourselves that Jesus is on our side as we do the opposite of what he commanded. That is nowhere clearer than when it comes to our attitudes about marriage. By this, I don't mean—to be sure—our idealized notions of what marriage ought to be, but rather what happens to our Christian conviction when marriages begin to hit turbulence or even to break apart.

* * * *

Evangelical Christians in North America like to tell ourselves that we are "countercultural," standing outside the mainstream of society, bearing witness for Christ. The reality, though, is quite different when we look at the actual data rather than our own slogans about ourselves. On the one hand, the entrepreneurial nature of American evangelicalism, centered on personal conversion and suspicious of institutions, has had the freedom to establish bonds with like-minded believers for the cause of missions and church-planting in ways never possible in the bureaucracies of other churches, with their byzantine structures and glacial pace. On the other hand, this "free market ecclesiology" can easily make it marketable to the point of eclipsing the very distinctiveness it has to offer to the world in the first place.

The fact is, the popular caricature of Western Christians as censorious scolds, standing athwart culture with a kind of embittered separatism, is negative, but not true. The problem for us is that the reality is not any better. There are some ways in which Western Christianity does run counter to the prevailing culture—our views on sexual morality and in the practice of charitable giving, for example. In other areas, such as the actual practice of sexual integrity, the data show that we are only as countercultural as we want to be. As one observer noted, the culture war is mostly an illusion since the church is gladly enmeshed in the same therapeutic, consumerist milieu of autonomous individualism that gave us the Sexual Revolution in the first place.[35] In terms of pornography, premarital sex, and many other issues, this scholar argues, if evangelical Christians are fighting, we are fighting for the other side, whether we know it or not. This is probably nowhere more clearly seen than in the shockingly high numbers of those who make the trek from our baptisteries to the local divorce court. In fact, some studies show that areas where there are more evangelical Christians have higher divorce rates than those without.[36]

Now, again, some of these statistics are misleading. After all, to ask someone in Bible Belt America who is over the age of forty if he or she is "born again" or an "evangelical Christian" is somewhat the equivalent of asking someone elsewhere if he or she is a patriot. To say otherwise would be to opt out of the social system, built as it is on nominal, cultural Christianity. Evangelical Christians tend to proliferate, at least in this country, in places of long-term economic struggle. These populations, studies show, marry earlier, marry more often, and divorce more frequently. Nonetheless, we could explain away these data points, showing others that demonstrate committed churchgoers are less likely to divorce than their secular peers in the same situation, but such would prove little. The very fact that this is a point of discussion is already a defeat for the idea that the gospel is transforming our subculture. Whatever the exact rates of divorce among Christians, they are far too similar, if not worse, than the general population.

Moreover, one need not look at statistics to see the cultural accommodation to a divorce culture within professing Christian circles. Notice how divorce is rarely even mentioned in the hubbub of culture war issues around us. Is this because the Bible does not speak to the matter? Hardly. The Bible addresses divorce far more extensively than many of the questions we confront loudly with a "Christian worldview." Leaders within the political sphere, and even within the church, have broken marriage vows, sometimes scandalously, with virtually no protest, or even moral evaluation, from the church. It is not that, in these cases, the church weighs and agonizes over these matters and comes to a different set of conclusions, but rather that there is virtually no moral analysis at all.

Years ago, I came across a list of quotations on the family from various articles and sermons across the denominational spectrum. The most impressive was from a pastor within my tradition, speaking at a 1980s-era conference organized by the organization I now lead. This pastor prophetically charged evangelical Christians with relegating the issue of divorce to "descriptive statements in which we are drowning" at the expense of "normative statements, a divine word, a prophetic word, an authoritative word, a transcendent word from God." This leader displayed what impressed me as some of the most remarkable pastoral courage I had seen on this point as he laid out the carnage left in gospel churches by rampant divorce, noting what this does to our global witness for Christ. The leader did not attack "the culture" or his political opponents but lamented instead that divorce was the only great issue where his own church tradition was "tongue-tied" with a "mutinous silence." As I read these words, I was sobered to contemplate how this leader's warnings were still true, many decades later. I was about to quote these remarks in a speech until I looked to find the author's name, only to realize that, by the time I was reading the statement, he himself was divorced.

Now, as I will discuss a bit further down in this text, there are a variety of views among conservative Protestant Christians about when, if ever, it is biblically permissible to divorce or to remarry after divorce.[37] Nonetheless, even the most expansive view of the biblical exceptions would rule out most of the divorces in modern American culture. How can Christians—whether on the Right or the Left culturally or politically—speak to issues of social justice and the common good without addressing what is no doubt the leading cause of "orphans and widows" (James 1:27) in our midst? How can we speak with any moral credibility at all about "family values" while speaking in muted tones on the issue of divorce and at full-volume on other matters? One survey of the preaching in a very conservative Christian denomination shows a distinct "softening" of preaching when it comes to divorce, often related to pastoral comments on forgiveness and "second chances" for those who have been divorced and remarried.[38] Forgiveness and second chances are precisely right, and ought to be at the center of our preaching. But what needs to be "forgiven" if it is not first seen to be sin? Would we pronounce "forgiveness" to adulterous spouses in our congregations who do not see adultery as wrong or, if wrong, as necessary in their situations? No. We would proclaim full forgiveness in Christ, but we would call for repentance, including an agreement with God that the sin is, in fact, sin. When it comes to divorce, though, often our churches speak in terms of "divorce care" ministries and "single again" Bible studies (both of which are commendable and missiologically appropriate), but rarely in the context of prophetic preaching and congregational discipline.

Some of this is a reaction to the censorious and condemnatory attitudes of many Christians, especially in previous generations, to those who have been divorced. When divorce was uncommon, those who had experienced it (regardless of whether they were the initiators of the divorce, or just the victims of it) were marginalized, sometimes treated as pariahs. As one woman who had been abandoned by her husband put it to me, "I wanted the gospel so badly, but the unspoken message to me seemed to be that divorce is the unforgivable sin." Such is out of step with the gospel, and a correcting of this is necessary for any church focused on the cross of Jesus Christ. We should offer full forgiveness and justification for any person who entrusts himself or herself to the atoning Jesus Christ. That does not explain, though, why we would not warn people away from a sin for which the wages are death, and the temporal consequences ruinous. Nor does it explain why we are willing to speak of all of us as sinners but not willing to speak of this—in many, if not most, cases—as itself sin, sin for which Christ died and for which we need forgiveness. Some of the issue here is that of pastoral courage, or lack thereof. One can watch the way that Christian national leaders can pivot away from any moral consideration of divorce the minute someone they "need" in terms of fundraising or political influence is unrepentantly divorced and remarried. The same often happens, just at a less noticeable level, in local congregations. And this is tragic, but easy enough to understand. Who wishes to speak to an issue, in the hard tones with which the Bible speaks to it, that affects virtually every family in the pews? John the Baptist telling Herod he could not have another man's wife is a quite rare profile in courage in almost any era. Rarely do cultural influence-makers need more than a handful of silver platters to silence the voices they don't want to hear.

The shift in evangelical attitudes toward marital permanence does not seem to have come through any kind of theological reflection or conversation at all. Instead, our approach to divorce seems to have meandered just a bit behind the mainstream of American cultural patterns of acceptance of "one spouse at a time" as a sad, but normal, part of life. We have grown accustomed to a divorce culture the way that, perhaps, our own future grandchildren or great-grandchildren may become accustomed to polygamy or artificially intelligent sex robots. Will they be more countercultural than we are? Many Christians don't register the same alarm when it comes to divorce as they do other aspects of family decline because they have seen divorce so often that it seems almost "normal" to them. This is precisely the problem. One poet of the last century was right to say, "Whoever considers as normal the order of things in which the strong triumph and the weak fail, and life ends with death, accepts the devil's rule."[39] The devil's rule is all about us when it comes to what we think of the tearing apart of the embedded picture of the gospel—the Christ-church one-flesh union—all around us. Some would tell us that when it comes to a divorce culture, we cannot "turn back the clock," but as Neil Postman warned us a generation ago, "in some respects the clock is wrong."[40] In order to bring a word of liberation, we must be willing to say so.

This is even more thorny when we move from the cultural terrain to the personal. I remember years ago, a commentator, tongue in cheek, addressing the abortion debate, with rising numbers of Americans opposed to abortion. She said: "Most Americans are pro-life with three exceptions: rape, incest, and my situation."[41] Her point was that moral abstractions could show up rather easily in answers to questions from a polling firm. When, though, a "pro-life" man has a pregnant teenage daughter or a "pro-life" woman finds herself to be pregnant in the middle of medical school, sometimes these abstractions are easily tossed aside. The same is true in this case. Moral commitments to the permanence of marriage are always readily assumed. In our culture, it is the rare couple—even among unbelievers—who do not pledge at the wedding to remain together "until death do us part." It's also true that divorce is often a deeply painful issue for those who have had nothing to do with the conflicts in the marriage whatsoever. How many children are, right now, shuttling back and forth between a mother and a stepfather and a father and a stepmother? And how many of them are suppressing a palpable sense of guilt—as if somehow they could have kept their parents' marriage together—or else a simmering rage at the parents who could not keep their childhood homes together?

* * * *

So how did we get here? Some would suggest that the problem lies in early marriage rates. Those regions where the typical person delays marriage until well into the twenties or even into the thirties tend to have lower rates of divorce than regions with higher rates of very young marriage. To some degree, this is no doubt true. We would all agree that there are many people who are too young to marry, which is why, were one of my sons to announce that he, in high school, is engaged, I would step in to veto the notion. And yet, marriage rates throughout history and all over the world have been much younger than ours are now. That's not just the case in the distant Isaac-and-Rebekah past. My grandmother was married in the 1940s at the age of fourteen. She was not pregnant, and there was no scandal involved, in her little community in Mississippi. She was also in a culture which—for all of its many social and moral and structural evils—did not see much divorce. Those lacking maturity to rough out the difficulties of marriage—whatever their age—should not marry. And yet, delaying marriage indefinitely does not seem to solve the problem.

Delayed marriage is a reality in our cultural ecosystem. In some ways, this could be good, if it means a person preparing himself or herself for marriage, spending the time it takes to discipline himself to be a faithful husband, or herself a faithful wife. Often, though, delayed marriage is about something quite different from this. To some degree, marriage is often delayed due to the extension of adolescence, a fear of "grown-up" commitments and responsibilities. This is not though, I believe, the primary reason marriage time lines have inched up and up on the chronological scale. Instead, this is probably most often due to an idealization of marriage. In a culture in which marriage is about finding the one soul mate who can meet every need, forever in the haze of romance, then one will often search endlessly for such a person, never finding him or her. When one adds to this the lack of social bonds that might make divorce rare, we end up with an awful predicament: seeking to determine who, out of billions of possibilities, is "the One," while also making sure that this partner will never leave or cause pain. That's an impossible mission. No wonder some secretly see marrying, whomever they marry, as "settling." If, though, we see marriage as sharing a cross, as bearing suffering together, walking together on a pilgrimage toward the New Jerusalem, the picture changes dramatically.

Yes, those who delay marriage in our culture have lower divorce rates than those who marry young, but often they do so by opting out of marriage altogether or by cohabiting sometimes with multiple partners through their young adulthoods. This hardly does away with divorce; it just keeps divorce out of the court system as people experience serial, kind-of "marriages," just without the commitment or the accountability. Many of these people often suffer multiple cases of what we might call common-law divorces. So these statistics are quite confused. I cannot claim to have solved the problem of highway car accidents simply by pointing to reduced rates of such accidents in my town if in fact people have stopped buying cars altogether. And this would be especially absurd if, in this scenario, people are having just as many accidents on motorcycles. Yes, literally and technically, the car accident problem would then be resolved, but to no substantive end. One can certainly understand why those who have lived through the trauma of divorce—often in the lives of their own parents—would seek to protect themselves by avoiding the arena of divorce, marriage itself, but this is hardly the solution.

After one of the many studies on divorce came out showing higher rates of divorce in more culturally conservative states, I had an exchange via text message with a sociologist friend about the results. He blamed country music. I think he was mostly kidding me—knowing that I am a fan of old-school outlaw country—but not entirely. Country music, with its roots in the folk songs of the Appalachian and southern regions of the United States, illustrates, he said, that southerners have a more "romanticized" view of marriage than other Americans. I responded that southerners have a more romanticized view of *everything* than other Americans. Country music, it seemed to me, was actually less problematic than other forms of popular music, which idealize not marriage but adolescent, hormonal experiences of romance. At least the older forms of country music would speak lyrically to marriages lasting into old age, and, even when they (frequently) dealt with divorce, many of these songs lament the divorce, sometimes in haunting terms. I had to admit, though, that my friend was not totally wrong. Country music is indeed problematic when it comes to the divorce culture. This is not, though, due to its vision of marriage (which is often remarkably good) but in its tacit acceptance of a Bible Belt gospel.

Secularized conservative evangelicals in Tennessee are in a much worse place than secularized liberal Episcopalians in Connecticut. First of all, the Connecticut Episcopalian has a greater sense of economic stability and social capital. The secularized evangelicals, moreover, don't know that they are secularizing. The Connecticut nominal Episcopalian is in a region that has been secularizing since well before his or her grandparents were ever born out of Puritanism, with its strong commitment to social structures and community solidarity. There is no illusion of Christendom for this person. The southern evangelical, though, is also secularizing—accepting as normal what his ancestors would have seen as scandal—but is secularizing out of revivalism. The need for a "personal relationship with Jesus Christ" is, in my view, both biblical and necessary. But if this is disconnected from a sense of belonging within the church, it can easily lead to an almost-gospel of "praying to receive Christ" with no sense of Christ's lordship over one's life or accountability to Christ's church. When that is added to biblical illiteracy and theological minimalism, the result is disastrous, both for persons and for marriages and families.

If the Christian life is mostly about my individual emotional experience with God, then this pattern of life easily enough translates into marriages that are about my emotional experience with my spouse. When that sense of revivalist mysticism is added to a "Christian" culture in which no church will notice or care what I do, so long as I say the right words about Jesus and vote for the right candidates, it feels natural enough to believe—as Paul denounced in Romans 6:1—that my divorce is just one more thing for God to forgive, and forgiving is his job. A sense of "Christianity" without theological definition, ecclesial identity, and community accountability does indeed lead into a perfect storm of divorce culture: an idealized view of marriage in which my spouse will always be "the one" to meet my needs, and an individualized view of the gospel in which Jesus exists to meet my needs just as my spouse does, except for eternity.

My sociologist friend might well be right that country music illustrates the problem, except that it is not the songs about divorce and adultery that do so, but the gospel song at the end of it all. In some ways, these closing songs at a concert that was otherwise full of choruses celebrating getting drunk and being cheated on, represent the very best aspects of Bible Belt revivalism: namely, that no one is too far gone for redemption. But the worst aspects are there too—Jesus is my Savior but doesn't tell me what to do. This feeds directly into a view of the gospel and a view of the gospel icon of marriage that are disturbingly similar. Both views are built off a kind of emotional commitment, one at the altar call and one at the wedding altar, of "I Surrender All," without a serious "counting of the cost" of either one. Nominal Christianity empowers this much easier than does secularism or paganism because with nominal Christianity one has the social pressure for marriage without strong community and discipleship. The gospel doesn't propel a divorce culture, but an almost-gospel certainly does.

For Christians, this is more than just a social problem or even an issue of personal hurt and crisis. The prophet Malachi looked to the future for the day when, as he said to the people of God, "the Lord whom you seek will suddenly come to his temple" (Mal. 3:1). This would seem to be good news for a people disappointed that the rebuilding of the temple after exile did not usher in the messianic time they were expecting. And yet Malachi wrote this in warning, not in reassurance, asking "who can endure the day of his coming, and who can stand when he appears?" (Mal. 3:2).

What would prompt such hard words from the prophet? He wrote that it was because of the breaking of the covenant, by the people of Judah. This was expressed in two ways. The first is straightforwardly spiritual. "For Judah has profaned the sanctuary of the LORD, which he loves, and has married the daughter of a foreign god" (Mal. 2:11). As was the case repeatedly, the nation slinked into idolatry. And, as he also did repeatedly, God compared this idolatry with a violation of marriage vows. This culture of spiritual "divorce" was linked, inextricably, to a culture of literal divorce. The second grievance God had against his people was this: "You cover the LORD's altar with tears, with weeping and groaning because he no longer regards the offering or accepts it with favor from your hand. But you say, 'Why does he not?' Because the LORD was witness between you and the wife of your youth, to whom you have been faithless, though she is your companion and your wife by covenant" (Mal. 2:13–14). This was a matter of social injustice, for which God comprehensively indicted his people in this prophet's book and elsewhere, but it was more than that.

The divorcing of these marriages was no more just a matter of individual vows breaking apart than the idolatry in the temple was just a matter of misused space. Of marriage, the prophet proclaimed: "Did he not make them one with a portion of the Spirit in their union? And what was the one God seeking? Godly offspring" (Mal. 2:15). These marriages were not just about personal love and commitment (although they were that), and they were not just about social breakdown (although they were that too). Each marriage was, mysteriously, a matter of spiritual union. God made these couples one, and dispensed his Spirit into the union. He is, therefore, a witness against those who have wrongly divorced their wives, just as he is elsewhere spoken of as a witness against those who mistreat their workers or the poor (Mal. 3:5; James 5:4). The message from God was not one of mere judgment but of a warning to those who were not yet in the situation. "So guard yourselves in your spirit, and let none of you be faithless to the wife of your youth" (Mal. 2:15). And then God pronounced, once again, his verdict on a divorce culture. "For the man who does not love his wife but divorces her, says the Lord, the God of Israel, covers his garment with violence, says the Lord of hosts" (Mal. 2:16). The breaking of marriage vows, God says, is an act of violence.

* * * *

As Malachi promised, God did come into his temple, though not the way his people expected. He provided a new temple—in the flesh of his Son Jesus—whereby God would tabernacle with his people (John 1:14). Some would see Jesus as the "sweeter side of God," talking as he does against being judgmental or retaliatory. I once heard a man threaten to beat up someone by saying, "I'm going to go Old Testament on you." Jesus is indeed the embodiment of the grace and forgiveness of God, but the cross shows us that this is not at the expense of God's holiness and justice. Jesus' teaching is consistent with this as well. Jesus offered mercy—startlingly so to the culture around him—to the Samaritan woman at the well, but in so doing he uncovered her five failed marriages and her current cohabitation

(John 4:16–17). In order to draw her to his grace, he must show her why she needed it. The same is true for us.

Nowhere is the reality of Jesus more at odds with the sentimental caricature of him than in his teaching on the permanence of marriage. The Pharisees came to Jesus "in order to test him," on the question of divorce (Mark 10:1–11). Since the religious leaders often "tested" Jesus by attempting to put him at odds with popular opinion (on, for example, whether to pay taxes to Caesar or on whether there would be a resurrection), one might conclude that the topic of divorce was as personally sensitive in the first century as it is today. The Pharisees appealed to Scripture—to the Mosaic law permitting divorce (Deut. 24:1–4). Jesus, though, taught that the Law of Moses was a temporary measure, meant to rein in the consequences of hearts that were too hardened to hear God's voice on this matter (Mark 10:5). Citing Genesis, Jesus said that God's design was monogamy and permanence of the one-flesh union of male and female (Mark 10:6–7). "So they are no longer two but one flesh," he said. "What therefore God has joined together let not man separate" (Mark 10:8–9). This prompted a follow-up interrogation by his disciples, but Jesus did not back down, and, if anything, ratcheted up the rhetoric. "Whoever divorces his wife and marries another commits adultery against her," he said, "and if she divorces her husband and marries another, she commits adultery" (Mark 10:11–12).

So does this mean that there is never a cause for divorce, or that those divorced must remain celibate and unmarried? Some Christians believe so. The Roman Catholic Church historically has taught that those who are divorced and remarried are in a state of perpetual adultery, unless the first marriage is recognized by the church not to have been a genuine marriage and thus annulled, and so those in this state have not been admitted to communion. Many Protestants agree with this assessment. I do not. Matthew's account of Jesus' words include what many call an "exception clause" to the question of adultery in the case of remarriage after divorce: "except in the case of sexual immorality" (Matt. 19:9). Some would argue that this merely means that in the case of sexual immorality, one is an adulterer already, even before the divorce and remarriage. I think this assumes too much on the text, and doesn't see the ways in which, throughout the Old Testament, sexual infidelity can indeed sever the one-flesh union.

The apostle Paul also wrote to the church at Corinth about the plight of those who have been abandoned by unbelieving spouses. It is not difficult to see why a Christian might assume that, having come to faith in Christ, he could divorce his spouse to which he was joined before coming to faith. He might easily conclude: I am a "new creation," aren't I? I did not marry this person; the "old me" did, and that old self is crucified with Christ and no longer alive. Paul though, like Jesus, treated marriage as a creation institution, one that remains until death. Moreover, one might have worried that remaining in a marriage with an unbeliever would be the same situation as the believer marrying an unbeliever, a case of being "unequally yoked" (2 Cor. 6:14). This is not the case though, the apostle said. God sanctifies the union through the believing spouse (1 Cor. 7:13–14). One shouldn't seek a divorce because one's spouse isn't a Christian (1 Cor. 7:12). The marriage is real, and can even be, relatively speaking, holy. Some, though, had been abandoned by their spouses after their conversion to Christ. They are, he said, "not bound" (1 Cor. 7:15), which implies that they are now free, as the Bible directs for those whose spouses are dead, to remarry in the Lord. Again, these exceptions are not universally held, but I believe them to be biblically accurate. The one-flesh union may be dissolved in the cases of unrepentant sexual breaking of the marriage bond or by the abandonment of that bond. In such cases, the divorce is no sin for the "innocent party," and that person may remarry without sin. Let me qualify these a bit more.

Sexual immorality is not here exclusively adultery. The word *porneia* includes a broader sense of sexual uncleanness. I believe that Jesus here *permits* divorce in some cases of such immorality, but he does not *mandate* divorce, here or elsewhere. If your spouse has cheated on you, the first step should be, just as it is within the broader church when it comes to the full range of sin, to reconcile the relationship

(Matt. 18:15–18). If the cheating spouse repents, the years to come may be difficult in restoring trust and establishing boundaries, but the marriage is intact. In some cases, the spouse will not respond and the innocent party needs then to take the matter to their church, again to call the erring one back to repentance (Matt. 18:17). Only when the spouse is clearly unrepentant, usually over an extended period of time, is the situation irrevocable, and thus grounds for the formal recognition of what is already a fact: the dissolution of the marriage. If you find text messages of a sexual nature between your husband and your best friend, your natural response might be to call a divorce attorney. At first, though, call your husband to repentance. Such marriages can be saved, and often should be.

Moreover, "abandonment" is more, in my view, than simply the walking away from the physical location of the home. Paul is speaking of a marriage in which the other partner has determined that the marriage is over. This is obvious to see in the case where, for instance, a man's wife leaves him and refuses to come home, saying that she's "moving on" with her life. I believe abandonment would also include, for instance, abusive behavior that makes the home an unsafe environment for a person or his or her children. If you are being abused, or if your children are in danger of being abused, leave the home immediately. The abuse calls for the response both of the civil authorities (Rom. 13:1-4) and the church. Call the police, first, to establish physical safety and temporal justice, and then call the leadership of your church. Do not, under any circumstances, put your children at risk of physical or sexual predation. The church, if suspecting such abuse, should also alert the civil authorities and also act to respond spiritually to this matter. Such satanic behavior toward the vulnerable makes a home uninhabitable and thus, in my view, clearly constitutes abandonment. Someone escaping such abuse is not in sin to divorce the abusive spouse and is, in my view, free to remarry.

Some would say that this abandonment exception applies only to those with an "unbelieving" spouse, and yet the New Testament does not categorize "believing" merely as those who are formally aligned with a church. The one who is unrepentant in sin may or may not be personally regenerate; we cannot know the heart. That person, though, is to be, finally, where there is no repentance shown, treated "as a Gentile and a tax collector" (Matt. 18:17). That doesn't mean irredeemable (consider how Jesus treated sinners and Gentiles and tax collectors!); it does mean that the person is to be considered outside of the people of God. If the person repents, then "you have gained your brother" (Matt. 18:15).

These exceptions are not individually determined. I cannot, in the middle of a marital crisis, conclude on my own that, for instance, my spouse's sexual immorality is irrevocable. Marriage is to be part of the discipline of the church. In an era of rampant autonomous individualism, we do not see how one's marriage—or one's divorce—should be anyone else's business. The Scripture declares it to be (1 Cor. 5:1–5). Church discipline is not—as I will elaborate later—simply, as we often think, summed up in the final step of excommunication (indeed, such cases ought to be rare). The goal of discipline is formative and restorative. That means that the church ought to start resisting divorce long before it starts by, among other things, only marrying those who are accountable to the church.

Marriage is a creation institution; it is not reserved only for believers. Unbelievers can and should marry, if they meet the Genesis 2 requirements. Such is a matter of statecraft, though, not of the church. The state has an interest in, among other things, safeguarding children, by holding mothers and fathers accountable to their vows and to the next generation. These unions are the business of the larger society in ways that other relationships aren't. When those marriages dissolve, the state rightly exercises authority. Our divorce laws, as they are, are often unjust, but think of the lack of justice there would be if we had no divorce laws at all. People would still leave their marriages, but with no restraints on the wreckage that could be caused through financial deprivation, child custody, and a thousand other contingencies. A divorce lawyer who advertises to entice people to divorce for his financial gain is wrong, but the attorney seeing to it that an abandoned spouse is not left destitute or that a sexually-abusive spouse doesn't gain custody of a child can be working for justice. Divorce is only possible in a fallen world, but in this fallen world there are often those who experience divorce as victims, not as perpetrators. These people have divorce foisted upon them, and they need protection.

The church, though, holds authority only over those who are united to it through the gospel (1 Cor. 5:9–13). Every marriage that the church solemnizes should be a marriage the church takes as its responsibility. When I, as a new groom, sign the state's marriage license, I am stating that I am accountable to the civil state should I break these vows. When I, as a Christian, marry within the church, I should have the same expectation of the church. The problem is that many go to the church at the start of a marriage—because it's expected that one would be married by a priest or a minister, or because the church is a beautiful venue for the photographs—but go only to the courts when the marriage dissolves. Churches should, then, marry only those who are accountable to the church—as well as to the state—and to the gathered witnesses for the keeping of their vows.

The "marrying parson" who will marry anyone, who stands where the wedding coordinator tells him to, reads his script and dutifully signs the paperwork for whatever couple shows up, should resign the ministry and do an honest day's work as a justice of the peace rather than as steward of the mysteries of God. We should gladly render to Caesar what belongs to Caesar, but the image imprinted on the marriage union isn't that of Caesar and his court but of Christ and his church. This means also that the church should work to prepare couples for the difficulties of marriage. If anyone should evaporate the sentimental idealization of marriage, it should be the church. That's especially true in an era in which that idealization is perhaps the leading driver of divorce. We should talk openly about what is at stake in divorce, not just emotionally but morally before God. And we should provide mentors—older, established couples who can guide others through challenges—for those struggling in their marriages.

What would happen if churches really took our biblical responsibilities seriously to care for marriages within the body and to hold accountable those who would hurt others by their vow-breaking? What would happen in one local congregation if a couple felt free to come forward and ask for prayer from the whole body over their faltering marriage, without feeling embarrassed or shamed or judged? What would happen if abuse were, in every one of our churches, not ever covered over, but in every case were dealt with in terms of civil justice and in terms of ecclesial accountability? What would happen if single mothers in our community—many of them abandoned or divorced by men—were treated as the Bible tells us to treat widows, cared for by the entire congregation spiritually, emotionally, socially, and, where needed, economically? What would happen is that we just might demonstrate to the outside world what we in fact are called to be: not a civic club or a political precinct or a self-improvement society but a community formed by a cross.

* * * *

What should couples themselves do to work against a creeping divorce culture in their own marriages? Again, it is best if this starts at the very beginning of the marriage. Really believe your vows, that this is not just a "love contract" but a permanent union. Divorce should not be silently hidden away as your last resort. If divorce is an option for you—even a last resort—it will happen. No marriage that is not—consciously and unconsciously—committed to permanence can survive. Even if it remains legally intact, such a marriage will not flourish. That's especially true when a culture of choice gives us the illusion that there's always the chance for a better spouse, a better marriage, a better life, if you could just go out looking for such things. When a couple in premarital counseling asks me if they should craft a prenuptial agreement, I almost always stop to more closely examine what is happening that they would be negotiating a divorce before the marriage. If the groom cannot trust the bride, or vice-versa, with money, how can they trust each other with their lives, their children, their future? Conclude that your options are not to be married to this person or to someone else, but to be married to this person in the pattern of the cross or to this person in the tumult of self. Our approach to marriage ought to resemble something akin to the answer given by one celebrity musician's wife when asked by reporters what the "secret" was to staying married as long as they had. "The main reason is that neither of us has died." For her, divorce was not the option they had avoided, but was not an option at all. That is, in fact, the key to a long marriage.

I remember early in my marriage talking to a friend about a couple we knew that had been driven apart by an affair. "If Maria ever cheated on me, I would be crushed," I said. "But I still wouldn't divorce her. I would take her back a thousand times, if I had to." My friend said, "Why don't you tell her that?" I chafed a bit. I didn't want to tell my wife that I would stay with her, even if she had an affair with another man. What would then keep her from having an affair? Well, it might be that what keeps her from having an affair is the knowledge that she has a husband so committed to their marriage that he would still love her, even if she had an affair. In marriage, only by laying down your weapons, can you really find the love you will need to withstand whatever battles lie ahead.

Behind that sense of permanence, though, is an ongoing struggle to learn how to love each other. Again, this does not mean simply the feeling of love, but the other-directed, self-sacrificial love that God demonstrated in sending his Son to the cross for us (John 3:16). Some will say, "Love is a decision, not a feeling." That's not quite right, though I affirm the point they are trying to make here, namely that one does not always "feel" like one is in love. But love is not a decision in the sense that it merely is a coldly rational choice. Look at the exuberance of the Song of Solomon. You press through difficult times in order to build a future together that will be less difficult. You choose to stay together when you don't feel like it, in order to "feel like it" at a later time. As a matter of fact, only when I give up my demand to constantly feel in love can I actually ever feel love for more than a fleeting moment. That requires commitment, fidelity, and the self-sacrifice we see in the cross.

A couple should not go into a marriage expecting not to fight. Even Jesus and his bride, the church, had disagreements, including about the most central truth of his mission, the cross. This analogy is not one-to-one, of course, because in the Christ-church union, unlike your marriage or mine, there is one sinless, infinitely wise spouse. When Christ and the church disagree, the outcome is easy enough to see. Christ is right; the church is wrong. That's not the case with marriages between fallen people. Often the solution to a disagreement is not to settle who is right and who is wrong, but to remind ourselves that we are, as Jesus put it, not two any longer but one. When my wife loses an argument with me, I haven't "won," and vice-versa. Even with the limitations on the analogy, we can glean from Jesus' response to disagreement from his church—especially Simon Peter, one of the foundation stones. Jesus does not avoid the conflict, at any turn, but he also knows his disciples well enough not to crush them with his words. The way of Christ will draw us toward patient engagement and away from the typical pathways many couples face: cold withdrawal from each other or angry rage, sexual bartering, threats to leave, and so forth. Couples who have disagreements shouldn't conclude that this means their marriage is necessarily imperiled. Often, the marriage in real jeopardy is the one in which there are no arguments at all—because one or both of the spouses just don't care enough anymore to fight. You will have disagreements.

The way to move forward is to plan ahead for those disagreements. Fight your arguments ahead of time when you feel the most affectionate toward one another. Few want to do this. Why would you want to ruin a perfect weekend away by bringing up what is triggered for you when your husband says, "You're just like your mother!" That's exactly the time to do so, just as the harvest is the time for the wise ant to store up for the winter (Prov. 6:8–10; 30:25). The tempers are cool, at those moments, and the affections are warm. These conversations need not be argumentative at all, but actually can be fun and playful—laughing at your own foibles, and showing how you want to love each other by reading what goes through the others mind or heart in certain situations. Many divorces could perhaps be avoided if couples would just reverse the timing of their planning sessions together. Plan your romantic getaways during a fight, and plan how you will fight on your romantic getaways.

Even beyond arguments, a marriage must prepare for times of stress that can wreck the unity of marriage. Building strong bonds between you, learning in small ways what to do when one of you faces disappointment, can help build the kind of resilience needed when one day you face stillbirth, liver cancer, a grown child in prison, or dementia. Learning to bear with each other, to forgive and to show patience, is about more than just "getting along," but about kindling a love strong enough to withstand suffering, the sort of love necessary to make it to the edge of the Jordan River together.

Watch for warning signals. Watch when you find yourself feeling or showing contempt for your spouse. Watch when you find yourself looking to escape away from your spouse, for comfort from the outside world, rather than the other way around. Watch when you find your sexual interactions becoming less frequent, and ask why that is. And do not, then, be afraid to ask for help. There is no shame in saying, "My marriage is in trouble." Everybody's marriage is in trouble at some point or another. Those who know their marriage is in trouble are the ones who can fight to save it.

We can work to prevent divorce within the church, and we can seek to reconcile separated or even divorced couples, but the reality is that many of us will still be divorced, and many of those remarried to other people. How do we respond to those already divorced? The question is not whether there are many in this situation who are blameless, and have biblical warrant to make exactly the decisions they made. I believe there are indeed. The question is what about those many situations, probably the vast majority, in which the divorce was in fact sinful, in which the remarriage was not allowable in Scripture. Again, we must look to the cross. We do not offer condemnation to the world. We do not liberate consciences though—many of them burdened down by guilt after divorcing when they shouldn't have— by avoiding the subject. We speak honestly about divorce not just in terms of therapy but in terms of its violation of God's holiness.

We don't stop there, though. Jesus came to save sinners, not the righteous, and he calls all of us to repentance. What does repentance look like in these situations? Take the worst-case scenario of the unbiblical divorced and remarried couple. They have, in fact, committed an adulterous act in the remarriage (Matt. 5:31–32). What now would we have them to do? Do they repent of this adultery by divorcing again? How can they repent of sin by repeating it, abandoning yet another spouse, breaking yet another set of vows? No. The Scripture does in many of these cases see the act of severing a marriage, and entering another, as an adulterous act. This does not mean that, once entered into, they are not marriages. The Samaritan woman at the well had five "husbands"—and Jesus uses that word.

A Christian entering into a marriage with a non-Christian is forbidden by Scripture. They are treated as real marriages, though. The person who repents of wrongly marrying an unbeliever does not follow Jesus by divorcing that spouse, but by remaining faithful (1 Cor. 7:12–17; 1 Pet. 3:1–2). We don't remedy our past sins by adding new ones. The person or the couple who are repentant of divorces or remarriages that weren't biblically allowed cannot go back and alter the past. They can, though, commit to "go, and . . . sin no more" (John 8:11), by acknowledging their own culpability, claiming full pardon through the atoning work of Christ, and working to remain, from now on, faithful to whatever vows they have made. Many of these persons and couples can then serve Christ, as many do, from their broken places.

One writer said long ago that he was suspicious "of fat revolutionaries and recently divorced marriage counselors."[42] True enough. But there are many on the far side of such divorces. In many cases, they may be the ones who equip and mentor younger people by saying, "Don't go in the direction I went, but if you already have, here's the path home." They know what's at stake, and they know, in this area, what all of us should know in many areas: what it means to be forgiven much.

* * * *

A divorce culture is built off of the assumption that a divorce can actually give a "new start." Those who are divorced can tell you that there really is not such a thing as an ex-husband or an ex-wife, even though such may be true legally or even morally. One can divorce a person, but one cannot divorce the history one had together. That's why some of the hurting divorced people in our pews are grieving, not just over a failed marriage, or over the loneliness of being, as we so callously put it, "single again." Many are grieving because they thought at the end of the divorce there would be a "new start." The next marriage will be the one that meets all their needs, but the old marriage lingers, in the psyche and in the conscience. A covenant cannot be just packed up in boxes and moved out the door.

A church that is anchored in the gospel of the cross will be a church that can say to the couple in crisis: "Stay married. Don't divorce," can say to the wrongly divorcing person: "Repent of this sin against your family and your God," and can say to the repentant divorced person: "God is not angry at you; you are forgiven," all at the same time. We can get there only when families and churches and pastors and leaders love divorced people more than we fear being unpopular with them. And it can only happen when we frame what marriage is in terms of the cross.

As one marriage researcher puts it, one reason modern marriage is so difficult is what she calls *the porcupine's dilemma*, defined as "the desire to achiever deep intimacy while remaining invulnerable to pain."[43] We see on the cross that such intimacy is impossible. We gain true communion only in vulnerability, only by surrendering the illusion that we can be impervious to hurt. This same researcher notes that one driving factor behind marital breakdown is the "all-or-nothing" ideal, that marriage must mean everything in order to be "good." When this doesn't happen—and all utopias short of heaven disappoint—all that's left is bitterness and resentment. The cross should point us to the fact that marriage will not, and cannot, be that for us. If we have a Wedding Feast before us, we should expect marriage to point us to that, but not to be that. Marriage is to teach us to hunger for the communion of God's kingdom, not to replace it.

The cross shows us the permanence of marriage, in a covenant sealed with blood. The cross also shows us that the nature of marriage is the sacrifice of self. That means we give ourselves to each other. We do not wield the threat of divorce as a means of self-protection. Instead, we build marriages that, as best we can, reflect the one-flesh union of Christ and his church. And then we run to that cross-shaped gospel even when we fail. The bride of Christ needs no prenuptial agreement. The bride of Christ needs no divorce lawyer. The bride of Christ needs no hyphenated name.

CHAPTER TEN
Children Are a Blessing,
Not a Burden

I DIDN'T KNOW WHY I was disrupting the natural-food grocery store, but I was. As I walked down the aisles of the earth-friendly, locally sourced, natural-food shop here in my city, the stares of my fellow customers were as ubiquitous as the word *artisanal* on the signs and labels around me. Some people would glare and then quickly look down, as if embarrassed for me. For a nanosecond, I wondered if, like in one of those awkward nightmares, I had forgotten to wear clothes. I looked down, and then around, before realizing what the spectacle was all about. They were walking beside and behind and in front of my cart: my five children. One woman, carrying her unbleached, recycled carton of cage-free eggs, cleared her throat and asked, "Are all these yours?" When I said "yes," she sighed and kind of rolled her eyes. I shrugged and said, "What can I say? We use organic birth control."

I can hardly turn this account into some sort of culture war clash of caricatures, though that would be easy enough to do. That's not accurate though. These reactions are hardly the contrast between a Cro-Magnon conservative Christian bound to outbreed the opposition versus the anti-family hostility of granola-rolling hippie throwbacks. First of all, the caricatures probably wouldn't hold up. There are some Christians (the majority of them in the history of the church, in fact) who have opposed artificial contraception altogether, but I'm not one of them. And, more recently, there have been Christians who believe that trusting God's sovereignty means having as many babies as one could possibly conceive and birth; I'm not one of them either.

If all the customers there knew about Christians and children were what they had seen on some reality television program, where people put minivans on their bridal registries, then they might see our brood as more bizarre than we actually are. At the same time, if I were to talk to the progressive shoppers in the aisles around me, I imagine we would find more agreement on family than I might expect. Moreover, their attitude toward my children isn't cordoned away in progressive secular pockets. I've been asked, "Don't you know what's causing that?" by people at revival meetings, not just by people wearing tie-dye T-shirts. The truth is, I was wrong to be annoyed by the bewilderment with which my neighbors saw all of my children—because I should have understood those attitudes. After all, I once shared them. And sometimes I still do.

There are, of course, major differences between the way people in various subcultures view children. Some have pointed out that one can see the basic cultural ideology, and rate of secularization, in a city based on the ratio of children's parks to pet boutiques. I am sure there's some truth to that. But it is not quite the case that more "conservative" areas are necessarily more "pro-family" or "pro-child." Many of the places that have lots of children around have children born out of wedlock or in complicated custody arrangements navigating different houses every weekend. Even more than that, it's become almost routine for older people, even within conservative Christian churches, to tell newly married couples (sometimes even in the receiving line at the wedding) not to have children too soon because "you want to enjoy your marriage first." That seemed normal to me when I married. As a matter of fact, my most ominous fear in those first few years of marriage would be that we might have an "accident" and my wife would end up pregnant before we were "ready." In order to ensure this, we spent the first several months of marriage using three different forms of "protection," just in case one or two of them failed. Two lines on a pregnancy test would have been as terrifying to me at the time as seeing a cigarette-smoking clown holding a knife outside my window at night.

Years later, when my wife and I decided we were "ready," and that we could "afford" children, we spent month after month with the disappointment of one blank pregnancy test after another, followed by a season of miscarriages. Eventually, the doctors told us they doubted we could ever bring a child fully to term. I know how to hide it well enough, so you probably wouldn't have noticed this had you known me then, but I was seething with rage. Underneath the surface of my life was anger, at myself, at my wife, at God. All my plans for myself seemed to be wrecked. As I said to my wife one night after one of the miscarriages, "I'm now realizing that we are going to die alone." I spent the first part of our marriage believing we were entitled not to have children, and then the second part of our marriage believing we were entitled to have children. I was wrong in both cases. As I've detailed elsewhere, God intervened in our lives, wrecking me and reconstructing me in all sorts of ways, making me realize what an awful father I would have been if children had been as easy to birth as they had been to avoid.[44] But I can hardly present myself as a "I once was lost but now I'm found" sort of testimony when it comes to the blessing of children.

My wife and I did eventually have the children we desperately prayed not to have too soon and then desperately prayed to have, at all, first by adoption and then through the more typical way. When I turned forty, I was exhausted. I was in a high-pressure job leading a large academic institution, plus preaching every Sunday and Wednesday, teaching multiple classes ranging from Sunday school to doctoral-level theology, plus writing books and articles and speaking all over the country. Plus, I was a husband and a father of, at the time, four boys. The older two children had special needs related to their early deprivations in a foreign orphanage that sapped much energy. The younger two were close together, and a blur of energy. I had just, it seemed, grown confident that I knew what I was doing in my primary job and, to some degree, as a father. After a long series of board meetings, I came home one night and collapsed on the couch. My wife stood over the edge of the sofa and said, with an almost apologetic tone, "I've been trying to think of when would be the least bad time to tell you this, but, I'm pregnant." My response was to place the pillow over my face and groan. Mind you, by that time I had written a book and a shelf full of articles on the goodness of children. Keep in mind that by this time nothing was a greater joy for me than spending time with my sons. Even after all of that, my word to my wife with a "surprise" baby on the way was just another version of the "Don't you know what's causing that?" routine I had so long despised and preached against. Here I was, a kinder, gentler, theologically trained Planned Parenthood.

* * * *

At one level, nothing seems as innocent, as non-threatening, as warm-hearted, as the idea of children. At another level, nothing can be scarier than the responsibilities we have with children. The people who warn against not having children too soon are not insane. One of the greatest challenges we have in the social order today is from those who disrupt the pattern of life that moves from personal maturity to marriage to childbearing, putting the children before one or both of the others. Many of the parents who sigh when they see an adult daughter or daughter-in-law pregnant are not so much cynical as they are worried about what will happen, if this marriage falters or if post-partum depression becomes too pronounced or he goes through a mid-life crisis and takes off for Florida with a stripper. What will happen, these potential grandparents, might wonder, if they can't afford all these mouths to feed? Will they all then end up back here, in the spare bedrooms? These are not unreasonable fears. Moreover, we must do more than simply look at declining birthrates and demographic data before concluding whether our society is friendly or unfriendly to children. There's quite a difference between the real and perceived social and economic cost of a family of six children among cotton-picking sharecroppers in 1926 rural Tennessee and what there would be for the same family of suburban service workers in contemporary Nashville. There's also a very different personal cost. The stress levels of a young mother—alone with her husband and children in a city to which they've been transferred for work—are quite different than those felt by her grandmother, who would have had far greater financial and even medical burdens, but who also had an extended family and a community of other young mothers just steps from her front door.

Even accounting for all of that, though, we cannot deny that the Bible seems to have a decidedly different view of children than the common one of our age, whether spoken or unspoken. "Behold, children are a heritage from the LORD, the fruit of the womb a reward," the Bible says. "Like arrows in the hand of a warrior are the children of one's youth" (Ps. 127:3–4). The Bible repeatedly presents the stories of those who cannot have children and yet are blessed by God with a child. This is sometimes the result of anguished prayer (Hannah, for example, in 1 Samuel 1) and sometimes the result of a surprising word from God (the case of Sarah with Isaac). In his original mandate for the creation, God said that humanity would multiply and fill the earth; this was seen as a blessing of the world, not a curse upon it. One might conclude that this is due to the agrarian nature of the Israelite economy. Children were fellow workers in the fields and thus a blessing the way farm equipment might be considered a "blessing." But there's more to this than that. Indeed, even in perhaps the harshest, darkest time of early Israel's life—their sojourn in Egypt—God saw as blessing the fact that the "people of Israel were fruitful and increased greatly; they multiplied and grew exceedingly strong so that the land was full of them" (Exod. 1:7). Pharaoh saw things differently, saw the children of this people as a burden to be managed, and, in due time, destroyed. The crushing economic burdens he put on this people though did not dissuade them since "the more they were oppressed, the more they multiplied and the more they spread abroad" so that the "Egyptians were in dread of the people of Israel" (Exod. 1:12). Even when the Egyptian government mandated lethal violence against male children, the people were undeterred, with midwives practicing civil disobedience against the destruction of the children. "So God dealt well with the midwives. And the people multiplied and grew very strong" (Exod. 1:20). God's blessing on the midwives, defying the fury of Pharaoh for not eliminating children, is, counterintuitively, to give them children (Exod. 1:21).

The fact that children are seen biblically as a blessing does not mean that the Bible idealizes children. In our cultural schizophrenia, we both fear and idealize babies. At least in families with means, children are given rooms decorated more elaborately than a sultan's would have been in a previous era. Children are expected to be good and kind, often in popular culture the wise voices that see what the adults miss. Even the shocking accounts of cruelty by children, such as in the novel *The Lord of the Flies*, are alarming precisely because they upend the expectation of idealized childhood, and thus are a signal that something has gone terribly wrong. As Flannery O'Connor once noted, though, "Stories of pious children tend to be false."[45] The Bible does speak of small children with a kind of relative innocence, as not yet knowing good from evil (Deut. 1:39; 1 Kings 3:7–9), and yet does not at all shy away from the sin and cruelty possible for children. David, looking at his own sin, pronounced that "in sin did my mother conceive me" (Ps. 51:5). From Cain and Abel onward, the arrival of children has brought with it the possibility not just of joy but also of sin or suffering. Even with such a realistic view of human nature, though, the Scripture sees the arrival of children as joy and blessing.

That joy and blessing are not just for what we call "nuclear families." Yes, there are specific instructions given to mothers and to fathers. Those who would argue that a nuclear family unmoored from a larger extended family is a modern innovation are quite right. But this does not mean that the nuclear family itself is an unbiblical innovation. Within the extended household, the relationship between father, mother, and children is still the foundational unit.[46] And yet, as we give instruction to mothers and fathers, and future mothers and fathers, some might ask, "What about Christians without children?" The truth is, though, there is no such thing as a Christian without children. You are part of the church, the household of God, a household into which, in every generation, God brings children. You either treat those children as part of your responsibility, as part of the body of Christ, or you will treat those children as, at least as far as you are concerned, orphans. That does not mean that every Christian is responsible to teach children's Sunday school, but it does mean that children are a sign of God's blessing and, if you're in Christ, that blessing is around you, whether you bear children biologically or not.

That's in some way easy for anyone to see. Even with all the differences we may have in our culture, the birth of a baby is seen, at least in the abstract, as a time of happiness and gratitude. In every era, the birth of a child can also be scary—maybe even more so in times when infant and maternal mortality were higher than they are now in the industrialized world. Nonetheless, cultural changes have shifted the way we see children, sometimes even in ways we don't fully recognize ourselves.

In every era, though, the birth of children turns out to be a "crisis," if we think of "crisis" as a turning point. Of course, birth is a "crisis" for the one being born, the first crisis of many that we experience. Even without memory of it, our birthday is marked year by year, noting that there was a time when we were not. The birth of a child is also a "crisis" for the parents of that child. In children, we experience a crisis of both joy and fear, no matter the circumstances. Even the most disenchanted secularist typically sees the birth of his or her own child in terms of awe and wonder. In listening to atheist and agnostic friends describe the birth of a child, the word that comes up most often is "miracle." Now, I understand that my friends here do not mean this literally—they do not believe in miracles, after all—but it is still instructive that this is the metaphor for which we so often grasp. At first glance, the birth of a child seems the furthest thing from a miracle. Reproduction is the most natural thing in the world. The species depends on it, and it happens every day. And yet, few can look into the face of his or her newborn baby and not well up with tears of gratitude and awed silence. At the same time, even under the best, most "planned" circumstances, the birth of a baby brings a note of unspoken terror. Who can look at a newborn baby and wonder whether or not we, as parents or as grandparents or as a church, will somehow fail this child?

Children bring with them the sense of our responsibilities, and with that the tremor of terror that we won't be able to live up to those responsibilities. For all of our talk about "pro-family" and "anti-family" or "pro-child" and "anti-child," debates. The real problem is not so much hostility to children as it is something much more basic: fear. We will almost all admit to some phobia or other: heights, snakes, public speaking. Few will acknowledge a phobia even more powerful, though often conflicted: the fear of babies. The fear is not unreasonable. It is the fear of giving up our lives for someone else.

With the birth of a child, and then at key moments in the growth of that child, we can feel this paradoxical sense of happiness and pain. Think, for instance, of when a child starts the first day of school, or when he leaves home for college, or when she walks down the aisle at her wedding. This is something akin to what C. S. Lewis called "joy"—the sort of longing mixed with both sweetness and pain that we can experience but not quite completely describe. We are taken, when we pay attention to what's happening, from the cradle straight to the cross. What we hope for in the birth of a new child is what we find ultimately at the cross. And what we fear most, at the birth of a new child, is what we find ultimately at the cross.

* * * *

Jesus' attitude toward marriage was, as we've noted, complicated somewhat by his call to take up the cross. Likewise, his attitude toward mothers and fathers was made more complex by the same factor. Jesus' attitude toward children, though, remains throughout the Scriptures uncomplicated. Jesus loves the little children. Even those not very familiar with religion at all can usually see in their mind's eye the picture of Jesus with children bustling around on his lap, arms outstretched to bless them. This picture comes from an account in the Gospels when the Bible tells us the crowds were pressing around Jesus, as they often did, this time with parents seeking out the sign-working Rabbi to bless their little ones (Mark 10:13–16). The parents who swarmed Jesus with their children may have just been the sort of parents who, like most of us, want the best for their children. They may have been like the parents in our era who hand their baby to a politician or a star athlete, to snap a picture. Or these parents may have been desperate. Their children may have been sick or injured. They may have been like several other parents in the Gospels who approached Jesus in desperation with their children at the precipice of death, seeking some help from the One they had heard could command demons and channel nature and even turn back disease and maybe even death itself.

The disciples held these parents and their offspring back. Jesus, Mark wrote, was "indignant" and rebuked them (Mark 10:14). Now, the Bible does not explain exactly why the disciples didn't want the children there, but it is probably not because they were child-hating misanthropes. They probably instead were merely attempting, as they often did, to keep the crowds from mobbing their teacher. The implication is present, though, that the disciples may have seen children as a distraction from their mission. The anger that flared in Jesus is one we see usually in the Gospels in only two areas: in the face of religious hypocrisy or in the exclusion of those the powerful deem not to matter (as in, for instance, Jesus' anger that the temple was a den of robbers rather than a house of prayer for all people). Moreover, we see Jesus repeatedly in the Gospels rebuking the disciples for their ideas of power and position and strength. This seems to be the exact same point Jesus is making here: "Truly, I say to you, whoever does not receive the kingdom of God like a child cannot enter it" (Mark 10:15).

In the Gospel of Mark, the welcoming of the children is placed in what seems to be a random conjunction of unrelated incidents. In the passage immediately before, Jesus addressed the ethics of divorce and remarriage, grounding the permanence and monogamy of marriage in God's creation design (Mark 10:1–13). Immediately after the welcoming of the children, Jesus is portrayed as telling a rich young man he must sell all his possessions and give everything to the poor in order to enter the kingdom (Mark 10:17–31). Overshadowing all of these incidents, though, is later in the chapter, in which Jesus told his disciples, "See, we are going up to Jerusalem, and the Son of Man will be delivered over to the chief priests and the scribes, and they will condemn him to death and deliver him over to the Gentiles" (Mark 10:33). The accounts before could seem to be disconnected vignettes of Jesus' love for marriage and babies and the poor, but they are connected, as is everything in the Gospels, by the entire point of Jesus' mission: "For even the Son of Man came not to be served but to serve, and to give his life as a ransom for many" (Mark 10:45). Jesus welcomed children because of the cross. In order to see then how children are part of our cross-bearing life, we must understand how Jesus views children in the first place and how the hostile powers of the old order view them. To understand children, we must understand the gospel.

What does Jesus mean when he says that no one can enter the kingdom unless one does so as a little child? First of all, he seems to mean that one can only come into spiritual life the same way we came into biological life: by sheer gift. One cannot enter the kingdom of God by means of "flesh and blood," Jesus told Nicodemus, but only by being born again (John 3:3). Nicodemus can be forgiven for taking Jesus too literally, wondering how it is that one can re-enter his mother's uterus in order to pass muster at Judgment. In some ways, Nicodemus, even in his ridiculous misunderstanding, was closer to Jesus' meaning than we often are. After all, for many of us, "born again" is simply a metaphor for a particular kind of Christian, one who has what we call a "personal relationship with Jesus Christ." The metaphor, though, tamed through familiarity, is meant to jar. The connection between new birth and birth itself is necessary to get the striking sense of our own helplessness to perform our way into God's new creation. We did nothing to earn our own birth, or to construct our own genetic code or time of conception. Sometimes an angry child will yell at his mother, "I didn't ask to be born!" That's true, of course, of all of us. Life is a gift.

Even in the means by which God designed the human race to march onward, we are shown over and over that we are not manufacturers of the next generation but receivers of something mysterious to us, uncontrollable by us. A child is conceived, at least in the natural order of things, not by an architectural act of will but in the joining of two people in an instant in which we are, arguably, the least in control of ourselves: the release of sexual union.[47] This sense of life as gift points us to even more ultimate realities. When God wished to communicate to people that he knew them better than they knew themselves, God did so by pointing to his knowledge of them in the womb. "Before I formed you in the womb I knew you," God said to Jeremiah (Jer. 1:5). "My frame was not hidden from you, when I was being made in secret," David sang to the Lord (Ps. 139:15). The same is true for our life in the kingdom. Through the cross of Christ, we were given, John says, "the right to become children of God, who were born not of blood nor of the will of the flesh nor of the will of man, but of God" (John 1:12–13). Whoever you are, whatever your situation, your story started with an act of grace, an act of grace that you could have done nothing to earn, because prior to it you did not even exist.

This brings us to what I believe is the central point of Jesus' metaphor of children inheriting the kingdom—that of vulnerable dependence. This is a point that Jesus made repeatedly—that we are those who must ask for daily bread, those who learn to cry out "Abba, Father." The language of childlikeness is especially evocative of that sort of dependence and vulnerability. Often, when a baby is born, a new parent will experience the fear that he or she might drop the baby by accident. "He just seems so fragile," a new mother might say of her son. "She just feels so delicate; I'm afraid I will break her," a new father might say of his daughter. The baby is indeed fragile. A human child cannot exist on his or her own. We must be "knit together," to use the biblical language, in our mothers' protective wombs, and then we must be dependent on our mothers for our food, for warmth, for the most basic protection from the elements. Our very first moments in life are demonstrable evidence of what we often spend the rest of our lives seeking to prove otherwise: that we are mortal, dependent creatures of flesh and blood. We are not gods but men and women, and we did not even start as men and women but as baby boys and girls.

This dependence is bound up with our life in the cross. The book of Hebrews says, in what I believe is one of the most important passages in all of Scripture, that a crucial aspect of Jesus' defeat of the devil is in the sharing of our humanity. Jesus is a human being, in solidarity with us. He can, therefore, serve as an offering for our sin, as a priest to represent us before God. The writer of Hebrews points back to the psalmist's claim that God has put "all things" under the feet of humanity and asks how this can be when we clearly do not see all things governed and ruled by humanity (Heb. 2:5–8). If this were so, we would not see human beings made homeless by hurricanes or suffocated by congestive heart failure or picked apart cell by cell by cancer. "But we see him who for a little while was made lower than the angels, namely Jesus, crowned with glory and honor because of the suffering of death, so that by the grace of God he might taste death for everyone" (Heb. 2:9). The glory and dominion we so crave—whether in our quest for wealth or for fame or for athletic prowess or by winning arguments—is all seen not in independence and swaggering confidence but in humiliating dependence, in the crucifixion of Jesus.

The moment the Bible identifies Jesus as crowned with authority, as bearing glory and honor, is the moment when he is the most dependent, the most powerless, the most seemingly useless to the outside world. It is the moment in which Jesus had to be helped with the carrying of his own instrument of torture. It is the moment when he was having his beard ripped from his face as he was beaten up by abusive Roman soldiers. This is the moment when Jesus was lifted up, not by his own power but by the power of those who were killing him; when Jesus said, "I thirst," as he could not even hydrate himself but must take sour vinegar from a sponge on the end of a stick. This is the moment where Jesus seemed to be displaying anything but "glory and honor."

At the cross, Jesus demonstrated that the weakness of God is more powerful than the strength of the world, that dependence upon God is greater than the independence of self-effort. We are called to be conformed to that cross even in the way that we are born: not as self-sustaining producers but as frail, fragile children of dust. We are not promoted into the kingdom, and we are not recruited into the kingdom. We are "begotten" into the kingdom (1 John 5:1 KJV), born again to newness of life. And we arrive there just as we arrived in the first birth, carried by a power other than our own. In order to find the kingdom, we must find that weakness, again.

* * * *

No matter how strong or influential we think we may be, our kindergarten class pictures can show us otherwise. When we look at the image of ourselves as that young boy or girl, we can almost immediately feel all the fears and insecurities of that time. If we're honest, we will also admit that we are, in many ways, still that same person, still protecting ourselves from being hurt. That sense of vulnerability leaves us with conflicted feelings about ourselves, and thus about children, who remind us of where we started and where we must end up. On the one hand, vulnerability is exactly why most people love babies, whether human or animal. We may admire a tiger marching back and forth in its cage at a zoo, but the tiger cub will draw a crowd for a different reason, usually with several people sighing, "He's so cute!" For the same reason, advertisers will use images of babies and toddlers for scenes for which they would never think of featuring adults. The babies are non-threatening. They cannot hurt us, at least not in that way. Ironically enough, it is this same vulnerability that makes children so scary. They cannot hurt us physically, but they can be hurt by us. And we know that, sooner or later, they could break our hearts.

Moreover, in a fallen world in which human beings, like animals, seek to protect ourselves from one another with displays of strength and aggression, small children seem oddly out of sync. Their vulnerability and dependence are thus used as a weapon to marginalize them, to make them invisible, when we do not want to see them. Children at their most vulnerable, in the womb of their mothers, are made much of when they are deemed to be "wanted." When they are deemed to be intrusive, they are made invisible by the use of clinical language such as "embryo" or "fetus" or "product of conception," in order to make violence against them more palatable to the conscience. The children of refugees and immigrants are likewise made invisible by language—often presented culturally or politically as parasites or as "anchors" for their parents to draw welfare benefits from a wealthier country. No matter how civilized we may believe ourselves to be, we can see what happens when a child happens to be in the category of both unpopular and defenseless, and the results are tragic. The way of the cross is different.

Unfortunately, we will never create a true culture of welcoming children if we do not upend the priorities of our churches when it comes to power. Why is the church so constantly drawn to economic and political power? This is not only the case for the highest levels of the church—whether medieval popes or contemporary culture warriors—but also shows up in local assemblies. We are drawn to the conversion testimonies of celebrity athletes or beauty contestants or reality television stars because they bring a sense of weight and influence, on their own terms—a weight and influence they are, in our view, lending to the gospel. In how many congregations are decisions made on the basis of spoken or unspoken decisions about who gives the most money and who might, if he or she were rankled, withhold that money? In such situations, we can see where our true religion is, and it is summed up in the dollar sign of Mammon not in the cross beam of Jesus. The same principle is at work sometimes in the "excellence" with which we run our worship services, as though the outside world needs to see our inability to fumble. When the church prioritizes power, influence, access, expertise, invulnerability, how on earth can we see ourselves as little children? If all of our illusions were put away, and if we were to see where we are on the scale of the trillions of years in front of us, we would see that we are, in fact, embryos and fetuses in the kingdom of God. We are able to be hurt, but hemmed in all around by the protective embrace of our God. When we see children—whether those the world considers "impressive" or the ones the world considers "defective"—we do not see their "potential," as though their lives will matter when they are grown and "contributing to society." We can see instead our own potential—if we would put aside our vain pretensions to superiority over others, to self-confidence and expertise, and to simply hold out our hands and cry, "Abba, Father!" We must crucify our lust for power. Our Father doesn't love us because of what we might do, nor does he need us in order to accomplish his will, but he does want us to reach for him, as desperate and dependent children.

This sense of dependence not only expresses the goodness of children, but also defines the way we parent them. Much of what amounts to parenting counsel in this era—whether from the church or from the outside world—amounts to technique. We are told the strategies to employ—whether it be how to install a car seat or how to toilet train or how to set boundaries for dating. Much of this is worthy and needed, but it can lead us, unintentionally, to the idea that children are one more means of technology, that they are an operating system for which we learn the code. Christian parenting will include many of these strategies, to be sure, but true Christian parenting starts not when we know what to do, but when we do not. We lead our children in a cross-shaped way when we acknowledge that we do not know what to do but must rely on our own Father for grace and for power.

Sometimes people will ask me what I think is the best biblical counsel for parenting, expecting, I think, that I will turn to one of the familiar proverbs on discipline or perhaps to Deuteronomy on instruction. Instead, I choose the account of the people of Judah standing before a foreign army of massive power coming to wipe them out. Jehoshaphat, the leader of the people, reminded them of God's presence with them in the story of their redemption, of his covenant promises. But he does not do so in a sloganeering "We can do this!" sort of way. Instead, he prays aloud for God's intervention: "For we are powerless against this great horde that is coming against us. We do not know what to do, but our eyes are on you" (2 Chron. 20:12). Children—whether in a home or in a church—are not a marauding army threatening us (though it may sometimes feel like that), but nevertheless this passage holds a great deal of relevance for parenting. The Scripture tells us what was at stake for Jehoshaphat and Israel—not just their individual lives but those of "their little ones, their wives, and their children" (2 Chron. 20:13). What was at stake was the welfare of their families, and they were powerless. This has everything to do with parenting. No matter how many books or articles we read or godly examples we follow, every parent will eventually reach this point of powerlessness and despair. Knowing this, and turning in dependence upon God, is something of what it means to come before him as a little child. Therein is the kingdom of God.

That constant biblical call to cross-shaped dependence is why I've changed my mind about "baby dedications" in churches. Many of you will not understand what I'm referencing, especially if you come from a Christian communion that baptizes infants. My communion does not; we baptize only those who profess that they believe the gospel and seek to be disciples. As such, I cynically dismissed "baby dedications," times in a church service when parents would stand with their newborns to dedicate their lives to the Lord, as just a way to do a "dry baptism" for low-church Protestants. As the years have gone by, though, I have seen that these times of dedication fill an urgent need for families and for the church. This is not so much for the children as for their parents, and for the rest of the congregation. The parents crowding around Jesus wanted a word of blessing upon their little ones. In our hyper-naturalistic time, we tend to lose the sense of what a "blessing" is, other than a rote prayer before a meal or spiritual-sounding language that we use to mean "lucky." The Bible, though, is filled with blessings, blessings that are sometimes wrestled for, sometimes lied about for, sometimes given on a deathbed. A blessing is to commit another to the good purposes of the Lord. Rightly done, a dedication by parents of their children can be a signal that these children do not in fact "belong" to the parents but to the Lord. Moreover, it can be a sign to the rest of the congregation that the rearing of these children is not simply up to the parents on the platform but to all of the gathered body.

Years ago, I saw a cartoon in a Christian magazine of a mother standing beside a crime scene as her son was handcuffed and arrested by police. The crying woman is pictured screaming, "Oh son! Oh son! Where did your youth pastor go wrong!" The point of the cartoon was to lampoon the way that many Christian parents neglect the discipleship of their children, believing this can be outsourced to the "professionals" within the church. That is, of course, a major concern, and one the church should correct. But the opposite tendency must be confronted as well: the idea that parents must rear their children alone, that such is none of the church's business. No amount of expertise is enough for that. We need the grace of God, and we need each other.

* * * *

Children picture the kingdom in another way. The kingdom is the reign of God in the future, breaking backward into the present by the cross-rule of Jesus. Children likewise represent the future, and that is a blessing from God. Sometimes I will hear from Christians, or others who wonder if they should have children at all since, "I wouldn't want them to grow up in a world like this." I even knew of a young Christian couple planning to sterilize themselves before their wedding, so that they would not bring a child into a world of cultural decadence or environmental catastrophe or nuclear war. Most people do not act with such extreme behavior, but the fears we face for our children are bound up in the same reasons we have such hope for them: we cannot see the future they will inhabit. We don't want them to enter a world where they will suffer. This is—let me say this as diplomatically as I can—nonsense. We are the people of the cross. Jesus told us beforehand that the times we would face—no matter when or what they are—would be filled with trials and tribulations but also with the presence of the Spirit of Christ himself (Matt. 28:20).

We can address our worries about suffering for our children in the opposite way as well, by denying to ourselves such possibilities and reassuring ourselves that the gospel will make all things well for our children and their future. This attitude is summed up in a Bible passage that has become something of the new John 3:16 for American cultural Christianity: Jeremiah 29:11. This passage, "For I know the plans I have for you, declares the LORD, plans for welfare and not for evil, to give you a future and a hope," shows up on wall plaques, on social media memes, even on tattoos. I have seen this verse "claimed" fervently by people who haven't been in church since before the first Bush Administration, but who are quite confident that this is God's way of telling them that their future is bright. The idea that prosperity and flourishing are just right around the corner resonates well with a consumerist American culture where optimism itself is a marketing strategy. Many think this verse tells them to have confidence in themselves, to follow their hearts, knowing that God will make their life-plans successful. Anyone who could find this sort of message in the prophet Jeremiah has never read any verse of Jeremiah above or below this one. The book of Jeremiah is all about God disrupting his people's plans and upending their dreams, starting with those of Jeremiah himself. This verse says the same. The exiles had been carted off from their homeland to Babylon. God seemed distant. The situation seemed as though they had been raptured away to judgment and that God's blessing was for those "left behind" in Jerusalem. Jeremiah's prophecy made the opposite case: God would bless the nation through the exiles.

That's good news for the world. That's good news for the nation. But it is hardly good news for any individual in the situation. Those left in Jerusalem didn't like this message so they found "prophets" who would tell them that peace was just around the corner (proving that entrepreneurial religious hucksterism is not a uniquely modern or American phenomenon). For the exiles, the message wasn't a cheery one either, at least in any future they would see in the short term. In Jeremiah's letter, they were told that their return from exile wouldn't happen in their generation. They should, then, create new lives in Babylon. If the exiles had known that they were getting what they wanted—immediate deliverance—they might rationally have held off on marrying and having children until they were back home. If they knew there was no hope for their future as a people, they might likewise give up on the future altogether. Instead, God told them, they should have children because there was a future and a hope for them, even if it was too far off for them to see. When everything seemed chaotic and random, God had a purpose for them. The exile wouldn't be permanent.

In that sense, Jeremiah 29:11 applies to us. We, too, have a future and a hope, one that is bound up in the life of Christ. And yet, we do not have a generic Christ but a crucified One. Our plans may evaporate. Our dreams may be crushed. Our lives may be snuffed out. But God's gospel—good news for us, for our flourishing and not for our destruction—will march on. Now, the future waiting for us may well not be one that the culture around us prizes. In fact, our futures may be those that would cause us to tremble if we saw them in a crystal ball. But, long term, our future is cosigned with Christ. Our ancestors in Babylon could know, not from observing their situation, but by the promise of God, that there was a future for them. So they could have babies and rear families and trust their God. The same is true for us.

That "children are the future" sounds like a truism bordering on the banal. And yet, this is one of the most difficult truths for us to grasp. We know, rationally, that there was a time—a vast expanse of time—before us when we didn't exist. And we know that there will be another vast expanse of time after we have passed from this earthly life. Knowing this truth, though, is not the same as facing this truth. The Scriptures, especially the Psalms, include many passages about the shortness of life. We must learn to "number our days" (Ps. 90:12) in order that we may have wisdom for the present. We must see that our lives are like the flower of the field, flourishing one day and then gone (Ps. 103:13). The arrogance of all our plans for ourselves must be tempered by the knowledge that our life is just a mist "that appears for a little time and then vanishes" (James 4:14). We must be reminded of this so often because, left to ourselves, we sinfully imagine that we are independent, self-existing, and immortal. In short, we believe ourselves to be gods, forever unaccountable to the judgment bar of God. The cross reminds us otherwise. So, too, do babies. This is one of the reasons why our culture so often prizes youth and vitality, why people panic at the sight of a grey hair or a sagging stomach. We do not want to be reminded that we will die. And that's one reason why every generation tends to disparage the generation coming after. We do not want to be reminded that we are replaceable.

My wife is amused by how often I will, seemingly out of nowhere, say to her, "Do you realize that I am now older than my mother was when we married?" or "Can you believe that we are now ten years older than that Sunday school teacher at our home church was, the one we thought was ancient at the time?" I will sometimes look at my sixteen-year-old sons and reminisce on just how antiquated my own parents seemed when I was sixteen (although they were younger then than I am now!). When a friend of mine told me that his grown son and his wife were expecting a child, my first thought was to be happy for their family, but I'll admit that my second thought was that it made me feel old that my peer was now a grandfather. Children remind us of our coming obsolescence.[48] And that too is a grace. Children show us that our future is not bound up in our striving and our performance. This is crucial for us to realize if we are to be made whole.

The ancient fertility religions of Canaan were so bloodthirsty because they asked people to sacrifice their children in order to bring blessings on themselves. They were to mortgage the future for the sake of the present.[49] The valley of Gehenna, which Jesus used to picture the judgment of hell, was a garbage dump, filled with fires. But it was originally the place of pagan worship, where people sacrificed their children to the god Moloch (2 Kings 16:3; Jer. 32:35).[50] The desolation there, spanning even the biblical testaments, was such that the place was fit only for the burning of refuse. The sacrifice of children might seem to bring present stability, but in fact it led only to hell. In our time, very few would physically sacrifice the lives of their children, but many do so through neglect or abandonment or various other ways. In expecting our children to meet our present needs, instead of pouring ourselves out for our children's future, we get not the stability we seek but a shiver of hell.

One can see this sometimes in churches that refuse to cultivate younger leadership or who do not want the burden of dealing with crying babies or rowdy adolescents or unstable new believers. These churches, or denominations, sometimes become virtual gerontocracies, never seeming to notice that there are fewer and fewer younger people around. This can seem liberating, in the moment, for those who want no tension about what music should be played or what programs should be offered. The church can seem "just like home" because it is a vehicle of nostalgia rather than mission. But, without new life, it will die with its members. This is a witness not to the crucified and resurrected Christ but to the Darwinian leer of a lioness devouring her young.

When we see godly older people pouring their lives into younger generations and churches doing the same, there is almost always one common denominator: the older generation is remarkably free of bitterness and jealousy. The younger generation embraces these mentors not because of their perceived "relevance." These are, to the contrary, often those who do the least to pretend to still be young. Instead, the distinguishing factor is that they are not threatened by those who will replace them. They have a secure identity in Christ, so they are willing to decrease in perceived power and "usefulness" without feeling an existential threat. We find that at the cross.

* * * *

The future children bring is one of joy, but also of sacrifice, sacrifice but also of joy. This is the paradox of modern parenthood that one journalist calls "all joy and no fun," arguing that changing roles of mothers and fathers and children mean that children often remodel their parents' lives in fundamental ways, from their marriages and vocations to their habits and hobbies, and even their own sense of self.[51] This is true, and while this may be heightened by modern parenthood it is hardly unique to it. Look at the biblical witness to the heights of fulfillment a child can bring to a parent, say, in the Proverbs, and to the depths of agony in, say, David's lament over his son Absalom. Much of this is due to the fact that we just cannot see as we are parenting how everything is going to turn out.

I once had a couple ask me to reassure them that they could adopt without "too much risk." When I pressed on what they meant, the husband told me that adoption and foster care were scary to him because "you never know who is going to show up." Now, I'm the first to admit that adoption and foster care bring with them special challenges, and those who step into such arenas should be equipped for them. But it is also true that no matter how a child comes—whether by adoption, foster care, or biological reproduction—"You never know who is going to show up."

A child is not a replicant of one of his parents, nor is he a mixture of replications from the two of his parents, as though he were 60 percent his mother and 40 percent his father. Every human being is unique—with unique gifts, weak points, callings, besetting sins, personality types, and so on. One of the reasons parents are sometimes frustrated with their children is that the children are not mere copies of their parents, with the same tendencies, hopes, aspirations, and interests.

Jesus taught us about family when he welcomed the little children, and he kept teaching us all the way to the Place of the Skull. Following his triumphal entry into Jerusalem, Jesus told his disciples, "Unless a grain of wheat falls into the earth and dies, it remains alone; but if it dies, it bears much fruit. Whoever loves his life loses it, and whoever hates his life in this world will keep it for eternal life" (John 12:24–25). He said that his time of glory had come, that he would be lifted up and would thereby draw all people to himself. This was, John wrote, "to show by what kind of death he was going to die" (John 12:33). He would not draw the world to himself by his teaching or by his miracles but by the sacrifice of himself. That's, of course, exactly what the cross did. After his resurrection, Jesus ascended to his Father and poured out the Spirit, a Spirit that went out on a search-and-rescue operation that drew together people from every conceivable tribe and nation, down through the centuries, joining us all together in one new household, all of us finding our new lives in the crucified Christ. The love between Christ and his church, consummated at the cross, was fruitful, and it multiplies. The bride of Christ did not know "who was going to show up" when the union consummated at the cross started to bear fruit. That's, as a matter of fact, where most of the fights and tensions of the New Testament emerge. Jewish Christians were learning to live with these Gentile newcomers, and vice versa. The cross means that the future is about self-sacrifice, not self-preservation.

Those who hope their children will make up for whatever they feel they "missed out" on in life—whether that's in terms of education or career or spiritual vitality—will inevitably be disappointed. Our children do not need to be "successes" in the way the world defines success. A child certainly does not exist in order to make up some real or perceived deficiency in the parent. Some parents idolize their children, with the parents finding their sense of identity in the life of the child. And some parents abandon their children literally. Some parents abandon their children to be shaped by their peer group or by the ambient culture or by the child's own appetites. None of these is the way of the cross.

Children are also difficult because nothing seems to expose what the self actually is more than bearing responsibility to lead a child to adulthood. When I was an adolescent, I was a parenting expert. I would never say this aloud, but I could tell you everything I thought my parents—especially my father—was doing wrong in rearing me. I expected him to be not just mature but omniscient and omnipotent. When he made (what I considered to be) mistakes, I found it mindboggling. As a father myself, though, I've heard myself saying aloud to my children some of the very things I thought were stupid when I heard my own father say them to me. I understand now why, for instance, he needed several days to recuperate from family vacation. "If he has this time off," I would think at the time, "Why don't we stay gone all of those days? Why on earth would we come home for him to sleep on the couch?" I get it now. More importantly, though, I now realize that a child's view of what it means to be an adult just isn't accurate.

We often assume that one acts like an adult because one feels like an adult. In truth, the reverse is true. One never really feels like a grown-up. No matter how one matures, we never get to the point of feeling confident in all our choices and actions. In many ways, we all still feel like scared and confused children. When one is a parent, though, one must nonetheless make decisions and bear responsibility. We must lay down our lives for the children God has given us. We cannot evade or resent the time and energy and maturity and financial responsibility demanded of us by the realities of adulthood and parenthood. We also, though, mustn't act as though we can bear all of that by our own power, especially since—as we have seen—children often show us just how powerless we can be.

Babies are a blessing, not a burden. Yes, babies will keep one from living out all of one's dreams for self-actualization. God doesn't want us self-actualized. He wants us blessed. There's a difference. And churches filled with people who fear babies because they want more freedom to pursue the American Dream will not be gospel-centered, evangelistic churches. The self-interest that sears over the joy of birth will also sear over the joy of new birth. We should never equate fertility with spirituality. That's the old error of Canaanite religion. God is going to lead some believers, perhaps many, not to marry so that, like the apostle Paul and many of the great missionaries of the church, they can devote themselves totally to gospel service. Others will marry but will not be blessed with large families, or with children at all. But, at the same time, can't we insist that our view of children be dictated more by the book of Proverbs rather than Madison Avenue or Wall Street?

There are signs that, at least in some small ways, the predominant Christian view of children is starting to reconnect with more ancient wisdom. Some of this might have to do with the place of

Christianity in Western culture. A previous generation of American Christians often sought desperately not to seem "freakish" to American culture, in order to win America for Christ. Thus, we saw much emphasis on "God and country" patriotism and "cultural relevance" and a downplaying of some of the deeper aspects of Christian doctrine and spirituality. Increasingly, though, it is harder and harder not to seem "freakish" in American culture, merely by holding on to the most base-level commitments of Christian ethics. If being married and staying married already marginalizes Christians from their peer groups, embracing a different view of children is not that far a step to take. If you are already outside the borders of what American culture considers the "good life," maybe it doesn't seem so odd to delay children until marriage and to celebrate children within marriage.

We are not guaranteed that our children will follow us in the gospel. God often starts off with new growth, bringing in those whose families never knew the Lord, even as some who grew up hearing the gospel fall away. But we have a biblical mandate to do two things at once: to share the gospel with all persons and to recognize that evangelism often includes raising up children in the nurture and admonition of the Lord. If we miss that point, our churches and families will absorb the message of much of the culture around us, a message that sees self as central and children as a nuisance. The growth of gospel Christianity means calling sinners to repentance and nurturing our children. We hold fast to the gospel in the revival tent, and at the dinner table, both.

I started out adulthood deeply fearful of children. I knew they were expensive. I didn't know how expensive—in both money and in anxiety and in emotional energy. I also didn't know the joy that could come with a little hand gripping mine. I didn't know the glory one could see in baptizing one's child as one's brother in Christ. I didn't know that children would be spiritual warfare, and that the warfare would be as sweet as it would be tough. Children, whether in the family or in the church, represent newness of life, the ongoing providence of God for the future. That's why the demonic powers so often come against children (from Pharaoh to Herod to the sex trafficking and abortion industries). When we embrace children, we share in the joy of the future. Children point us to the truth that the world has a future, and that the church has a future. God has yet more to do for the sons of Adam and the daughters of Eve. We can therefore rejuvenate and laugh and play, seeing right in front of us the gracious sign that we are not the pinnacle of life. We are bridging the way to the future, and God is there too. We also, though, open ourselves up to hurt. That's because parenting, whether familial or ecclesial, is not an economic transaction.

Parenting is living sacrifice, unconditional love. We bless our children not by weighing them down with expectations we couldn't bear ourselves, and not by leaving them to find their own way through the thicket of life. We bless our children by modeling maturity and by modeling childlikeness. We bless our children by keeping our promises, as best we can, but also by forgiving them, forgiving each other, and forgiving ourselves. And we bless the future by showing that love is greater than power, that a baby's cry is more hopeful than an army's siren. That's because the cross is more powerful than the crowd. A child can show us that grace is better than will, the future is better than the past, and that Christ is better than the self. A child can show us that we enter the kingdom not as conquering victors but as newborn infants. That's because we were brought into the kingdom not by our successes but by another's obedience. We could not earn that. We could only receive it. "What man and woman, if they ever gave serious thought to what having children inevitably involves, would ever have them?" asked Frederick Buechner. "Yet what man and woman, once having had them and loved them, would ever want it otherwise?" Buechner imagined what it would be like to wish away magically the pain associated with someone he loves. He couldn't do it, "because the pain is so much a part of the love that the love would be vastly diminished, unrecognizable, without it."[52] Indeed, love for one's children without pain would be as unrecognizable as a resur-rected Christ without nail scars.

* * * *

As scared as I was of having children "too early," and as scared as I was of having children "too late," God prepared, through all of that, Maria and me to hear from our doctor that, based on what he saw in an ultrasound, he thought that late-coming child might have Down syndrome. By that time, God had enabled us to be at peace with that, to be ready to bear whatever sacrifices would be needed, to rejoice in this new life. We didn't know what was awaiting us, but we didn't with the others either. When the doctor told us this, we looked at each other and knew that this child would be a gift. His worth and value wouldn't be based upon whether this age saw him as having "power" or "success" but instead upon the fact that this child was made in the image of God. We prayed that through our son we would see better, and bear witness better to, the gospel we had embraced of a Christ who was crucified in weakness and yet lives by the power of God.

Several weeks before the due date, on a Sunday morning as I was about to preach, I noticed during one of the opening hymns that my wife wasn't in her normal pew at our church. I slipped out during the offering and found her in the foyer. "Oh, I didn't want to bother you before you preached," she said. "My water has broken, but I know I'm a while away from giving birth. You go ahead and preach and then we'll go to the hospital." I told her she was insane, ran up to our minister of music to tell him he was preaching that day, and whisked her off to the hospital. A couple of hours later, he was here. He didn't have Down syndrome. The doctors were just as wrong as they were when they told us we wouldn't have children. Someone said, "You must feel like you dodged a bullet." No, not really. He didn't have Down syndrome, but someday he'll have something else. Maybe he will get sick or get hurt or lose his way, and we will be there, maybe reminding ourselves all along that he is a gift, that a child has upended our plans before, and we found that our plans needed upending. He interrupted one of our Sundays, but he didn't interrupt our lives.

Earlier, I wrote that children are a blessing, not a burden. That's not really true. As with many other things in the Christian life, this is not an "either/or" but a "both/and." Children are a paradox in that children are both a blessing and a burden. In fact, they are a blessing because they are a burden, and a burden because they are a blessing. The burden is the blessing. The gospel, in fact, redefines the very concept of "blessing" in Jesus' Sermon on the Mount. This applies not only to how we view our own sense of happiness, but also how we define happiness as it relates to the children around us, whether our own or the next generation within the church. "The ancients were afraid to display their happiness for fear the gods would punish them. We moderns are afraid to display our unhappiness for fear our neighbors will disapprove of us," Eugene Peterson writes. "The ancient world never expected to be happy and was sometimes surprised by little episodes of it. The modern world expects to be happy all the time and is full of resentment when it isn't. And then Jesus appears and says, 'Blessed are you.'"[53] That's a paradox, to be sure, but one that we should find familiar. After all, we start and end our lives at just such a paradox: at the cross.

To find a future, we must stop our pretending and protecting, and become as little children. As we do so, we will find that we will love the children among us. We will love to see the newness of life—the signs of the future—we see as new believers come to Christ, as we bear their burdens and seek to disciple them to maturity. In so doing, we might see that the kingdom of God is not a lonely capsule for isolated individuals but, as the prophet Micah called it, "like sheep in a fold, like a flock in its pasture, a noisy multitude of men" (Mic. 2:12). If we picture this rightly, this dependence, this vulnerability, this hope for the future, it just might be that the culture around us will look at this bustling, unruly church and ask, "Don't you know what's causing that?"

And we will say, "Yes. Yes we do."

Chapter Eleven
Parenting with the End in View

SHOULD I BAPTIZE MY SON, or should I ground him? That was the decision I wrestled with for days. And in the end, I did both. My teenage son had professed faith in Christ and had gone through our church's process toward baptism. The baptism was scheduled for the upcoming Sunday, but on the Friday beforehand, he broke a behavioral rule that, in our house, meant the loss of certain privileges. The offense here wasn't scandalous, just fairly typical adolescent disobedience. Still, I was torn. I knew he should be baptized. And I knew he should be grounded. It just felt awkward and confusing to say, "Welcome to the kingdom of God, and, by the way, you're grounded for the rest of the week."

The reason this was hard for me is because I was having trouble in the moment seeing both the gospel and the discipline of children. If I had chosen one or the other of these options, I would have, inadvertently, taught heresy to my son. If I had ignored the misbehavior, because it was baptism week, I probably would have taught a kind of cheap grace, in which one can use the holy things of God to evade consequences for actions. On the other hand, if I had postponed the baptism, I would have been signaling something even worse: that baptized Christians don't sin (so we should wait for a week when he wasn't a sinner in order to baptize him). Whichever way I turned, I found a frowning Saint Paul, disapproving of me, asking which part of Romans or Galatians or Ephesians I couldn't understand.

I was, though, standing in two very different spheres of accountability. As a minister of the gospel of Jesus Christ, I had one set of responsibilities. As the father of my child, I had others. The final decision was to say, "As my brother in Christ, I baptize you into newness of life. As your Dad, I ground you for up to three days." I was trying to ensure that he was grounded in the faith. In this case, that seemed to me that he should be grounded, in the faith.

The trouble was that I couldn't get through that impasse unless I stopped looking microscopically at the moment. My anger at his misbehavior made me want to say, "No way am I just pretending this didn't happen and baptizing you." My fatherly affection made me want to say, "Let's not ruin this special milestone with discipline." In order to move forward, I had to look telescopically at what I hoped that week would contribute to my son as an adult, as a servant of Christ, as maybe one day a father himself. To discipline rightly, I had to keep the end in view. But that is sometimes the most difficult thing to fathom when a parent is in the middle of toilet training a toddler or when a church is attempting to teach the Bible to a troubled adolescent.

* * * *

The apostle Paul wrote, "Children, obey your parents in the Lord, for this is right" (Eph. 6:1). This could seem to be just a timeless abstraction, a moral truism. And yet, Paul went on to set this directive in context. "'Honor your father and mother' (this is the first commandment with a promise) 'that it may go well with you and that you may live long in the land'" (Eph. 6:2–3). Apart from the gospel, this could seem to be a transaction: obey your parents and you get to live a long time. In fact, I can remember as a child hearing this text preached just that way. The pastor asked an elderly lady to stand and to give her age (again: pastors, don't do this). She was quite old. "See?" he said. "Mrs. Flossie here must have really obeyed her parents when she was a child. Look at how old she is now!" We children knew this woman to be the grouchiest, most curmudgeonly person we knew, the sort of person for whom the general message to us was not "Jesus Loves You" but "You Kids Get Off of My Lawn." To emulate her seemed like a death sentence, not a reward. "How much do I need to ignore my parents in order to live maybe to middle-age, but happy?" I thought.

That is, of course, not at all, what the Bible teaches. The Scripture is not saying that this commandment of God comes with a promise and the others do not, but rather that this is the first commandment that embeds within its command the promise itself. "To live long in the land" is not about extending one's mortal life in the "land" of the United States or wherever you happen to live. The commandments are about how Israel—as a people—was to live in the land of promise, to which God was bringing them after their slavery in Egypt, just as he promised Abraham. The commandments were not about God restricting his people's freedom or joy. He was instead preparing them, disciplining them, for their future.

The discipline our ancestors endured, which prepared them for the land, included teaching, the setting of boundaries, and the intervention of God to retrieve his people when they were wandering toward idolatry or covenant breaking. God's discipline was seen both in the way he provided for his children (by leading the way for them through the desert, by sending manna and water) but also by the way he did not give them everything for which they asked. "And he humbled you and let you hunger and fed you with manna, which you did not know, nor did your fathers know, that he might make you know that man does not live by bread alone, but man lives by every word that comes from the mouth of the LORD" (Deut. 8:3). Again, this is not God's punishment of his people—for that he would have wiped them away. This discipline was to shape in them the skills and habits and affections they would need in the land (knowing the lordship of God, that they are dependent upon him, and so on). We ought to expect this, the Bible says, as those who were disciplined—to varying degrees of competency—by our own parents. But the reverse is true as well. Parents are taught to dramatically reenact God in, for instance, the teaching of their children. Speaking of the words of God, Moses told the people, "You shall teach them diligently to your children, and shall talk of them when you sit in your house, and when you walk by the way, and when you lie down, and when you rise" (Deut. 6:7). This was precisely what God said that he had done, teaching his people his way, from Egypt through the wilderness to the Land of Promise and beyond. There was, and is, a goal in mind: "that you may do them in the land to which you are going over, to possess it" (Deut. 6:1).

In his Ephesians letter, Paul here made a connection between the importance of father–mother honoring not just because it is abstractly morally right (although it is), but also as a means of preparation for the future. After all, we too are being prepared for a Land of Promise, for the new creation that is to come. We honor parents not because of obligation but because we have glory waiting for us. Just as our parents are to train us for a future we can't fully anticipate as adults, our Father God is preparing us, in Christ, for a future we can't even imagine. And we cultivate the next generation because we desire that future for them as well.

In this, once again, the family structure unveils something to us about the mystery of the kingdom of God. The book of Hebrews ties the discipline of families and children to that of God with his people. The context, it seems, is a church reeling from both external threats of social marginalization and their own ongoing internal struggles with sin, all pointing toward the temptation just to give up on following Christ, to go back to their old lives. The author of Hebrews quoted for them the Old Testament words, "My son, do not regard lightly the discipline of the Lord, nor be weary when reproved by him. For the Lord disciplines the one he loves, and chastises every son whom he receives" (Heb. 12:5–6). One of the reasons we find discipline so hard in our households is that we do not really understand God's discipline of us. First of all, our problem is often that we think of "discipline" as punitive or wholly corrective. Discipline is the response to something gone wrong, in this view. It is the unpleasant aspect of parenting. A mother might complain about her husband, "He gets to do all the fun stuff of parenting, while I am forced to be the disciplinarian." What she means, of course, is that his passivity means she must be the one to correct misbehavior. With that, she's rightly frustrated. The same is true within the larger body of Christ. The New Testament speaks of church discipline. Usually when we think of this, if we do, we think of the last step of Matthew 18:15–20, of the expulsion of an unrepentant person caught in scandal from the church. That may well be a part of discipline, but that's not the whole of it. Discipline is the order of the church, the disciple-making commission of the people of God. Most discipline within the church is what some have called "formative" rather than "restorative," what we might call "positive" rather than "negative." That's because discipline goes beyond punishment and rebuke. Formation and correction go together. The same is true within the family.

You might object when you start reading a chapter on parenting and see that we are conversing here about discipline. "Parenting is about more than discipline," you might be saying. "What about love and affection and nurture?" You're exactly right. But love and affection and nurture are discipline. Put aside for a moment the punitive connotations of discipline and think of the way we might use the word for an athlete training for a competition. "She really has discipline," we might say. "She practices every morning and evening; she eats the right foods; she learns skills from other, more accomplished people in her field." All of that is discipline—from her sleeping when her peers are out partying to her parents standing on the sidelines cheering her on. All of these practices are what shape and guide her for her athletic future. The same is true for the church, and for the family.

Hugging a child is a discipline. Saying "I love you" is a discipline. Reading a bedtime story is a discipline. You may say, "Those things just come naturally for me, because I love my child." That may be true, but it is probably not true that you feel like doing these things all of the time, every day. Sometimes you must say to yourself, "I'm exhausted. I want to go to bed. But I'm going to sing 'Jesus Loves Me' to my child, and pray with him by his bed." That's discipline. You are not just showing affection to your child in the moment but building rhythms and practices that, over a long period of time, come to show that child that he is loved, and how to love others. Maybe it's really easy for you to say "I love you" to your spouse or your parents at the end of a phone conversation. That's only true because of countless "practices" at this, so that it now seems second nature for you in your family. Think of, though, how difficult it can be to say "I love you" to someone new, for the first time, either a potential love interest or even the person you've just met in the seat next to you at church, when the pastor says, "Turn to the person next to you and say, 'I love you'" (note to pastors: please don't do this either).

Discipline is discipleship. Through life together, we communicate what we expect of one another, and we train up a new generation with the affections, intuitions, and skills they will need for the future. Teaching the Bible is discipline. Modeling how to pray is discipline. Singing songs together is discipline. Toilet training is discipline. Driver's education is discipline. Showing an older adolescent how to apply for a job is discipline. And yes, correcting behaviors that aren't consistent with life in the family, or life in eternity, is part of discipline as well.

For the Christian, the Bible turns us repeatedly to the discipline we receive from our Father God as an analog for the discipline we are to give, and receive, within the family. The book of Hebrews, for instance, includes a section telling the church that, just as their earthly fathers disciplined them, so God disciplines them. The writer tells them that if they are not disciplined, they are, in fact, not sons but illegitimate children (Heb. 12:5–11). In so doing, the author points to several Old Testament passages about God disciplining his people, Israel, "the way a man disciplines his son." Now, again, if we see this passage in the frame of a punitive sense of discipline, we can easily get the wrong idea, a wrong idea many of us are prone to anyway.

Whenever a sin in my life is especially obvious to me, I often will find that I stop praying. When I examine why that is, it's because I think, subconsciously, that God is angry with me. Part of this is because I grew up with some in my extended family who, when they were angry, would simply stop speaking, and some others who would erupt into long lectures of how he or she had been wronged. I learned—was "disciplined" to—withdraw from that sort of conflict. Unless I pay attention, I will see that I'm doing that with God as well. I assume that my sin means that God is angry with me, that his discipline means that God will do something to me, to "get back" at me for my transgression. Never am I further away from the gospel than at these times.

In those moments, I don't understand what discipline, in fact, is. It may seem in those moments as though I am filled with shame, and that's true enough, but I am simultaneously filled with pride. I believe that my sin is shocking and disappointing to God, such that he will withdraw himself from me, as though the rest of my life before God I am standing there sinless. I am seeing myself not as a beloved son, but as a servant, earning my wages. When my Bible is read, my prayers are said, the people around me are adequately loved and forgiven, the commandments adequately kept, then I can come boldly before the throne of grace, is what I'm thinking. And, if not, then God is sulking somewhere in the universe, daring me to come near him so he can strike me down. Now, that's not the gospel I have received, or that I believe. The real issue there is a misunderstanding—one that I must constantly battle in my own psyche—of the cross itself.

* * * *

If you are in Christ, God is not angry with you. That's not because God is proud of your accomplishments or your compliance. All that is as filthy rags before a holy God. God is happy with you because you are embedded in the life of Christ. You are represented by a high priest who has lived your life for you, and is living his life through you. God is not, and cannot, be angry with him. Yes, justice will be done for every sin against God or against one another. At that cross, that has already happened for you. You are not under God's wrath, but standing in his grace. Jesus bore the day of God's vengeance so that you would stand, right now, in the eternal Jubilee, in the everlasting year of God's favor. To think of God's discipline as some sort of "karma" looking to knock you down is going to skew the way that you nurture and direct the next generation. This sort of thinking also empties the cross of its power.

We think either that God is a doltish grandfather who will leave us in our sin, or we think of God as an abusive stepfather seeking to strike us down. Neither of those images are accurate. Discipline here is not punishment, nor is it the venting of anger. The discourse on God's discipline in Hebrews is an *encouragement*, not a threat. The author was demonstrating to the people that they are not alone, they are ringed about with a great cloud of witnesses, as they run toward a goal. This passage is teaching that God is active all around you, and, just as we see in the book of Romans, in all of that he is working for "the good," namely to conform you to the image of Christ (Rom. 8:28–29). If you want to see God's discipline in your life, recall a conversation you had with someone who encouraged you to keep going when you were ready to give up. That's God's discipline. Recall a situation where you learned, maybe through help from some wise mentors, how to walk away from a self-destructive habit. That's God's discipline. Remember when you heard a song or a hymn that filled you with the realization that you are loved by God. That's God's discipline. And, also, remember when you wanted badly something that never came to you, no matter how you tried to get it, something that would have changed your life in ways you couldn't even see at the time. That's God's discipline too. And all of this is with a goal in mind. Paul looked long term at the entry into the land. The book of Hebrews looked also short term toward holiness and maturity.

The discipline of God is, while unpleasant at the time, "for our good, so that we may share his holiness" (Heb. 12:10). The end result is the "peaceful fruit of righteousness to those who have been trained by it" (Heb. 12:11), to keep us from the direction we so often want to go: toward immorality or bitterness, to, like Esau before us, squander our inheritance for a single meal (Heb. 12:14–17). Just as God did with his children Israel, God is intervening in our lives, putting us through areas of toughening, providentially averting us from catastrophic decisions that can seem right in the moment. This should be reflected in the discipline of cross-shaped families as well. But in order to pursue this, we must have a goal in mind; we must have a vision of the future.

First, we must have a sense of a short-term goal, and by short-term, I mean the next seventy-five years of the child's life, or, maybe, the next several generations ahead. A key aspect of this goal is that of maturity. We are, the Bible says, to "grow up . . . into Christ" (Eph. 4:15). The goal of ministry is to "present everyone mature" (Col. 1:28). At first glance, maturity would seem to be a contradiction of what Jesus told us: that we are to be as "little children." How on Earth, we may ask, can we be both mature and childlike at the same time? In reality, though, our culture does indeed keep childlikeness and maturity together, just in the opposite way that God intends. The Bible tells us to be "wise as to what is good and innocent as to what is evil" (Rom. 16:19). The culture says the reverse.

A generation ago, one sociologist warned of the "disappearance of childhood," which he saw illustrated in the changing nature of children's sports. He wrote: "Except for the inner city, where games are still under the control of the youths who play them, the games of American youth have become increasingly official, mock-professional, and extremely serious."[54] Frenetic activity is easy; maturity is costly. Maturity means self-control over one's own immediate desires and impulses for the sake of others. This is lost when adults evade the "grown-up" responsibilities of childrearing or discipleship altogether. This is also lost when parents treat their children as peers or, even worse, as a studio audience before whom to perform. In many cases, the children bear the responsibilities of adulthood so that the adults can relive the feelings of childhood. Popular culture in our age prizes youth as the source of authenticity and relevance, and downgrades authority. Sometimes this is for good reason, as when—as did young Josiah—a younger generation rights the sclerotic ways of an unfaithful older generation.

Culturally, the backlash against the idea of the "strict" father is because of the capriciousness and abuse of countless fathers. The problem is not, sometimes, what we are rebelling against but rather where we turn next, after the rebellion is over. "All of us who have been angry at the fathers rejoiced at first when the fathers lost authority, but the picture becomes more somber when we realize that the forces that destroyed the father will not be satisfied and are moving toward the mother," writes poet Robert Bly. "Mothers are discounted everywhere. When mothers and fathers are both dismembered, we will have a society of orphans, or, more exactly, a culture of adolescent orphans."[55] One would be hard-pressed to find a more apt metaphor for our time that that of the "Age of the Adolescent Orphan."

More often, though, the Bible sees the older—parents, extended family, the elders and teachers of the church—as accountable for cultivating the wisdom to see what the younger ones will need, long before the younger ones actually see the relevance of these things. Deuteronomy, then, instructs parents to teach the Word of the Lord to their children. The book of Proverbs is a series of instructions from a father to a son. Paul wrote to his son in the faith, Timothy, directing him away from "youthful lusts" and toward maturity (2 Tim. 2:22). The goal is maturity, and the means to get there is wisdom.

Wisdom, biblically defined, is a way of walking in the world, of learning to rule as an heir to the kingdom. This is a different sort of wisdom, though, than that of the world, which is knowledge for the sake of power or expertise. The wisdom of God, the wisdom toward which we are growing up in Christ, is that of "the foolishness" of the cross (1 Cor. 1:18–31). This means that, more than a storehouse of facts embedded in the brain (although, again, this is important) we should work to cultivate the sorts of intuitions that can recognize the beauty of holiness, and to recoil from the ugliness of the will to power. A parent, or a church, need not be an expert on culture to train up wise children who can discern good from evil. Yes, we should be aware of what is happening around us, and seek to be able to frame it in Christian terms, but far more important is that we shape our children's imaginations by the storyline of Scripture, just by the way we locate ourselves in it and refer back to it to see where we are in our pilgrimage through life. It is less important that your child has a Christian worldview than that your child has a Christian world, the world of the biblical text that calls us to Christ and him crucified. What we want, in the end, is not so much children who can deconstruct every argument so much as children who know to say, "If I have to choose between this and Jesus, I choose Jesus."

We don't then shy away from the dark aspects of human existence. Part of the power of temptation, after all, is to mystify sin as that which is forbidden and thus desirable (see the serpent's line of questioning in Genesis 3). The sin is then presented as being free from future consequences (again, see the snake's words). The Bible takes the opposite approach. God never glorifies sin. He tells us about it honestly, including the fact that it is often temporarily pleasurable (Heb. 11:25), and then he shows us the wages sin demands. The father's counsel to his son in Proverbs 7 about sexual immorality is like this. The father describes in poetic detail what leads up to such an encounter, why it would seem to be desirable, but then he gives the telescopic view of the sin, including the deadly end. Christian children will be confronted with all sorts of dark realities, sometimes much earlier than we would choose, from conversations with school-mates or from a variety of other ways. A Christian parent should not act disgruntled by questions about such things, but instead should—in the context of relationship—give insight as to how the cross points us to a different way.

There are many things we shelter our children from before they are ready for them. God prepared his people with the "tutor" of the law for centuries before disclosing "in the fullness of time" the mystery of Christ (Gal. 4:4). Jesus did the same. He told his disciples early on, "Come follow me" and "Come and see," and gradually unveiled the cross. In some ways, though, we walk our children through the cultural ecosystem around us as if it were a four-dimensional book of Ecclesiastes: "Sex. Drink. Money. Power. It's all out there, but it's all vanity in the end." We want so badly to protect them from the world. But, like Ecclesiastes, we want to leave them with more than this. We want to leave them with a word of exhortation at the end that says: "Remember also your Creator in the days of your youth" (Eccl. 12:1). We want to train them—to form them—to walk in the world with the wisdom from above. Formation of children means teaching not just to the intellect or to the will, but to the conscience. That means knowing the goodness of God, the strength of his promises, our place in the story, but also the wisdom to see to it "that we would not be outwitted by Satan; for we are not ignorant of his designs" (2 Cor. 2:11).

Wisdom and maturity is about training up kings and queens to rule. Solomon, for instance, the son of David, demonstrated his child-like dependence on God when he was told he could ask God for any one thing. He asked for wisdom, because he said he was a young child who needed to "discern between good and evil" in order to "govern this your great people" (1 Kings 3:9). Much of this is quite practical.

Solomon understood human nature well enough, for instance, to know which mother was lying to him in a kidnapping case. To some degree, the wisdom we pass on will be about the practical matters of how to make one's way in the world—how to read a text, how to mow a lawn, how to develop a work ethic, how to see the rhythm of cause and effect. Much of the Proverbs, for instance, is about such matters. We are training for the future by showing—through instruction and through habits and through the imagination—what it would look like to, by the Spirit, rule over whatever arena God puts the child in, rather than the child being ruled by himself or by the satanic powers.

The longer-term goal, though, is to prepare our children for the next trillion years. Most of our children will not be, like Solomon, high-ranking government officials (though some will). Yet every single one of us, in Christ, is a future galactic world-emperor, a joint-heir with Christ, in the boot camp of our sojourn in this present age. We suffer with Christ in order to be glorified with him (Rom. 8:17). Jesus said that those who are faithful in small things will be put over many things (Matt. 25:23). In Christ Jesus, we see one who is "greater than Solomon" (Matt. 12:42), and in the mystery of Christ "are hidden all the treasures of wisdom and knowledge" (Col. 2:3). We are leading our children to actually grow up into Christ. When we are disciplined for the future, meaning our eternal future, we actually join Jesus in his own discipline.

That sounds blasphemous to speak of Jesus as having been disciplined, but, again, this is because we picture an unruly Jesus being spanked by Joseph. That's not what I mean by discipline. Jesus did not walk straight from the manger to the cross, but instead in his humanity "learned obedience through what he suffered" (Heb. 5:8). It can be disconcerting to read Old Testament promises that the New Testament fulfills in Christ mentioning discipline. "When he commits iniquity, I will discipline him with the rod of men, with the stripes of the sons of men," God told David of his coming son (2 Sam. 7:14). Jesus, of course, has no iniquity. Jesus, though, was the start of a new humanity, a representative for all of us who are found in him. Jesus is not corrected by God because he submits and delights in all of the words of God. But in the formative sense, Jesus, in his humanity, is indeed disciplined (shaped, discipled) by God, and he disciplined himself, readying himself for the climax of his ministry: the offering of himself for his people.

Jesus obeyed his parents and "grew and became strong, filled with wisdom" (Luke 2:40). He embedded in his heart the Word of God, probably through the teaching of Mary and Joseph and the extended family, such that he was able to turn immediately to the text of Isaiah he wanted to reference in the synagogue, and he was able to see how this text on the kingdom was fulfilled in him. To understand God's discipline of us, we must see that we are disciplined *in Christ*. God said that he disciplined his people Israel—especially in the exodus and the wilderness wandering. That story of Israel came to fulfillment in Jesus himself. Moreover, much of the discipline language of the Old Testament is in reference to the coming king of the throne of David. God said to David that he would build a house for David's son, and give him the kingdom forever. "I will be to him a father, and he shall be to me a son" (2 Sam. 7:14). "When he commits iniquity, I will discipline him with the rod of men, with the stripes of the son of men, but my steadfast love will not depart from him" (2 Sam. 7:14–15). That same language is used in the Psalms, when God revealed his kinship with the Davidic king; part of that is seen in his discipline (Ps. 89:30–37).

To understand, then, what discipline is, we must understand who we are in Christ. The entire point of these passages is not about God's rage at you, or at his people. In fact, it is just the reverse. Remember, God said that he was disciplining his people—by both providing bread and water when they were starving in the wilderness and by allowing them to hunger in the first place—so that they would know, when they came into the land of promise, that "man does not live by bread alone, but, by every word that proceeds from the mouth of God" (Deut. 8:3). This is precisely because God receives them as his children, and precisely because he has a future for them (Deut. 8:5–20). If God did not see his people as his children, he would leave them, as he did the other nations, to walk in their own way. But because God had a future for his people, he trained them—sometimes in ways that seemed hard or inexplicable at the time. Jesus stepped into this, and summed it all up in himself. He was prepared for the cross through the testing in the desert, and never wavered from his identity or his inheritance. The one who thinks himself too good for discipline thinks himself to be greater than Jesus himself. When we disciple and raise up the next generation, we are calling them to that, calling them to him. That means calling them to a cross.

So, if that is the end-goal, how do we get there? We do that by seeing how God fathers us for the future, and attempting to do likewise. In Christ, God fathers us first by affirming that sense of belonging. Speaking of the formation of the coming King, God said, "I will be to him a Father, and he shall be to me a son" (2 Sam. 7:14). The discipline God speaks of in reference to Christ is bound up in that. He loves his Son. He sees his Son. He delights in his Son. God disciplines us precisely because he is treating us "as sons" rather than as "illegitimate children" (Heb. 12:8). Receiving this discipline as sons and daughters reinforces that we belong to God, as members of his family. In our families, some of this sense of identity and belonging is formed in the traditions and rhythms we share together. One of the best examples is seen in the mundane practice of sharing meals together. Family dinner may seem to be second nature in your home, but notice what happens if schedules become so convoluted that family dinners start to be skipped. Before you know it, they are gone, with everyone scarfing down his or her food alone while staring a screen. But coming together for meals is about more than what studies show best equip children to be well balanced (although we care about their flourishing). It is about imitating Jesus, who initiates his people into the family by a regular gathering around the Lord's Table. As parents, we are seeking to show our children that our end goal for them is a Wedding Feast, not Esau's scarfed, lonely meal.

* * * *

If we, as parents, are driven by self, we will expect our children to reflect us back to ourselves, rather than seeking to shape and form their identities. The child will just become an extension of the parents. Those shaped by the cross, though, will pour themselves out for the next generation in order to say to the child, "Who are you?" and "How did God gift you?" The love of a parent is seldom seen any clearer than when a parent exerts the effort to affirm the gifts and callings of a child, especially when those gifts are different than those of the parent. A hard-driven, corporate-lawyer-of-a-mother shows love to her daughter who is struggling in school when that mother doesn't expect her child to be the same as she, but delights to see her child come alive in a pottery class or on the tennis court. This sense of belonging means verbal affirmations of "I love you" (as God does, repeatedly, from the skies in the earthly mission of Jesus), but also in narrating back to the child what you see in him or her. The message we send is not just "I love you," but "I love *you*"—I know who you are, I see you, and I am pleased with you.

In the biblical world, this sense of belonging was, in some ways, more easily conveyed because children were with their parents working in the field or constructing a house or fishing a lake. A child could see how he belonged to the family because he was not just a "consumer" but an actual part of the household economy. The reverse is often true in our context. Parents are absent from much of their children's lives, and they compensate for feeling guilty by buying their children more and more consumer goods. A modern American family will not, of course, usually have the same sort of family burden-sharing as an ancient Middle Eastern family (and in most ways, that is for the better), but there are nonetheless ways that a family can include every part of the household as part of the family's mission together. In our home, this starts as soon as a child is old enough to do almost anything at all, with him being given a small chore to do that is his responsibility. A very small child might be given a trash can in a bathroom to check every day, to empty its contents into the larger trash can in the kitchen. It would, of course, be easier to just do that myself than to teach him to do it, and to clean up the trail of refuse he leaves behind in the trek from one room to the other. The main point, though, is not to get a task done, and is really not even to teach him to work (although that's of course important), but to say to him, "You're one of us. We need you." Our Father disciplines us in this way, by gifting us for service in the church, by inviting us into his mission. In fact, one of the most important aspects of our discipline from our Father is our learning to do small things in order that we may one day be given more authority over bigger things (Luke 16:10; 19:17). As important as we often think our careers or vocations or ministries are, their actual purpose is just to train us to do what we could not imagine now in the coming kingdom of Christ. God is just having us empty the little trash can into the bigger trash can, in order to say to us, "You are part of this family; you belong."

That also includes making sure that the children see that the family is on mission, together, with the resurrected Christ. Some families have a "family mission statement." That sounds a bit too corporate for our household (but if it works for you, have at it), but it matters to us that our children see their parents caring for others—spiritually, physically, emotionally. The best thing my children can learn from me is that I am part of the church, by seeing me sing in worship and serving the body of Christ and the world with the gospel. Some Christians worry obsessively over what their spiritual gifts are, taking written surveys and personality profiles. The Bible never insists that it's important that we know what our gifts are—at least not in the way that they are often portrayed in these assessments, with our skills and giftings ranked from greatest to least. What is important is that we serve, and that the church sees those gifts. Some of the most effective servants of Christ's church have never thought about what their gifts are; they are simply focused on building up the gifts of others. The important question is not whether you can answer what your spiritual gift is, but whether your children could answer that about you. That's discipline too.

One of the ways that we cultivate this sense of belonging is by recognizing in our discipleship and our discipline that our children are not agriculture or machinery but persons. This means that each one of them will possess unique strengths and vulnerabilities. In a technocratic age, however, we assume that everything is a matter of technique, including the rearing of children. Hence, we often act as though, if we would just put the right "five steps" to work, we could redirect a strong-willed child or accomplish toilet training without tears (from baby or parent). Yes, there are some general principles that apply to all children as children and to all people as people. Some general principles are true for all human beings, but often many specifics—what sort of sleep or feeding regimens are maintained, what type of schooling is chosen, and when it's started, and so on—can be child-specific and family-specific and, if universalized, can cause harm.

One parents a Joseph differently than a Samson, a David differently than a Jeremiah, or a Peter differently than a John. You may have one child who is more nonchalant about moral distinctions and another with an overly sensitive conscience. You may have one who conforms too quickly with his peer group and another who harshly judges his own or others' sins. These require different sets of instructions, boundaries, and corrections. With one of my sons, I often have to say, "This matters! Beware of this!" and with another I must constantly say, "Sinning doesn't mean that you're not a Christian; it means that the Spirit is leading you toward Christlikeness. You're forgiven, so let it go." We must bear the burdens of each child, in unique ways. This reflects the Fatherhood of God who "knows our frame; he remembers that we are dust" (Ps. 103:14).

With that sense of belonging also comes the stability of authority. One of our sons was, as a toddler, especially given to temper tantrums. My wife and I stopped then, as we were getting ready one day, to hear the morning television program announce that a parenting expert would be on after the commercial break, to talk about fits and how to stop them. This was exactly the kind of expertise we needed, badly.

We listened as the parenting expert explained that tantrums were not a discipline matter at all, just a communication problem. A child breaks down, the expert said, when he feels as though he isn't being heard or understood by his parent. Parents should then let tantrums happen, without correcting them. The host asked about what to do if the child were throwing a fit in a grocery store, say, because the parents wouldn't buy him a cookie he demanded. The same applies, the expert said. The parent should lean down, at eye level with the child, take his head in the parent's hand, look into the child's eye, and repeat over and over again gently: "You want a cookie . . . You want a cookie . . . You want a cookie." The child would soon see, the expert said, that the parents understood him, and the tantrum would stop, even without buying him what he wanted.

Now, Maria and I were not—and are not—parenting experts, but we did have some inkling that the sort of behavior we empowered when our child was small—in this case, anger and lack of self-control—wouldn't stop with the smallness of the child, but would grow with him, perhaps into something enormous. We feared that, though the expert's advice sounded simple and easy, were we to follow it we would one day be looking into the stubble-covered face of a young man, repeating gently, "You just robbed a liquor store . . . You just robbed a liquor store . . . You just robbed a liquor store." We knew we couldn't go that direction, although we weren't sure exactly what our alternative would be.

The sort of discipline the expert offered in that interview was what many would call "permissive" parenting, one that sees the fundamental issue of human nature as a lack of information or nurture rather than the more radical problem Christians and others recognize. The parents, in this case, are not so much "the authority" as the facilitators, helping the child to tap into his own, already-formed inner resources to redirect his behavior. Many Christians, including those who would ridicule this form of parenting, actually practice it. They may see themselves as strong authorities in their home, but exercise that authority sporadically or inconsistently or with a different vision altogether of what authority is. Psychologists and behavioral scientists have differentiated between "permissive" parenting and "authoritative" parenting, but in recent years more of them are also making, rightly, the distinction between "authoritative" parenting and "authoritarian" parenting. Authoritative parenting sees the clear direction of the child's moral and spiritual formation as the responsibility of the parents. Authoritarian parenting, though, can often seem to be "maintaining authority and order," when in reality children are simply cowed into compliance. That is not the authority we have found in Christ.

Our problem is, though, that apart from the cross we often confuse authority with power. As a matter of fact, when we replace authority with power *or* when we replace authority with no authority, we tend to have the same result. Authority is not raw power. If someone in the workplace, in a department not yours and of a lower rank, tells you how you are going to do a project, you might well respond, "You don't have the authority to tell me what to do." What you do not mean is that the person is incapable of speaking words of instruction. You mean that he doesn't have the right to direct you. But suppose he were to brandish a gun, and tell you to comply or be shot. You might then do what he says, but that still doesn't mean that he now has authority to do it. He just has the raw power to force compliance. That's not what authority is. Authority, biblically defined, is not synonymous with "power." It does not express one's ability to do something, but expresses one's right and responsibility to do it as well.

Authority also presupposes accountability. When we remove the stability that comes from wise, loving adult authority—or when we make that authority the result of sheer strength—we will very soon end up with children who idolize power, either to get the power they think necessary to hold back the chaos or to put themselves in the place of importance they've seen power signify. These children will want a strongman, or to be one. If children believe that authority is about whoever has the most power at the time, they will eventually see that the devil has more power than they do. We, though, have escaped, Jesus told us, from the grip of a strongman. As a matter of fact, he tied up this strongman and plundered his house (Mark 3:27).

The devil uses power to tempt and seduce. How, though, do we overcome the power of the devil? It is not by matching raw power with raw power. We overcome the accuser through what the world thinks is weakness: the word of our testimony and the blood of the Lamb (Rev. 12:11). Authority is all about pouring oneself out for another. Jesus said that his authority is seen in the fact that he lays his own life down that he may take it up again (John 10:18). The sign of authority is not size or influence or age or title but a cross.

* * * *

A Christian vision of parenting calls us away both from passivity and from domineering. It is key that the Scriptures teach us both for children to be obedient to their parents, and, simultaneously, for parents not to "provoke not your children" to anger, but bring them up in the "nurture and admonition of the Lord" (Eph. 6:4 KJV). In truth, there's no such thing as an "undisciplined" family, or an "undisciplined" church, or even an "undisciplined" person. Everyone is disciplined—trained, formed, and corrected toward certain inclinations and behaviors. The question is what we are disciplined toward, not whether we are disciplined. Parents who walk past their child torturing a puppy, without comment, is not a picture of a family neglecting discipline. In fact, they are disciplining their son to see that cruelty and violence, at least toward defenseless animals, is not a momentous enough matter to intervene. That child is being shaped and formed, by that lack of correction, toward an expected future, albeit one that is awful.

Many times as parents we do precisely what our Father never does, and will never do. James wrote, "Let no one say when he is tempted, 'I am being tempted by God,' for God cannot be tempted with evil, and he himself tempts no one" (James 1:13). Paul wrote that "God is faithful, and he will not let you be tempted beyond your ability, but with the temptation he will also provide the way of escape, that you may be able to endure it" (1 Cor. 10:13). That's why God through the Law of Moses treated his people as a tightly governed child "under guardians and managers until the date set by his father" (Gal. 4:2). He carefully works us toward maturity, seeing that we're faithful in small things before putting us over many things. In the same way, a parent should strive to start with very restrictive boundaries of freedom and responsibility and then gradually prepare the child for greater and greater freedom and responsibility. Often, parents wish instead to give little attention to boundaries when the consequences don't immediately disrupt their lives and then to move in after patterns are established by an entire childhood. Other parents wish to keep the boundaries restrictive, infantilizing the child. This is the sort of parent who calls her son's military superior to complain about his treatment at boot camp or her daughter's college dean to take issue with a grade.

Often, a parent's lack of adequate boundaries is rooted in peer pressure—not the pressure of the child's peers on him or her but the pressure of the parent's peers on the parent.

The parent doesn't want to deprive his or her child of what the world around would say children need. Or the parent shies away from such boundaries for fear of losing favor with his or her child. This is not only wrong-headed, but also shortsighted. Your children will soon recognize that you do not have a longer-term view for them than they have for themselves. If you train them to see you as a means to the end of indulging their appetites, they will ultimately choose their appetites over you. Again, remember the sad example of the priest Eli, whose sons took from the fat of the offerings, and then, fully matured, rebelled to their father's great grief (1 Sam. 2:12–21; 4:16–18).

Disciplining our children is not just about correcting misbehavior but also about training them in what's to be loved and prioritized. That means discipling ourselves to care about our children's best interest more than our own. We should care, then, not as much about what our children think of us in the moment, but how they will view us when it matters most—looking backward from their own deathbeds a lifetime from now, and beyond that, as subjects before the Judgment Seat of Christ. That sort of self-sacrificial parenting requires wisdom, patience, and a willingness to, when necessary, be unpopular. Yes, children will complain, at first, about any boundary markers in their lives. So did we, and all those before us, when we were delivered from our respective Pharaohs into a Father's house.

At the same time, though, some are tempted to image God poorly through a discipline that is harsh or arbitrary. Parents are to raise their children "in the nurture and admonition of the Lord," the Scripture commands, but are also not to "exasperate" their children. Walking away from such exasperation starts with a house in which correction and rebuke is not the primary mode of interaction. God's household is not dour and withholding, but full of joy. Some parents interact with their children so much in correction and rebuke that they mimic the older brother of Jesus' parable instead of the joy-filled father who plans a party for his returning son (Luke 15:11–32). Some parents believe they are holy, when instead they are signaling to their children that the kingdom of Christ is a tedious seminar of Pharisees, not a household of those who bask in the favor and liberation of our God (Luke 4:18–19). If laughter and joy are not part of our families, something is wrong.

Some parents see corrective discipline as the venting of a parent's own anger or frustration. Indeed, many who are lax in discipline in small things, then "explode" in yelling at their children when they reach a certain (often undefined) point. Children are hardly able to hear authority in parents who have clearly lost control of their own impulses by their frantic screaming. If, as the Bible teaches, discipline is about the future of the child, and not about the parent's self-expression, then we should discipline when we are the calmest and most in possession of self-control. If you are given to yelling or anger, first discipline yourself. It may be that you should say to your child, "We are going to talk about this, but first I am going for a walk." Calming yourself down before addressing the problem does not divert discipline but instead affirms it. Certainly, if there is ever abuse of a child in your home, no matter who is carrying out that abuse, the civil authorities should be called immediately. The abuse of children, in a home or in a church, should not be excused, ignored, or tolerated for even a nanosecond. But even in situations not approaching abuse, the anger of the parent can, sadly, still be the defining characteristic of the home. This is not the way it should be.

Nor should we assume that just because a parent doesn't yell and scream that he or she has a temper under control. Sometimes—even perfectly legitimate—means of corrective discipline, such as sending a child to his room, can communicate something quite different from the fatherly discipline of God through the gospel. Again, this can be a good strategy if one means a short period of isolation in order to prompt the child to calm down or to reflect on the gravity of the situation. Extended periods of such isolation, though, remove the child from the life of the family. That is not the biblical pattern, of discipline and restoration, but instead a means of removing the child from the very means of discipleship that he (and we) so desperately need. God's discipline seeks not to isolate and marginalize but to drive the erring sheep back into the sheepfold with his voice, to welcome the prodigal son back to the table, not to keep him away.

For some parents, the expectations of their children are so rigid that no child can meet them. Sometimes this is because, unlike God himself, parents are unable to see the difference between immaturity and rebellion. Yes, small issues of lack of discipline can lead to large issues later, but that doesn't mean that everything a child is doing is worthy of immediate response. God rebukes his people for their lack of maturity, in many instances. Those who should be teachers, in the early church, were still needing to be taught, needing the "milk" of basic instruction rather than the "solid food" of those who are "mature," and who have "their powers of discernment trained by constant practice to distinguish good from evil" (Heb. 5:11–14). The author of Hebrews, though, did not put them into teaching authority before they were ready, nor did he shove solid food into the mouth of a baby who had not yet learned to chew. Instead, he taught, and sought to bring them up to the maturity to which they were called. Moreover, God, unlike the inscrutable gods of the other nations, revealed exactly what he expected of his people. One did not need to speculate about what God found good or right or pleasing to him.

God is also not harsh with us in our discipline. The commandments of the Lord are "not burdensome" (1 John 5:3). A child who concludes that she cannot figure out what her parents expect is a child who will soon give up trying. A child who concludes that he can never meet his parents' expectations will also give up trying. I think immediately of one situation of a legalistic father who was constantly needling his children about everything, disciplining them much too drastically and beyond what was called for by the infraction. Some of this man's children ended up in ongoing rebellion against everything that reminded them of him, while some of them lived out lives so cowed down that they could barely stand to speak to a clerk in a store in response to a greeting. Now, it could be, of course, that the personalities of these children were such that this would have been the outcome anyway, but God forbid that our angry, harsh discipline should be what sparks or exacerbates such.

Instruction is not chiefly about imparting information or moral standards, although we want to inculcate knowledge and a moral compass. Discipline is not about compliance but about repentance. Correction is necessary, but correction is about repentance, not about punishment. Punishment is hell. Hell has fallen on us at the cross, and we bear it no more. Discipline bears resemblance to hell, only in one way: that both display actions have consequences and that we must give an account of who we are and what we've done. But discipline is not hell; it's grace. Discipline is a temporary hardship for the sake of our good, yielding the "peaceful fruit of righteousness to those who have been trained by it" (Heb. 12:11). To do so, we must often surrender notions of what "success" looks like for our child. We should pray, first and foremost, not that our child gets into a good school, or finds an esteemed career, or even that he or she would have a stable family one day. We should pray that, more than anything, our child will leave an exit hole in a graveyard one day because he or she has learned to hear the voice of Christ.

Moral credibility is gained not, though, by hiding our sins and failings from our children, but by repenting of them before our children. We do not sacrifice our credibility when we say to our children, "I was wrong" or "Will you forgive me?" In order to discipline our children, we must be disciplined ourselves. In order to parent our children, we must be Fathered ourselves. In order to carry the gospel to our children, we must cling to the gospel ourselves. The cross, then, must not only be the focus in how we teach and train and discipline but when we stumble as well. We will never get this completely right. You will feel like a failure most of the time as a parent or as a leader of the next generation, even when you are not failing. Unlike the Father, we are not all-holy, and we are not all-knowing. Though our goal is to act in the long-term, best interest of our children, we will often lose sight of what that is or not know in the first place.

That is, of course, what parenting and discipline are all about. The end goal is not that our children will behave better. In fact, a well-behaved person is sometimes the closest to hell. If a person learns to cower in front of whomever seems most powerful at the moment, well, the devil seems quite powerful in this time-between-the-times. Even worse, a person who learns to obey without learning to repent is someone who will either despair or who will try to establish his own righteousness. This, of course, never actually brings about righteousness because the one who has broken the law at one point is a lawbreaker, and "whoever keeps the whole law but fails in one point has become accountable of all of it" (James 2:10). The point of discipline is not to learn behavior so much as it is to learn repentance. There's a reason the apostle Paul's admonition on parents and children is in the context of spiritual warfare—the truth that we do not "wrestle against flesh and blood" (Eph. 6:12). The goal of our parenting is not compliance—children who learn to yield to a stronger power. The goal of our parenting is the right kind of fighting. We want children who love the kingdom God is promising, and who kick back against the occupying force of this present darkness. We discipline not so that we can teach our children what to do and not to do, so much as we discipline to teach them where to go when they fail at that, or rather to Whom they should go. That requires a parenting that keeps the gospel in view—where justice and love, truth and grace, meet in the crucified Christ.

Perhaps the best way to see this is in Jesus' own "parenting" of his apostles. His discipline of them is right at the forefront of his ministry, hence the word "disciples" we use for them. We tend to think of parenthood simply in terms of God the Father, but God is fathering us through Christ Jesus. Like earthly fathers, Jesus models (except perfectly) the fatherliness of God with those around him. The Gospels are filled with examples of this, but one that immediately comes to mind is Jesus' interaction with his disciples at Caesarea Philippi, after Simon Peter confessed that Jesus is the Christ, the Son of the living God. Jesus affirmed Peter's confession with an unveiling of the future: "On this rock I will build my church, and the gates of hell shall not prevail against it," not just in the big, cosmic sweep of it all but particularly with Peter's role in it. Strikingly, though, after this triumph teaching about the coming kingdom, Jesus turned, as he always did, right back to the cross, as he "began to show his disciples that he must go to Jerusalem and suffer many things from the elders and chief priests and scribes, and be killed, and on the third day be raised" (Matt. 16:21–22). In this Jesus both praised and affirmed those who discipled ("Blessed are you, Simon Bar-Jonah . . .") and also corrected, in this case sharply ("Get behind me, Satan . . ."). Jesus, though, isn't shocked by Peter's ignorant accidental Satanism, or by his future sin. He knew he would betray him three times. He doesn't drive him into sin or hiding. He says to him, "When you have turned again, strengthen your brothers" (Luke 22:32). If parents and church leaders and mentors could get a grasp of what Jesus is doing here, how here he is modeling himself after his Father, we just might see what it means to parent with a cross on our backs, and with a kingdom in view.

* * * *

We want our children to flourish in the world. We want our children to look back on us with love and respect. But we should want, most of all, that our children will look back and see that our only self-identity was this: "What could wash away our sin? Nothing but the blood of Jesus." We should parent in such a way that our children see that our hope for them is not that they are "successful enough" to look good to our peers, nor is it that they are well-behaved enough not to keep us awake at night, but that they are, like us, alive to God through Jesus Christ. We should hope that they should see us, and themselves, as simultaneously sinful and justified, as sometimes grounded but always baptized. For that, we need a cross.

Chapter Twelve

Family Tensions, Family Traumas

A FRIEND OF MINE, WHOSE children are a bit older than my own, recently dropped his firstborn son off at college. My friend said that he left his son's dormitory room and wept bitterly, despite the fact that the college was just a few miles from his front doorstep. An older Christian man came upon my friend and asked if he was alright. My friend said that his emotions weren't so much due to sentimentality, although there was some of that, as much as to guilt. My friend is a musician, who must spend much of his time touring on the road. "I realize now that I had such a limited amount of time with my son," my friend said. "And I was gone so much. Why wasn't I home with him more? And when I was home why did I ever waste time watching television?" The older man looked at my friend and said, "Oh, the Lord redeems all of that."

My friend said that one sentence was liberating. The man did not do what he expected—reassure him. "If he had told me that I had been a good father, I would have just rationalized that he didn't know the whole situation," my friend said. "And if he said my absence didn't matter, I wouldn't have believed him." Instead, this wise stranger pointed to the cross. The Lord can redeem this story, by joining it to the redeeming work of the cross. Instead of a word of reassurance regarding my friend's performance, he offered something better: a word of grace.

I listened carefully, because while I haven't reached the "empty nest" yet, even partially, I know all too well what it means to feel like a parenting failure. None of us will make it through life without hurting and being hurt by others. Often those hurts will happen within the context of family—sometimes from people grievously long gone, sometimes from people who are annoyingly, persistently still here.

* * * *

Jesus told us to expect tumult and suffering. The apostle Peter, likewise, told the churches to which he wrote, "Do not be surprised at the fiery trial when it comes upon you, to test you, as though something strange were happening to you" (1 Pet. 4:12). The sense of God's presence and purpose behind pain, though, does not lead to a Stoic fatalism or a kind of Buddhist calm in the face of evil and hurt. The cross makes it clear that evil is real, and calls for the judgment of God. The cross also makes it clear that none of us need be undone ultimately by what has been done to us, or, sometimes even worse, by what we have done to others.

Knowing how to apply the cross-shaped nature of our gospel to our often confusing family lives and situations, though, can be difficult, especially when what troubles us can range sometimes from mild tension to real trauma. How do we know how to walk toward the future God has for us in the gospel when what ought to be the most secure element of our identities—our families—fractures or even falls? Some of this will mean walking through the ordinary tensions of the family, and some of it will be about looking backward and forward at the very real traumas we face. As Jesus moved toward the cross, he had many who knew something of what he was about, and were actively seeking to kill him. There were others, though, who just did not yet understand, failing to see who he was and what he was saying. Neither derailed Jesus' trek to the cross, nor did he confuse the one with the other.

Working often with families formed through adoption, I regularly hear from grown children who were adopted talking about the difficulties that come along with sorting through identity questions. One of these Christians said to me, "You just can't imagine what it is like to sit across a table from people who are a mystery to you, to think to yourself, 'I am nothing like you! How did I end up in this family."

I said that, to some degree, what she was experiencing was due to the adoption, but a great deal more of it is far more universal than that. "I actually do know what that's like," I said. "It's called Thanksgiving."

As much as we idealize family, this idealism tends to fade when we deal with the very real frictions that can happen between members of a family with different personalities and different perspectives. Some of this is just navigating what conversations to bring up and which to avoid. Some of it is more serious: family members who are hostile to your faith, for instance. Or maybe you are someone who thought you were an empty nester, now dealing with a son or daughter back in his old bedroom, maybe with a spouse or a partner or some children now in tow. That's difficult enough with one's family of origin, where at least one has had the training ground of a lifetime to know, as they say, "where the bodies are buried." When one adds to that the mix of in-laws, often with their own very confusing dynamics, unspoken feuds and peace treaties, and complicated backstories, this can become even more fraught. How do we then carry the cross when tensions inevitably come?

First, the gospel calls us to *peace*. Yes, Jesus tells us that he brings a sword of division, and that this sometimes splits up families

(Matt. 10:34–37). But there's a difference between gospel division and carnal division (1 Cor. 1:10–17). The Spirit brings about peace (Gal. 5:22), and the sons of God are called to be peacemakers (Matt. 5:9) so we should "strive for peace with everyone" (Heb. 12:14). Often the divisiveness that happens within extended families is about conflicting spiritual worldviews, but occasionally the divisiveness is not about an unbelieving family member persecuting a Christian, but rather because a Christian decides to go ahead and, at the family table, sort the wheat from the weeds right now, rather than, as Jesus told us, waiting for Judgment Day (Matt. 13:29–30). Yes, the gospel exposes sin, but not for the purpose of condemnation (John 3:17). The gospel strategically exposes sin in order to point to Christ. Antagonizing unbelieving family members because they think or feel like unbelievers is not the way of the cross.

Some Christians think their belligerence is actually a sign of holiness. They leave the Christmas table saying, "See, if you're not being opposed, then you're not with Christ!" Sometimes, of course, divisions must come. But think of the qualifications Jesus gives for his church's leaders—that they must not be "quarrelsome" and they must be "well thought of by outsiders" (1 Tim. 3:3, 7). That's in the same list as not being a heretic or a drunk. Your presence should be, as much as possible, one of peace and tranquility. The gospel you believe ought to be what disrupts.

Moreover, the Scripture calls us to *honor*. We are to fear God, to obey the king, and to honor (notice this) everyone (1 Pet. 2:17). If cousin Hattie Jo does tequila shots in her car outside the family gathering just to take the edge off of her cocaine, well, she still bears the imprint of the God you adore. You cannot do the will of God by opposing the will of God. That is, you cannot evangelize, for example, your unbelieving father and mother by disrespecting them. God tells us to honor those to whom honor is due. That means showing, everywhere possible, respect and gratitude.

This calls also for *humility*. Part of the reason for many of our tensions within extended families is because we see differences over

Jesus as of the same sort as our differences over foreign policy in the Middle East, or the chances of our favorite sports team to make the playoffs this year, or who deserves the most gratitude for preparing the family meal. As Christians, we cannot be those who, like the professional polarizers in our culture around us, value having the last word. Jesus, not once, sought to prove he was right. And he was accused of everything from being a drunk to being a demoniac. He rejected Satan's temptation to force a visible vindication—by throwing himself from the temple pinnacle and being theatrically rescued by God—waiting instead for God to vindicate him at the empty tomb.

We often veer toward Satanism with our extended families—especially those who are nominal Christians or unbelievers—because we pride ourselves on knowing the truth of the gospel. That's why we feel rage when Uncle Ronnie pontificates that "many roads lead to God." Uncle Ronnie is wrong, but we must not want to prove ourselves right more than we want him resurrected. We find ourselves here when we forget just how it was that we came to Christ in the first place. This wasn't our brilliance, like being accepted into an Ivy League university, or our exertion of will, like learning a winning chess strategy. "What do you have that you did not receive?" the apostle Paul asked. "If you then received it, why do you boast as though you did not receive it?" (1 Cor. 4:7). Satan wants to destroy you through this primal flaw, pride (1 Pet. 5:7–9; 1 Tim. 3:6). He doesn't care if that pride comes through looking around the family table and figuring out how much more money you make than your second cousin-in-law or whether it comes by looking around the table and saying, "Thank you Lord that I am not like these publicans." The end result is the same (Prov. 29:23). Unless you're in an exceptionally sanctified family, you're going to see failing marriages, parenting crises, and a thousand other shards of the curse (and you're going to experience many of these personally as well). If your response is to puff up as you compare yourself with others, there's a Satanist at your family gathering, and you're it.

This calls then also for *maturity*. If we are following the way of the cross, we will follow the path Jesus took: from temptation to suffering to crucifixion and then ultimately to glory. Often we think of those tests as big, monumental things, but they rarely are. God might bring you to maturity in Christ by your fighting lions before the emperor or standing with a John 3:16 sign before tanks in the streets of Beijing. More likely, though, this testing will be in those seemingly little places of temptation—like whether you will bear patiently with the belching brother-in-law at the end of the table who wants to talk about how the Cubans killed President Kennedy or about how he can make you rich by joining his multilevel marketing business selling herbal laxatives. One of the questions we must ask ourselves is whether the tension we feel should be attributed to our own immaturity, and sometimes the answer is yes.

In any case, though, see the tensions around you as more than something you would undo if only you were part of a different family. They will always be here. Remember also that the cross points us to a Day of Judgment when we will give an account for every idle (that means seemingly tiny, insignificant, or unmemorable) thought, word, or deed. We will see then that the Spirit has led us to carry our crosses into every possible arena in which to live out the gospel, including Aunt Flossie's dining room table.

Here I am using the word *tension* to speak to those everyday frictions that require patience and wisdom, but which don't usually threaten the family itself, while speaking of "trauma" as those experiences of harm and hurt that imperil one's very sense of self and community. Sometimes the line between the two is fuzzy, especially when it relates to relationships between parents and wayward children. I don't like the phrase "prodigal children" much because it tends to presume that the children are the ones who have gone away to the far country while the parents have stayed at home. That's not Jesus' point, though. All of us are prodigals—just at different places in our redemption stories. It would be just as accurate, often, to speak of "prodigal parents" and "prodigal brothers and sisters" and "prodigal churches." Of course, there is also a wide spectrum in what we see as "wandering children," ranging from families that are intact and love one another, but where the children have not received the faith tradition of their parents, to situations in which the children express resentment and hatred toward their parents, and even are involved in dangerous or socially destructive behaviors. There is a special kind of agony that comes, though, when a parent—whether a literal parent or a spiritual parent—sees a child wandering away from the way he or she was taught and into self-destruction. If, as the apostle John wrote, "I have no greater joy than to hear that my children are walking in the truth" (3 John 4), then surely the mirror image of that is true as well.

Sometimes this hurt is intensified by an inadequate sense of sin and grace, not on the part of the "prodigals" but on the part of those waiting for them to return. Some parents can feel a kind of betrayal, as though the child's unbelief is itself an act of hatred directed toward the parent, because the child owes his family his own conversion and discipleship. A parent may act shocked that a child would rebel— "How could he do this after the way he was raised?" or "What a lack of gratitude she has for us when we have done all this for her!" If you are finding yourself thinking this way, realize what is happening. You are missing what God has revealed to us at the cross. The reality is, you are not just dealing with a "prodigal child," but God is dealing with a "prodigal cosmos."

* * * *

Sin and rebellion against God is universal (with the only exception being Jesus) in the entire stream of the human race, including you. All of our stories include our awareness of God, our awareness of his revelation in our consciences, and nonetheless our turning away in ingratitude toward the self and the idols we can construct (Rom. 1:18–23). Knowing this about ourselves is essential to relating well to those who disappoint us with their disbelief or rebellion. To be shocked that our child, or our mentored protégé, could commit any sin, or walk in any path, is a sign that we do not really get what the cross has taught us about human sin and the human heart.

Sometimes—usually unspoken—there is a feeling of betrayal by God himself, for not intervening to save the child. Often, this is rooted in a transactional view of what childrearing is all about. Some parents in our contemporary milieu, as I observed earlier, think of childrearing as the equivalent of raising cattle or programming code into a computer, a relatively simple matter of cause and effect, input and output. Christians sometimes adopt the exact same viewpoint, even early in life, watching a fussy baby and judging her parents for not putting her on the sort of sleep-schedule that would ensure contentment. This becomes even more pronounced when Christians do the same with a spiritual mechanism instead of a technical one. "Train up a child in the way he should go; even when he is old he will not depart from it" (Prov. 22:6) is a passage many parents of wayward children will "claim" as a "promise" that God will, in the end, save their child. This, of course, is not what the book of Proverbs teaches.

There is no prosperity gospel of parenting. The text, as do many of the proverbs, speaks of a general principle: parents' direction of their children is formative, in some way, for the rest of their lives. That's certainly true. This does not mean, though, that a child reared in a Christian home will inevitably turn out to be a Christian, even if that child was reared in a very good Christian home. In many cases, a child who grew up with the Bible and hymns and the warm eco-system of the gospel all around him will nevertheless walk away from all of it. Sometimes this is—like the prodigal in Jesus' parable—for a short period of time, as he is trying to find an identity distinct from his parents. Sometimes it is for life.

This does not mean that the parents' gospel instruction and modeling was all for naught. We are all confronted—for good or for ill—with our backgrounds, sometimes increasingly as we age or in moments we least expect. Many who grew up in Christian homes are not Christian but are, as Flannery O'Connor would put it, "Christ-haunted." That is to say, their affections and hidden intuitions keep drawing them into a confrontation with the Christ they do not want to find. Sometimes this "Christ-haunting" becomes a poltergeist, noisily prodding the conscience from embedded memories of old Sunday school songs or family Bible readings or the example of a parent who prayed with him at night. Sometimes this leads to conversion, maybe even long after the parents are dead. Sometimes it does not. Knowledge of facts, and even immersion in the things of God, does not guarantee new birth. The guards who witnessed the events of the resurrection, Matthew tells us in one of the most subtly disturbing passages in all of the Bible, were given a "sufficient sum of money" to deny what they had seen with their own eyes: that the most momentous event in cosmic history had, in fact, happened. What on earth could be a "sufficient sum" to do that? We do know, though, that the Spirit can convict anyone of sin and bring anyone to faith in Christ, even after years of running. The Spirit blows where he wills, and we cannot track him. We can only see the leaves as they scatter in his wake (John 3:8).

Sometimes what parents experience is not a sense of entitlement but a wrong-headed sense of guilt. Either they spend all of their time second-guessing their own parenting decisions or failures or omissions from days long past, or they feel guilty for the way they are presently handling the situations of a child in active or passive rebellion. I will never forget an older man, an impressive, godly Christian, who once came to my office and broke into tears, saying that he feared he was going to hell. He clearly held to the gospel, so I asked why he would think this. He said that he knew that Jesus said that whoever denied him before men, he would deny before his Father in heaven (Matt. 10:33). And this man believed that he regularly denied Christ.

When I pressed him on this, he explained that his grown daughter, not a Christian, was involved in a long-term, sexual, cohabiting relationship outside of marriage, and that she had a little boy through that union. Guilt-ridden, he told me his daughter knows what her parents think about the morality of marriage and sexuality, but that he does not always turn to the topic when they are together. He also explained he regularly visits his daughter, and that they have "normal" father/daughter conversations, often filled with laughter. And I learned, that he is involved, almost constantly, in the life of his grandson. What this man didn't realize is that he was living out life heroically. He was a Christian model for parenting and grand-parenting, but he felt as though he was denying Christ because every conversation with his daughter was not a sparring match over biblical texts on sexual morality. This is the sad result of the kind of adver-sary culture, in which the church in our zeal to defend the faith has sometimes unintentionally presented the picture that our interactions with unbelievers ought to be constant arguments. This is not how God dealt with us.

In truth, sometimes people turn around as the result of losing an argument, but I rarely see that. Usually, a word is strategically spoken, bearing witness to Christ, and then the one giving that word has the patience to wait for the Spirit to apply the word. As Jesus taught us, "The kingdom of God is as if a man should scatter seed on the ground. He sleeps and rises night and day, and the seed sprouts and grows; he knows not how" (Mark 4:26–27). This seems too slow and plodding for some of us. We want to win an argument, see our children saved, and then move on with our lives. That is not, though, how God works. Many years ago, I experienced a broken relationship with a friend (as much my fault, or more, than his), but, at the time, he would not respond to notes I had sent apologizing for my part in the disagreement.

In talking to a wise older man, I said how haunted I was by guilt in this unresolved conflict. The older man said, "I think the problem is that you are a narrative thinker and you want narrative closure here. You want a plot resolution, and you just have to realize that your life is not a book. You may not ever see 'closure' here, and you should trust God with the plot." He was exactly right. Almost as soon as I saw this, and said to God that I accepted the fact that I may never see this friendship reconciled, my old-and-now-new friend contacted me, with apologies accepted and apologies of his own to offer. That is not a prescription for forcing God to act, just the reverse. In my case, though, I think God wanted me to crucify my need for a life of "plot-line consistency" before I would experience the grace of resolution.

Most people—including prodigal family members—wrestle with the gospel, as all of us do, for long periods of time before they walk toward Christ, if they do. In many cases, the precipitating factor is not a lost argument but instead exactly what it was in the parable of the prodigal: a crisis.

A group of researchers some time ago did an experiment in which they read the parable of the prodigal son to groups in various places around the world: Asia, Africa, Eastern Europe, the Middle East, North America. The researchers would then ask people in each of these settings to recount back for them the story. There was one detail that people in the developing world always mentioned that those in the developed nations always left out: the famine. The son, you will remember, took his inheritance, went to the far country where he spent and squandered it. He only "came to himself" and came home after, Jesus said, "a severe famine arose in that country, and he began to be in need" (Luke 15:14). Those in affluent contexts didn't remember this part of the story because it seemed to them to be a minor detail. For those who lived regularly with the threat of famine, this seemed to be a major part of the story.[56] It is indeed. When dealing with those who are wandering away from the faith, we must recognize that sometimes they will not start evaluating the deep questions of their lives until they find themselves in a situation in which they don't know what to do. We must be the sort of parents and grandparents and churches that have kept open every possible connection: so that our prodigals will know how to get back home, and know that we will meet them at the road, already planning a homecoming party.

That requires, though, a death to self. The pain over a wayward child is real, and ought to be present in the life driven by the Spirit.

Jesus wept over Jerusalem (Luke 19:42–44). The apostle Paul said that he wished he could himself be sent to hell and cut off from Christ "for the sake of my brothers, my kinsmen according to the flesh" (Rom. 9:3). This pain should not be confused, though, with our carnal demand that we display to the world around us what "blessed" and "successful" families we have. In many cases, the real tragedy in a family with rebellious children is not that their parents hurt for them, but that their parents are embarrassed by them. If "good" children were merely the result of technique, then we could boast of our own righteousness through the lives of our children. It is not.

The same is true in the opposite situation. If we think that something is deficient or shameful about a family with prodigals, then we must conclude that something is deficient or shameful about the Family of God. Families, though, are not about us and our presentation to the world. Sometimes what it may take for a child to see the cross in the lives of his parents is to hear those parents say, "No matter what you do. No matter where you go. You will always be our child, and we will always be glad to say so. We may not like what you are doing, but we are not ashamed of you." This is, after all, the same sort of kindness our Father showed to us, the kindness that brought us to repentance in the first place (Rom. 2:4).

Even in happy endings of such situations, rarely is there an obviously definitive darkness-to-light transition, no more than it is for any of us. God forgives people immediately upon faith and repentance. He then spends the rest of our lives shaping us and forming us, pulling us away from old habits and affections toward new ones. God is infinitely patient and gentle and kind with us. We must be as well. The son or daughter who, for example, has spent time in the far country of substance addiction, might suddenly have no more desire for the drugs he used to do, but this is unlikely. Usually, what ensues is a long struggle for holiness, often with some knocks and backslidings along the way. We should not despair over this, nor should we constantly hold over the head of a repentant child what it was he did "to us." If we really believe the gospel of the cross, then all of that is crucified and behind us. We should instead show patience and the same sort of lack of remembrance of old hurts that God himself has shown to us. "As far as the east is from the west, so far does he remove our transgressions from us," the psalmist sang of God (Ps. 103:12).

In the first of the Narnia stories, the brother Edmund commits mutiny against Aslan the King and against his siblings, allying himself with the evil White Witch, drawn along by her hypnotizing Turkish Delight. Eventually, of course, Edmund comes back. The other children see the lion walking and talking with the erstwhile rebel, though they cannot hear the conversation. Aslan approaches them, with Edmund. "Here is your brother," Aslan said. "And there is no need to talk to him about what is past."[57] That is all of our story. We are all Edmund. We should then show the same grace to those who have disappointed or sinned against us, even—maybe especially—if they are our own children.

* * * *

Sometimes Christians speak of being "pro-family" and of having "strong family values" as though this would be, to everyone, a positive picture of Christianity. For many, though, the idea of "family" is terrifying. Many people have found their deepest suffering, even profound trauma, at the hands of family members. One woman who had been through profound suffering at the hands of her stepfather told me that she didn't think she could ever be a Christian, and the cross is the reason why. She heard the gospel preached, about the account of Jesus crying out, "Father, forgive them, they do not know what they do" (Luke 23:34). If this is Christianity, she told me, she wanted nothing to do with it. She knew what she had experienced, and she could not simply wave that away as though it were nothing. I understand what she meant. If I thought that were the gospel, I wouldn't believe it either. But it's not.

Many throughout the centuries have sought to protect the reputation of God by downplaying his wrath. To some degree, the impulse here is good, because many have a false view of God as an angry, sullen, punitive Deity, not as the God of overflowing love Jesus revealed to us. God's wrath is not a temper tantrum. On the other hand, those who would point us away from the wrath of God do so at the peril of eclipsing God's own revelation of himself, as holy and just, the One who "does not leave the guilty unpunished" (Exod. 34:7 NIV). At the cross, the apostle Paul wrote, God "condemned sin in the flesh" (Rom. 8:3). This is important for us to know, especially those who have survived awful things in their backgrounds.

The skeptical woman I talked to was right in her intuitions. She was not vengeful. She knew, though, that someone who would cover over what had happened to her is someone unjust. God agrees with her. He embedded in our consciences the understanding that the one who "justifies the wicked" is evil, as is the one who "condemns the righteous" (Prov. 17:15). Indeed, a major obstacle to belief in God is precisely what this woman senses: the fear that many acts of horrifying injustice get covered over and are never brought to justice. That ought to trouble us even more than it does. Our innate sense of justice, and disposition to oppose injustice, is part of our most basic humanity, not due to the Fall but due to our creation in the image of God. This is true even of those who would claim to be horrified by the idea of a wrathful God.

The Civil War-era song "The Battle Hymn of the Republic" is direct with biblical imagery of God "trampling out the vintage where the grapes of wrath are stored" and wielding a "terrible, swift sword" against the evil of slavery. This is important because the Americans singing the song were reminding themselves that slavery was not merely a matter of regional conflict, but of moral accountability, an accountability that would have begged for resolution even if the war had not succeeded. Likewise, the civil rights movement grounded its non-violent resistance to Jim Crow wickedness in the same terms, with Martin Luther King Jr. speaking against the violence of the

Alabama police forces by saying: "We will leave them standing before their God and the world splattered with the blood and reeking with the stench of our Negro brothers." He was pointing to a Judgment Seat where evil is held to account. He was saying what, in the same era, the folk-singer Odetta would sing to the terrorist forces of the Ku Klux Klan: "You may run on for a long time, but, let me tell you: God Almighty's going to cut you down." All of this is grounded in the Scriptures themselves, both Old and New Testaments; God does not turn a blind eye to evil. If anything, the cross reaffirms that.

Sadly, this hurt woman's view of the gospel probably came from professing Christians who wrongly represent God as she described. To our shame, many do this especially as it relates to the most hidden, and most horrifying, acts of physical or psychic horror against defenseless children. How many times have we heard of silence against some shocking act of the abuse of a child or of a spouse or someone else being covered over by religious people, sometimes even churches, because the predator is "forgiven by the blood of Christ"? This sort of cheap grace is not the good news of Jesus Christ.

Wherever there is the abuse of the powerless by those in power over them, the church should demand accountability. Where such misdeeds are violations of the civil law, the church should immediately alert those with the commission, given by God, to "carry out God's wrath on the wrongdoer" (Rom. 13:4): that is, the civil authorities. Moreover, the church should do everything possible to see to it that predators do not use the spiritual cover of the name of Christ to commit their horrors. That includes the disclosure of any potential act of harm, and diligent cooperation with investigative bodies any time there is the suspicion of any harm to a child or a spouse or anyone else. Even as we do so, we know there are people walking about, maybe even in our own pews, who assume that because they were never caught in their physical or sexual or psychological abuse that this means they have escaped accountability. We should be the ones reminding such people that there is "nothing hidden that will not be made manifest, nor is anything secret that will not be known and come to light" (Luke 8:17), if not in this life, then in the one to come. At the cross, God's wrath and God's love come together; they do not cancel each other out.

The late Anglican pastor John Stott argued that he could never believe in God were it not for the cross. As he put it, in a world of such horrors—burned children and battered women and concentration camps and genocides—how could one believe in a God who was agnostic of all of that? Stott wrote that he had visited temples in Asia in which he stood before the statues of a placid, remote-looking Buddha, with arms crossed, eyes closed, softly smiling. His imagination was forced to turn away and to turn instead "to that lonely, twisted, tortured figure on the cross, nails through hands and feet, back lacerated, limbs wrenched, brow bleeding from thorn-pricks, mouth dry and intolerably thirsty, plunged in God-forsaken darkness. That is the God for me!"[58] Indeed, this is the God who is there. At the cross, Jesus aligned himself with those who are abused and maligned and powerless and ashamed. He stood with us, or hanged with us, there. And in that powerless act, he also delivered the deathblow to the reptilian power behind the evil every one of us has experienced. Jesus is not distant from your pain; he is crucified by it—with it and with you.

If you've experienced awful things, though, you may still wonder what the way forward is for you. How can you, you might ask, come to worship God as Father if you have never seen anything in a father but anger or violence or predation? It may well be, though, that you are being prepared by God to be the most likely to communicate to others what it means to have God as Father. You know what God is *not* like. And you may well long for, wish for, in the midst of your pain, a parent who loves you, accepts you, protects you. Frederick Buechner wrote once that Christianity is mostly wishful thinking. By this, he didn't mean that Christianity isn't true; quite the contrary. He wrote that even the part of us that, when something unspeakably horrible has been done, longs for something like a judgment or a hell is, he wrote, "reflect[ing] the wish that somewhere the score is being kept." The wish for a Father who is not like the horror you have known is not merely your imagination. You know the difference between what should be, and what has been for you. "Sometimes wishing is the wings the truth comes on," Buechner concluded. "Sometimes the truth is what sets us wishing for it."[59]

What has happened to us in our past, of course, shapes us, and that's especially true when terrible things have happened in what is to be the primal place of safety: the family. Some have concluded that this means that their lives are permanently, maybe even eternally, wrecked by the fear or the shame or the anger that has come out of what has been endured. Again, remember that you follow a crucified Christ. We cannot know why God permitted you to undergo what you have lived through. There are no answers for such mysteries, and it probably wouldn't help us much even if we had all of the answers to our questions of "why." Sometimes people misunderstand the famous passage "And we know that for those who love God all things work together for good, for those who are called according to his purpose" (Rom. 8:28). They wrongly assume that this is just another way of saying "Everything happens for a reason," or "What doesn't kill you makes you stronger." No. The Scripture does not say that everything that happens to you is good, by no means. The Scripture says that, in all things, *God* is at work for your good, to conform you to Christ. Crucifixion is not good. And yet, even in the cross, God was at work, turning evil against itself, defeating it with its own artillery. You cannot know why you've endured what you've endured. You can know, though, that you survived. You bear wounds, yes, and they make up part of who you are. When you first encounter the Lord Jesus at your resurrection, notice, though, his hands and his side. They still bear the marks of Roman spikes and spears (John 20:24–29). And yet, he is no victim. He is the triumphant Lion of Judah, the One who is the heir of the universe. In him so are you.

* * * *

So between now and then, how does one cope with the wounds of a family trauma? Perhaps you have the misunderstanding mentioned before of what forgiveness means. Forgiveness in light of the cross does not at all mean that sins are excused. As a matter of fact, the cross ensures what God had already said: every sin and every injustice will be judged either at the cross or in hell. Part of the confusion about what it means to forgive is that some would say that the gospel means we should forgive everyone, while others would say, no, that we are to forgive as God does: those who repent and apologize. The disagreement here is not so much over what the Scripture commands of us, namely to forgive in order that we may be forgiven (Matt. 6:14), but rather over what we mean when we say "forgiveness." Those who would say we should not forgive apart from the person who has harmed us repenting are including the idea of reconciliation in forgiveness, rather than mere nonretaliation. I would agree with them that you should not necessarily reconcile with someone who has harmed you. For one thing, depending on the circumstances, such a reconciliation could be harmful to you or to other people. Or, sometimes, the cost of the reconciliation, from the other person, is essentially that you help cover up whatever happened. This, obviously, you cannot do both for the sake of integrity of conscience and out of love of neighbor for those who could be next to be harmed. The Bible tells us to "live peaceably with all," but qualifies this with "if possible, so far as it depends on you" (Rom. 12:18). Sometimes this is not possible, because it does not all depend upon you.

Forgiveness, biblically speaking, does not, in my view, always result in reconciliation. Yes, God is reconciled to us when we repent and believe, coming into union with Christ. But, even before that, God is "kind to the ungrateful and the evil" (Luke 6:35). Forgiveness includes, even when not including reconciliation, a refusal to demand vigilante justice—to see to it that sins against me are avenged by *me*. That does not mean that justice is not done. When we are persecuted or reviled, we are told to "never avenge yourselves, but leave it to the wrath of God, for it is written, 'Vengeance is mine, I will repay'" (Rom. 12:19). This does not mean that one does not seek justice, only that we do not "repay . . . evil for evil" (Rom. 12:17). Calling the police when there has been a crime is not repaying evil for evil. Keeping one's child away from the home of an abusive grandparent is not repaying evil for evil. A church disciplining a neglectful husband or father is not repaying evil for evil.

Many believe that they are free from their pasts, simply because they do not feel angry toward those who have failed or hurt them. Sometimes this is because the pain itself has left the person numb. You might be angrier than you think you are, with your anger submerged deep within. First of all, note that anger itself is not a sin; personal retaliation is. Often, anger is not contradictory to being merciful to others but a part of being merciful to others.

A counselor told me that the thing he most often hears from those who were severely neglected or even abused by their parents is, "Well, they did the best that they knew how." This sounds commendable, and even spiritual, but in most of these cases, it is not forgiveness, but self-protection. The person doesn't want to face up to the fact that he or she had a parent who would be so unloving and cruel, so it is easier to rationalize away what happened. This does not, though, lead to healing, because it is hiding from the reality behind an idealized image.

If you've been through a disappointing or traumatic background, though, even a deep trauma, you need not hide that dark reality from yourself. In the cross, God has displayed and absorbed the scariest possibilities of fallen human existence. You cannot go back and undo the past. Sometimes those who wish that they had not lived through scary or traumatic family situations will replay the scenarios over and over again, asking, "What could I have done differently?" or "What if this detail had been different? Might I have avoided this catastrophe then?" Sometimes this is even in terms of blaming themselves for things they know, at the rational level, were not their fault (such as a child blaming himself for his parents' divorce or a wife blaming herself for her husband's affair). You can grieve over your past, but you cannot change it. You can also, though, know that while you are shaped by your past, you are not defined by it. Whoever has hurt you has really hurt you, but they have not defeated you. You have survived. Your life is hidden in Christ. Your future is not that of a victim but of a joint-heir with Christ. The poet Christian Wyman writes of the "mild merciful amnesia" of his life being interrupted by the realizations of what he has endured in the past. "How is it now, like ruins unearthed by ruin, my childhood should rise?" he writes. "Lord, suffer me to sing these wounds by which I am made and marred."[60] You may well feel marred by your wounds, but listen deeply into your life and see how you also have been made by them. Sing the wounds. By that I don't mean to sing them away with cheeriness, but sing them the way Jesus did Psalm 22 from the cross—with honest lament at the seeming absence of God while also clinging to the flashes of reminders of his presence.

The cross-shaped vision of reality means that the church must know how to lament, including when we talk about family. We can easily sing together in worship with the prophet Jeremiah, "Great is thy faithfulness" (Lam. 3:23 KJV), but hardly any other passage of the book. Who can conceive of singing in a worship service, again with Jeremiah: "You have wrapped yourself with a cloud so that no prayer can pass through. You have made us scum and garbage among the peoples" (Lam. 3:43–45)? Instead we often practice a forced cheeriness that is part of the ad hoc liturgy of many evangelical churches. As the service begins a grinning pastor or worship leader chirps, "It's great to see you today!" or "We're glad you're here!" As the worship service closes, the same toothy visage says, "See you next Sunday! Have a great week!" We tell ourselves this is because we are "joyful in the Lord." And yet, many hurting people wonder if the sort of giddiness and happiness that we associate with life in Christ has passed them by. People—including those who have been abandoned or hurt by those closest to them—assume that to be "Christian" is to learn to smile through it all. The cross speaks a different word, though.

Jesus said, "Blessed are those who mourn, for they shall be comforted" (Matt. 5:4). In the kingdom, we receive comfort in a different way than that prescribed by modern culture, certainly not by pretending we're happy. We are comforted when we see our brokenness, our sin, our desperate circumstances, and we grieve, weep, and cry out for deliverance. That's why James, the brother of our Lord, seems so out of step with the contemporary Christian ethos. "Be wretched and mourn and weep," he wrote. "Let your laughter be turned to mourning and your joy to gloom" (James 4:9). What would happen to a church leader who ended a worship service with, "Have a wretched day!" or "I hope your week is full of crying!" It would sound crazy. Jesus always does sound crazy to us, at first (John 7:15, 20). The truth is, though, few of us are as happy as we seem to be. Maybe the best thing we have to offer to the family is more tears, more cries for help, more confession of sin, more prayers of desperation that are too deep for words. Maybe then the lonely and the desperate among us will see that the gospel has not come for the happy but for the brokenhearted; not for the well but for the sick; not for the found but for the lost.

* * * *

Maybe, though, you have not so much lived through trauma, but you can look back on your family life and see the pain of regrets that you have, for things you have done or things you've left undone.

A few years ago, I felt my knees buckle as I knelt down during the closing hymn at the church where I preached at the time, to receive a trembling little four-year-old boy who took my hand and said, "Can you please pray that my Mama and Daddy don't get a divorce." I stifled tears as I heard in his voice, and saw in his face, the sense of powerlessness he felt. I steamed internally with self-righteous anger at these parents. How could they, I asked myself, put their own bickering—whatever it was about—over the security and identity of their own defenseless child? But then I felt a sense of horror hitting me not long after when I realized how, in the frenetic "busyness" of my ministry, I hadn't been home to pray with my own sons at dinner or at their bedtime in over a week. I was a failure. I needed repentance, and sought it, but I needed more than a course correction; I needed mercy.

Perhaps some of you look back on a parent, now dead, that you wish you had told that you loved. Maybe you look back on words you wish you could take back. Maybe you broke your wedding vows in an affair, or in abandoning your spouse. Maybe you left your children, or left them to the side as you poured your whole identity into your work. You cannot undo the past either. You can, if the family members you have disappointed or hurt are still living, apologize and ask for forgiveness. Do not, though, expect that they must immediately forgive you. A woman who had broken up her marriage with an affair with another man apologized to her grown children for what they were forced to live through in their childhood and then, when they didn't immediately accept her apology, went into a rage, quoting Scripture at them about their lack of forgiveness. This displays not repentance, but entitlement. We cannot micromanage the spiritual formation of other people's hearts. We can ask for forgiveness, but then we must give them the room to extend that forgiveness, or not.

It may be that your past, whether as the one hurt or the one hurting others, leads you to conclude that you are doomed to repeat all of your old patterns or all the old patterns that were imposed on you. You may look at your family and wonder, as one who has lived through brokenness, if you are predestined to break their home now. Such is not the case. Perhaps you feel, even now, the pull to walk away. Perhaps it seems too difficult, especially if you haven't had good models, to be a faithful brother or sister within the church, a faithful husband or wife, a faithful father or mother, a faithful grandfather or grandmother, a faithful son or daughter. The pull itself is no sign that you are doomed to dissolve the family. It is instead a call to spiritual warfare, to cry out for the Spirit, to walk in the way of the cross. It is a call to exercise, as J. R. R. Tolkien once wrote to his son who was growing cynical about the state of the church, "the virtue of loyalty, which indeed only becomes a virtue when one is under pressure to desert it."[61]

But again, you cannot go back and undo the past, even if you were to reconcile with an ex-spouse or start speaking to an estranged child or drop the lawsuit against your parents over your grandmother's will. Sometimes what leaves you paralyzed is the guilt and remorse and regret you feel looking backward on how you have fallen short of your duties to others in your family, and even how, in your selfishness, you have robbed yourself of lasting joy. Look to the cross.

That is far more painful than it sounds. When the Israelites were in the wilderness, wandering between the land of slavery and the land of promise, disobedient to the God who delivered them, they were cursed with an attack from fiery serpents. In their pain and dying, their leader, the prophet Moses, intervened with the Lord, who provided a vehicle of healing for them in a bronze serpent aloft on a pole. In order to be healed, they looked to the very image of what afflicted them: a snake, high and lifted up before them (Num. 21:4–9). Jesus said, "And as Moses lifted up the serpent in the wilderness, so must the Son of Man be lifted up, that whoever believes in him may have eternal life" (John 3:14–15). In order to be delivered, we must look to that which frightens us most, to that which exposes us for who we really are, in all of our sin and all our brokenness. We look to the crucified Christ, bearing for us the curse we have brought on ourselves, and upon him. That's true in every aspect of our lives, but is perhaps especially painful and difficult when it deals with our failures within our families, revealing as these often do the vast distance between who we are and who we pretend to be.

As Fleming Rutledge has rightly noted, one sometimes assumes that he, by his own power, comes to repentance and then God's grace is activated. In so doing, this person forgets that it is by God's grace that awareness of sin is awakened in the first place. "When this recognition dawns on us, *we are already standing within* God's grace," she wrote. "Were it not for the mercy of God surrounding us, we would have no perspective from which to view sin, for we would be entirely subject to it," Rutledge writes. "That is the reason for affirming that wherever sin is unmasked and confessed, *God's redemptive power is already present and acting.*"[62] This is indeed the case. If you are longing for deliverance from the hurts you have caused, or the hurt you endure, you are not waiting on God's grace to find you. God's grace is already there. As the wise man told my guilt-stricken empty-nester friend, "The Lord redeems all of that."

Chapter Thirteen
On Aging and the Family

MY SON SAMUEL, ABOUT THREE years old, at the time, wanted to have a theological conversation with me, and I'm afraid I didn't have the courage for it. Samuel carried around with him a ragged little stuffed toy baby owl, dirt stains clinging to its frayed cloth. He called his baby owl "Pengui," mistaking the bird for a penguin. We never corrected him, because who wants to debate ornithology with a toddler? This toy had been Samuel's constant companion since he was in the crib. The softness of the toy seemed to comfort him, as he would often rub Pengui up against his cheek when he was calming down after crying.

On this day, we had been the ones crying, after the death of someone close to our family. Hearing us talk about dying, Samuel started asking questions about death. I answered them all, confidently, from the Bible. I can still re-imagine what it was like to see those little brown eyes darting along as I talked about the promise of resurrection for all who trust Jesus, and I can still see what it was like to notice that they were suddenly filled with tears. "Daddy," he said, "if I go to heaven, can I take Pengui with me?" I sat still, my thoughts jogging ahead of me, trying to find a way to answer this without traumatizing my little son over, of all things, heaven. The idea of missing Pengui on a road trip sounded hellish to Samuel, much less for all of eternity. Finally I said, "Well, Samuel, heaven is perfect happiness in the presence of God. If, in the world to come, God knows that having Pengui with you will make you happy, then I am sure Pengui will be there."

I looked at my wife, with a wink, as if to say, "This is how you do it." An hour or so later, though, Samuel handed me a sheet of paper with scrawled pictures on it. The paper looked a lot like the "lists" he would give us for birthday or Christmas presents he wanted, I thought. And I was almost right. "What's this?" I asked, with the sort of sing-song voice a father gives to a child when he's been handed an art project. Samuel said, "Those are all the toys at the store that I also want to take to heaven with me when I die." I could hardly think of the words to say. Later that night, I lay awake in the bed, and said to my wife, "Do you realize what a failure I am as both a father and as a theologian? I basically lied to my son about the eschaton, and simultaneously taught him to store up on earth the treasures he wants to take to heaven. That's the exact opposite of what Jesus taught. That means that, in terms of parenting, I am literally anti-Christ." Maria laughed, and said that I should wash the imaginary "666" from my forehead. But I still slept uneasily, knowing that for all my self-image as a man of gospel courage, my Christian conviction couldn't stand up to a toy owlet.

What bothered me the most was not whatever confusing theology I had communicated. That would be gone from memory soon enough. What troubled me was that I had used Christianity, not in terms of bearing witness to the truth, but to quiet the questions of a little one. That may seem trifling, and yet this was the very point at which, as an adolescent, I had experienced a spiritual crisis of faith. As a teenager, I was looking around at the Bible-Belt cultural Christianity around me, and I started to wonder if anyone really believed this at all, or if the Christian faith I heard constantly preached and quoted was really just a prop for southern culture or conservative politics.

One of the things that provoked this crisis in me was the fact that I had recently been to several funerals. At these funerals, several times I saw in the casket at the front of the church a person I had never actually seen at church, whom I knew to be notorious for womanizing or drunkenness or just meanness to those around him. But despite all of this, at these funerals, everyone would say, though, as predictable as could be, "He's in a better place." or "He's with Jesus now." This was confusing. At every Sunday morning altar call, we were hellfire-and-brimstone revivalists. At every funeral, we were universalists. It was as though we believed in justification by embalming alone. I would slowly realize that I wasn't the only one who didn't believe what my neighbors were saying about the spiritual state of the deceased. They didn't believe it either. For them, these words of heaven and everlasting life were, at least at a funeral, just the sorts of things one was expected to say to the survivors, right along with "Doesn't he look natural?" and "If you need anything at all, call me." Christianity was a means to an end. I lived through that dark night of the soul and found Jesus on the other side. But here I was with my toddler, doing the same thing —trying to find a gospel useful enough to help him make it through the night.

* * * *

Over every conversation about the gospel, really every conversation about anything, looms the shadow of death. How do we make sense of our lives, if, in fact, we are going to age and wither and die? That's especially true when, as we are faced with mortality, we do precisely what a toddler would do: cling to our comforting toys all the more. "Set your minds on things that are above, not on things that are on earth," Paul wrote to the church at Colossae. "For you have died, and your life is hidden with Christ in God" (Col. 3:2–3). To convince myself that I am invulnerable and immortal, I too often grasp onto my financial stability or my family tranquility or my career success to keep my focus away from the fact that everything around me is transient and temporal, an evaporating mist. That reality has everything to do with the family—including the way we care for the aged among us, the way we drift onward into elderliness ourselves.

The difficulty in talking about the family as a way of carrying our crosses is that we might assume that "The Family" is one, static reality. By that I am not just referring to the differences between families and between the way families are structured in this fallen age. I mean that the family—our family and our place in it—changes over the span of our life cycle, sometimes in ways that can disorient us. If we pay attention, though, we can see that such changes can remind us—wherever we are in our lives—of our callings in the present, and our callings to a life beyond the veil of death.

To some degree, this is easiest when it comes to seeing the transitions from childhood to adulthood. We recognize as we mature, that the adults around us like to constantly, it seems, marvel at "how fast you're growing" or say things along the lines of, "Last time I saw you, you were just a baby! Look how big you are!" When we are children, we cannot imagine why time seems to have passed so quickly for adults when it seems to crawl by for us. Those of us who have children of our own will notice that older people will say to us, when our babies are still young, "Enjoy every minute; it goes by so fast." This seems to us like just another cliché, but in time we learn that, like most clichés, it has become a truism because it is true. We step back and wonder, "Where did this woman come from? She was my little girl just yesterday!" or "How did he suddenly become this man? Where is my little boy?" At the same time, we see those around us, our parents and our grandparents and our in-laws, moving a step or two ahead of us in the lifespan. We tend to largely ignore this until we see them start to stumble and to fall into decline. Then, we move both into the strain and stress of caring for those who have always been the ones to care for us, and in this we are reminded of what awaits us too: aging toward mortality.

Some studies suggest that the "forties" are the most difficult period of time for most people. Some scientists speak of a "U-turn" in terms of personal happiness, which is high in our twenties and into our thirties, then plummets at midlife, before, sometime in our fifties, spiking upward again. Some have suggested that this is because, at midlife, we start to see that what we hoped and planned for ourselves isn't going to happen the way we might have imagined it. Others, though, suggest that this is due to the inordinate stress that comes on people when, as many must do, they are simultaneously parenting their children and dealing with the problems that come with aging parents. What we are dealing with here is the encroachment of death. We notice this perhaps when our mother starts to forget things or when our father falls and breaks a hip in the shower, but, in truth, we are being prepared by our extended family, all along, for the process of aging, even before we recognize it.

Extended families are themselves a sign of both life and death. If you are married, take a minute to look at a photograph from your wedding. Chances are, standing there will not only be your spouse, but your parents along with his or her parents. If you are not married, do the same with some other milestone picture (graduation celebration, birthday party, etc.). There will be, most probably, multiple generations of family members around you. If you are like me, you might stop and calculate how old those family members were then. My parents seemed so old to me when I graduated high school, and when I married. When I look at those pictures, though, I am looking into young faces— and I realize that, though I feel internally the same as I did at nineteen, just with some emotional scars and lessons learned along the way—I am older now than they were then.

Thinking about this recently, I realized that in the amount of time between the age my parents were at my wedding and the age they are now, I will be retired. That time span seems like nothing, and yet in the same amount of time, I will be finished with what seems so massively important to me now, moving quickly toward the span of years the psalmist tells us we can, at best, expect: "For all our days pass away under your wrath; we bring our years to an end like a sigh. The years of our life are seventy, or even by reason of strength eighty; yet their span is but toil and trouble; they are soon gone, and we fly away" (Ps. 90:9–10). There are many ways that God has signaled to us that we are not ultimate, that we came from somewhere and we will, sooner than we think, return to the earth. One of those ways is by putting us in not just nuclear families of a peer-spouse and perhaps children, but in extended families, with people all across the spectrum of generations. We can see, if we choose to see, something of what it takes to mature, and we can see, if we choose to see, what awaits us in the fullness of time.

In some ways, the three- or four-generational family is in jeopardy. In a globalizing, increasingly mobile society there are rarely those who know their grandparents or other extended family members in the way that previous generations would have. Some families don't have grandparents and in-laws around in the same way because those figures have had to step in, often heroically, as parents. I cannot count how many faithful grandparents I know who are rearing their grandchildren in their homes (and in one case, their great-grandchildren). Sometimes this is because of a disability on the part of the child's parents, or because the parents have been killed. Sometimes this is because a parent abandoned the children, or is imprisoned, or is addicted to substances that render that parent incapable of caring for his child. In other cases, though, we simply live spread out across multiple counties or states or even time zones from extended family.

I noticed this phenomenon in my own life when, coming home from Christmas in my hometown, I noticed that my children seemed listless and depressed. They had spent over a week with their grandparents (whom they adore) running through the woods there at the home in which I grew up in Biloxi, Mississippi. They fished in the pond behind my parents' house and, like I did, spent hours exploring Pirates' Alley and eating hot beignets at Café du Monde in New Orleans. The atmosphere in the car on the way home, as we drove almost twelve hours, was funereal, not because a vacation was ending but because they were leaving their grandparents behind, for who knows how long.

I cannot say that I understand how they felt. My grandmother lived right next door, as I was growing up. My other set of grandparents lived not far away, and I would spend endless hours with them, walking down the beach near our home or camping on a creek bank somewhere in the woods or riding roller coasters at a state fair or a theme park. At Christmas, my grandparents would carry out the exact same rituals every time. My grandfather would be at the stove cooking oyster stew, and, when opening his presents, always shirts, he would put each shirt on, one on top of the other. Most of my days in "ordinary time" were spent with my grandmother, picking purple hull peas in her garden or harvesting dewberries or, of course, riding back and forth to church. My children know their grandparents, but they don't have that day-by-day experience. Fewer and fewer children do.

The Western industrialized world has changed from the way almost every previous culture knew it to be: agrarian hamlets with extended tribes working the same land as their fathers and mothers, and grandfathers and grandmothers. There's no easy fix to this. One cannot will away such changes. One can, though, know what it is that we have lost, and endeavor to find ways to ameliorate this.

A church I know has a ministry unlike any I have seen. The ministry is designed to serve women who work in a nearby strip club. And it works well because of how many times it has failed. The church initially sent women who were roughly the same age as the women who worked in these clubs, and the project was a debacle. The strippers assumed that these women, their own age, would think they were "better than us," since these would-be ministers were middle-class women living "respectable" lives. The next stage was an even worse disaster. The church trained and equipped older women to enter the strip clubs and build relationships, to evangelize and to serve. The strippers had negative reactions to most of these women because the women reminded them of their mothers, mothers with whom most of them had, at best, conflicted relationships. Even still, the church commendably did not give up on their mission field and sent a third cohort of women who were even older, and the ministry flourished. The women working in the strip club, some of them also prostituted out by predatory pimps, would confide in these old church ladies. The elderly women became their friends. Some of the strippers came to know Christ through their witness. Many more were given an exit route from the trafficking of the sex industry. The church leaders told me, "We saw a change when we sent in women who were not the age of the strippers' mothers, but the ages of their grandmothers. Almost all of them had conflict with their mothers, but they all loved and missed a grandmother. They felt as though a surrogate mother would judge them, but never a surrogate grandmother." There's much wisdom there. This is not simply true of those who dance nude for a living, but, to some degree, for almost all of us.

* * * *

There's a reason why parents and children, even in the best of situations, will have a certain degree of friction. Parents, after all, are given primary responsibility for the "nurture and admonition" of their children in the Lord (Eph. 6:4 KJV). Those who would suggest that we have overemphasized the nuclear family and underemphasized the extended family in our contemporary Western culture are quite right. The families of the biblical world—as the families of virtually every premodern culture—were extended and multigenerational. Calculating dates from the Bible is not a straightforward task since the language "son of . . ." in Scripture does not always mean, literally, the son of a father but the descendant of an ancestor. Jesus, for instance, is called the "son of Joseph" (John 6:42), but also the "son of David, the son of Abraham" (Matt. 1:1). That said, the Bible does make a clear distinction between the mother-father-child dynamic and that of the larger family just as it makes a clear distinction between the larger family and the tribe or the nation. As one Old

Testament theologian puts it, the biblical family is not a "dormitory with double-beds."[63]

Parents often marvel at how much more lax their parents are when it comes to a grandchild's misbehavior than they were with them when they were children. This is natural. The grandparents, after all, are not immediately responsible for discipline, and so can relate to their grandchildren in a different way, leaving the parents to be stricter on them. When I was a young father, I assumed that much of this relaxed grand-parenting mode came from the exhaustion of age or of being out of touch with the day-to-day needs of childrearing. I suppose that is true in some cases and in some ways, but it is probably more true that age and experience teach one how to better differentiate between immaturity and disobedience.

I knew a mother who was panicked at the fact that her child was still wetting the bed at the age of eight or nine, frantically casting about as to what to do. The child's grandmother said, "Why don't you talk to an adult who lives with the issue of bedwetting?" The mother said she didn't know anyone like that, who didn't face some other medical disability, to which the grandmother replied, "Exactly. He will grow out of it, sooner or later. Relax." Could grandparents be too relaxed? Of course. That's why many of them, when called upon to be primary caregiver, shift from that mode to "parent" mode almost immediately. A child, though, needs both—someone who must give immediate personal account, a parent, for one's formation and correction and a family member who is related just as closely by affection but more loosely by responsibility. We need this, in fact, not just in our families by nature, but also in our family by grace, the church.

A common saying in my Baptist tradition is, "God has no grand-children." What is meant by this saying is just another way of saying, "You must be born again" (John 3:7), that each person must come to faith in Christ and become thereby a child of God. One cannot be justified by God on account of his or her family legacy—because he or she was reared in a Christian family—if that person rejects, personally, the gospel. Those in other traditions would, I'm sure, not use that exact same language. But whether we would say that God has grandchildren, we do, in fact, need grandparents within the body of Christ. We need those mentors who can "parent" us—who can be involved close in, nurturing us through periods of doubt and rebuking us in periods of sin. But we also need those even older in the faith, those who might not be as personally involved with us, but who can love us and serve as mentors and role models. Our "mothers and fathers" in the faith often serve the exact same role as natural mothers and fathers—preparing us for life in Christ. Our "grandfathers and grandmothers" in the faith often do the same as our natural grandparents, telling us to stop worrying so much, to relax in the joy of the Lord, to grow old without bitterness or regret. We need both.

Moreover, the grandparent vocation is distinct and unique not only because of differing levels of responsibility, but also because a person usually finds his or her identity in relation to, and in some ways against, his or her mother or father. Years ago, I heard an elderly former government official saying in an interview what he had learned in the course of his career. One of those things was to never trust a politician who is a "junior" but who does not use the "junior" on his campaign signs. Such a person has too large an ego to serve, the elderly man said, since he is essentially asking the world to forget that he shares his father's name. I suppose that could sometimes be the case, but probably not usually. Most people who don't use the word "junior"—in whatever occupation—are simply trying to forge their own identity, to be their own person. In reality, that's true of all of us, whether we are officially "juniors" or not. The child grows to maturity partly by seeing where he or she starts and where his or her parents' identities leave off. This is an important part of the growth process, and one that, if short-circuited, can have serious consequences both on our flourishing and on our spiritual pilgrimages.

Often I will hear from young couples—usually young husbands—complaining about their in-law difficulties or about their own parents or extended families. Maybe they're a young couple whose parents or grandparents don't exactly approve of the way they are rearing their children, and would like to tell them all about how to do it better. Or, maybe they are new parents trying to discern how to teach transcendent priorities when every Christmas is Mammonpalooza at Aunt Judie's house.

Now, tension takes place whenever finite and sinful people come into contact with one another. Someone asks, "When is the baby due?" to an unpregnant woman, or somebody blasts one's favorite political figure . . . or, well, the examples can go on and on. Living in an extended family can be chaotic and confusing. Sometimes those grousing about the undue interference of parents or in-laws are wrongly maintaining a "no one can tell me what to do" sort of refusal of any counsel, including wise counsel. Some of the wisest advice we see in Scripture, after all, is not only the counsel of father to son throughout the book of Proverbs but that of Jethro to his son-in-law Moses, about the fact that Moses' responsibilities were too great to bear alone and that he should delegate some of this burden to others (Exod. 18:1–27). "So Moses listened to the voice of his father-in-law and did all that he had said," the Scripture tells us, commending the prophet for his reliance on the wisdom of his wife's family (Exod. 18:24). It takes discernment to tell the difference between one's indolence in refusing to take advice and one's indolence in refusing to lead one's own home instead of outsourcing that to whomever seems the most opinionated at the moment.

This is especially true, though, when the lines between childhood and adulthood become blurred. I've had young men tell me they feel like children when they go home to see their extended families. Their parents or parents-in-law dictate to them where to go, and for how much time. They highjack the rearing of their children ("Oh, come on! He can watch this one horror film! Don't be so strict!"). Some of these men just give in, and seethe in frustration. While there may be legitimate battles to fight here ("No, little Caleb is not watching the horror film with you."), sometimes the extended family treats the grown person as a child because that's how he or she acts the rest of the year. Sometimes this is attributed to the ongoing dependence of the (grown) child on the rest of the family, either emotionally or (far more commonly) financially.

This is why the Bible calls on one to leave father and mother, and to cleave to one's spouse (Gen. 2:24). Sometimes extended families interfere inordinately in their adult children's lives because they are controlling and meddling. In those cases, they should be gently rebuffed. In other cases, though, they interfere because they have not made the transition from seeing their child as a child to seeing their child as an adult. Often, this is because the child, and his or her family are still financially dependent on their parents, long after establishing his or her own household. There are, of course, reasons why this might be the case. A daughter may have a husband who has left, or a son may have been diagnosed suddenly with cancer. There could be a catastrophe where the in-laws become the primary support for a time. Sometimes, though, the young married couple simply start out taking financial subsidies from one set of parents or the other in order to live at the same level to which they are accustomed—that is, to the level at which their parents lived. Except in the case, though, of inherited wealth, very few parents of grown children lived as well as they do now when they were starting out their lives. Whatever their income and quality of life is now, it typically took years to achieve. Instead of expecting this immediately, the young new household should see the "lean years" together not as deprivation but as an adventure.

This is not the case, obviously, when there is real jeopardy of not having the means for the necessities of food or clothing or shelter or healthcare, but often the largest conflicts I see are not in those dire circumstances. Almost inevitably, the grown children who are subsidized by parents or in-laws will find the same dynamic at work as a church ministry that is subsidized by the state. Initially, this church group will say to themselves, "Just think of what we could do with our gospel-centered recovery ministry to addicts, if we could apply for government grants." When this happens, though, the state will almost always want the church to comply with its demands: to see to it, for instance, that sharing the gospel is not part of the recovery ministry, pulling out from it the very thing that was key to the ministry's success in the first place. "If you don't want Caesar's meddling," I will usually say to these churches, "Don't take Caesar's coin."

The same is true, almost always, with extended families. More often than not, as one makes decisions, follows though on them, and provides for a household, the extended family will come, maybe gradually, to see that they need not worry about constantly looking about for where to place the safety net. They will no longer worry as much about whether "our little boy" or "our little girl" will be alright, because they will gradually come to see that this is not, in fact, a "little boy" or a "little girl" but a responsible man or woman, leading a household.

This "leaving/cleaving" dynamic is true not only financially but also emotionally. Many marriages are strained because a husband or wife finds in a mother or father the primary source of counsel. This is good and right in most cases. We all need outside direction, and a parent, older and wiser, is often the right place to find this. The exception comes in the matter of "venting" about one's grievances or fears about a spouse. Rare is the mother or father who can keep objectivity about how he or she sees the son- or daughter-in-law in such a case. A son might tell his mother that his wife is flirtatious with other men, that he cannot take how she is headed toward an affair. He might then have a conversation with his wife, resolve a misunderstanding and never think anything more of it, while his mother worries about when she will hear that her son has been left for another man. Likewise, a daughter might tell her father that her husband never listens to her, that he is cold and inhuman. She and her husband might then fight and reconcile, with the husband repenting of his insensitivity and the wife apologizing for her anger. The wife may then forget all about the kerfuffle while her father does not. Leaving and cleaving means that certain boundaries are maintained, and that one's parents are not (again, except in extraordinary circumstances) the default source of comfort and help instead of one's spouse.

Leaving and cleaving does not, though, mean what is commonly practiced in modern Western society, where a nuclear family remains in an almost impermeable silo from the family of origin. This becomes especially relevant as extended family members age and, as is often the case, falter toward death. With longer lifespans due to modern medicine comes with it the expectation that more care will be needed, for longer periods of time, of parents and grandparents by their children. The Scripture commands us, included in the ten words with which God summarized his moral law to his people, "honor your father and your mother" (Exod. 20:12). As we have seen, the apostle Paul referenced this command in the context of children with their parents within the home (Eph. 6:1–2), but this is because childhood is where we first learn to honor our parents, not because honoring of father and mother concludes with adulthood. As a matter of fact, most of the biblical direction for honoring father and mother is not about small children at all, but to adults about their elderly parents. Moreover, most of this is not so much about an emotional expression of gratitude (although that is, of course, part of it) as it is in terms of what we might call economics. A child is to care for the parents who cared for him.

* * * *

Years ago, I was speaking at an event on a university campus devoted to the topic of "the sanctity of human life." I spent my time talking about the protection of children—the unborn, orphans, and other vulnerable little ones, with some parenthetical references about human dignity in the opposition of euthanasia.

After me, though, was a Middle-Eastern immigrant woman, who spent most of her time talking about the need to not grumble when changing the diapers of one's aged, infirm parents, but to remember that they changed one's diapers years before. I was thinking, rightly, about the sanctity of human life in terms of the most basic prohibitions against killing another person. My colleague—shaped in a culture much closer in this particular respect to that of the Bible—concentrated also on the need for one generation to physically and economically care for the next, and to do so practically and without grumbling. I was chastened by this.

If we are a people of the cross, this means that the gospel addresses our breaking of the law at every point—including that of honoring father and mother. If Jesus died for something, we cannot see such things as trifling matters or as nuisances to be resolved. As I mentioned earlier in this book, Jesus was careful to keep this law on our behalf even from the cross itself, as he made arrangements for the care of his mother (John 19:26–27). And Jesus charged the religious leaders with breaking the commandment of God because, in their zeal to maintain their external display of religiosity, they ignored the care of their aged parents. "For God commanded, 'Honor your father and your mother,' and, 'Whoever reviles father or mother must surely die,'" Jesus thundered. "But you say, 'If anyone tells his father or his mother, 'What you would have gained from me is given to God,'" he need not honor his father.' So for the sake of your tradition you have made void the word of God" (Matt. 15:4–6). These are sharp words. Jesus accused these scribes and Pharisees of doing an almost reverse-Sermon on the Mount. In the Sermon, Jesus would quote a commandment from the Law, followed by, "but I say to you." Jesus, though, intensified each commandment, showing how the commandment interrogated us internally as well as externally. These religious leaders, though, were saying, "but I say to you" while deescalating the demands of God's law, and, even worse, doing so without authority and under the pretense of service to God. We rarely ignore our elderly under such biblical gymnastics, but we often assume that what is most important are our own careers and families, sometimes at the expense of those to whom our very lives are indebted.

The Scripture, though, calls not only on children to care for their parents, but on the church to care for its elderly members. James wrote, "Religion that is pure and undefiled before the God the Father is this: to visit orphans and widows in their affliction, and to keep oneself unstained from the world" (James 1:27). James, the brother of our Lord Jesus, had seen this care for the most vulnerable among us, orphaned children and widowed women, up close. Joseph, after all, took into his own family a vulnerable child and a vulnerable woman: the refugee Jesus, on the run from the edict of Herod to murder all such children, and Mary, a woman pregnant outside of wedlock (Matt. 1:18–2:23). The New Testament apostles, almost immediately after the formation of the young church, gave direction as to how to provide not only for the widows among them, but the widows who were Gentiles and thus likely to be forgotten in a largely Jewish church (Acts 6:1–7).

The apostle Paul likewise detailed provisions to Timothy for how the church should provide for the widows among them (1 Tim. 5:3–16). Paul told Timothy that the one who will not "provide his relatives, and especially for members of his household" has "denied the faith and is worse than an unbeliever" (1 Tim. 5:8). I have heard this preached in reference to a man who would abandon his wife and children, leaving them to fend for themselves. This is, of course, applicable, but the reference goes far beyond just that. The immediate context is that of widows. A household is responsible for its relatives, not only as a matter of social order but because to do otherwise is worse than apostasy, the apostle contended. Nor does the apostle treat these widows as merely a personal, family responsibility. Those who do not have families, or who do not have families who will care for them, are not forgotten but have provision made for them by the church. This is, of course, consistent with God who, from the beginning of the canon, made provision in the structure of the economy of Israel for those who were widows and aged (Lev. 19:9; 23:22; Ruth 2:3, 17).

In our era, there are nursing homes and eldercare facilities filled with elderly people whose children have forgotten them, save perhaps to pay for their care. The situation is even worse for the elderly poor who are often destitute and without anyone to even remember them, much less care for them. The biblical call to honor mother and father does not mean that a family should not seek institutionalized care for an elderly loved one. I knew a man whose mother once told him to promise her two things: that he would never put her in a nursing home and that he would never put a "vault" around her casket when she died. She couldn't stand the thought of a nursing home, and the idea of a vault was awful because, "Honey, I would smother to death." The son said, "Mother, if you're smothering in there, something has gone terribly wrong in the first place." He refused to make those promises, and he was wise in this refusal. In many cases, those who keep an elderly relative or friend at home, when they are not able to adequately provide medical or other care for this person, are actually harming, not honoring, the elder. What this does mean, though, is that we cannot outsource the care of our elderly to some third party. A person's needs are not simply medical. A person needs affection and conversation and spiritual encouragement—the very same things one needs in every other stage of life. To allow an elderly person to languish in an institution alone, or, for that matter, to leave an elderly person alone in his or her home, without connection to others, to the Word of God and to the Lord's Table, is not just cruel but a repudiation of the gospel itself.

In some ways, the market-driven nature of the church in our era prepares us to abandon our elderly long before they are incapacitated. Increasingly, our churches are oriented, by music and by culture, toward one generation or the other. Older congregations signal in a multitude of ways—hymns chosen, traditions followed, even graphic design—that younger people are not wanted. Younger congregations do the same, in the same ways as well as with, for instance, the volume of the music in the service. Sometimes these tensions between generations will be inevitable and relatively innocuous, but when the old signal to the young, or the young to the old, "We do not need you," we are putting asunder what God has put together. The great crisis of the church in the next era may well be this: how do we share a common ministry to one another when we do not share a common hymnody with one another? Long before we put the elderly out of our sight in dark apartments or hospital rooms, we put them out of our sight in worship services and mission trips. Some congregations are, as I mentioned elsewhere, gerontocracies in which the older generations prize their nostalgic reenactments of the past more than they do the next generation. Those congregations or denominations will die. But we cannot make the opposite error—of congregations for whom the very sight of elderly people, in leadership or even at all, is seen as "off-brand." When that happens, we are well on our way to doing exactly what Jesus warned us about: devouring widows' houses even while we pray our long prayers (Mark 12:40; Luke 20:47).

* * * *

The changes in the life cycle are even seen in the way we think of the future, of eternal life itself. For years, I have spent time—along with many others—calling people away from the idea of heaven as the idle staring into a timeless light. If we are honest, I will often say, many of us secretly find the idea of heaven boring—a static existence for time without end. In reality, though, I have argued, the Bible does not speak of our future this way. We do not have an "afterlife"—as though our life now is our "life" and what follows is "after." We have instead the Christian hope of the resurrection of the body. What we have waiting for us is not an ethereal heaven but a joining of heaven to earth—a new creation. And with that comes an ongoing mission. The "crowns" we receive at judgment are not ornamental but signs of governing authority. Our eternal life is active—we will be reigning with Christ, judging angels (1 Cor. 6; 2–3; Rev. 20:6). "Rest," biblically defined, I will say, does not mean a cessation of activity but a clearing-away of enemies and obstacles (1 Kings 5:3–4; Heb. 4:1–13). I believe all of that now more than ever.

I often, though, think of what I learned from an older theologian—one who shares with me a new creation eschatology—about how, for him, he no longer dismisses the concept of heaven in terms of a cessation of activity, of "rest" in the classic sense, centered upon the Beatific Vision of God. He said that the idea of eternity as activity invigorated him when he was young, but the older he became the more he looked forward to tranquility, the less he looked forward to the adventure of whatever was to come in the hereafter and the more he looked forward to resting in peace. In fact, the Bible speaks of the life to come both in terms of tranquility and activity, of continuity and discontinuity. It is probably so that the elderly Christian who feels tired of life and wants merely to rest is acting not out of theological ignorance but out of the same natural longing that a traveler on a long journey would look forward to falling into bed and sleeping. After the sleep, though, the traveler is rejuvenated, ready for the next mission from his Lord.

It could be that we need both emphases. The tired, elderly Christian needs to be reminded, "Your work is not over. There is abundant life to come, with all that entails!" And, at the same time, the young, busy Christian needs to be reminded that activity itself does not equal life and that the Sabbath rest that awaits us should call us to "Be still, and know that I am God" (Ps. 46:10). This is especially true when, as the poet David Whyte remarked, we often see one another through the "blurred vision of velocity," in which we lose sight of anyone going at a slower pace than we are. This means, he rightly says, that we lose sight of those who are sick, those who are elderly, those who are children, and even "the parts of our own selves that limp a little, the vulnerabilities that actually give us color and character."[64] Eternity before us should remind us that a man's life does not consist in the abundance of his schedule. As long as we do not grasp this, we will continue to see the aged and the elderly as merely burdens to bear, not as what they are: future rulers of the universe, joint-heirs with Christ, in the embryo of elderliness.

To be sure, caring for elderly parents or grandparents or mentors can be taxing and trying. I saw my own grandmother harried as she cared, in her home, for her own mother, my great-grandmother, who lived to well over one hundred years old. She would not only attend to my great-grandmother all day but would then be awakened in the night by the elderly woman yelling loudly, "Jesus, Mary, and Joseph, I give you my heart and my soul!" (this was the Catholic side of my family). My grandmother would gently ask her to keep her voice down so she could sleep. When we next saw my great-grandmother, my wife said, "We're praying for you," to which the elderly woman glared at her daughter and said, "Well, I'm glad that *someone* still believes in prayer." My grandmother shrugged her shoulders and did not take this personally at all, any more than one would take personally a baby crying in frustration.

Sometimes we can see the need for this sense of patience with the very elderly—those who are, for instance, slipping into dementia—far more readily than we can see that this dynamic might be required much earlier. Often, a middle-aged child will notice that he or she is starting to have to help a parent make decisions about, for instance, where to move his or her stuff. Often, the grown child will say, "We've reversed roles!" I have even seen situations where grown children are dealing with their parents' tumultuous love-lives in their retirement complexes, with every conversation about who likes whom, and who is breaking up with whom. "It's just like middle school all over again," said one woman. "Except that the middle-schooler is my mother!" And not only is this true, but it can manifest in many different ways. Remember, after all, just how cruel and scary those years of the edge between childhood and adolescence could be. One observer noted the disequilibrium that could be felt by those who had spent their lives and careers achieving social and material status only to find in the anonymity of the eldercare facility all the cliques and rivalries of high school, "that there is a 'cool table' in the nursing home's dining room, and we have not been invited to sit there."[65]

As a matter of fact, the comparison is completely apt. If we live long enough, we will regress backward past the recapitulation of those awkward years into some stage of dependence and infancy. Some of this starts with the indignities—the three-star general who has fallen in his bathtub and recognizes that the medical technicians helping him up are talking to him with the unmistakable tone and cadence with which one talks to a small child. Often this degeneration can be startling to the one experiencing it, and to those who love that person. In some ways, it can threaten to almost unravel history, so we are not sure what now constitutes personal identity. The gentle, warm, family man who now, in his dementia, screams profanities at his wife, threatening to shoot her for trampling his rose garden, as she stands before him in the living room. The faithful Christian woman who led the missions efforts for her church now, in her confused mental state, reverts to her life as she knew it before she came to faith—mocking the "fairy-tales" of religion, seeming to deny even Christ himself. Such can be disorienting to family and friends to the point of desperation. And yet, such moments can also remind us that we are more than our cognition, that somewhere in the haze of confusion there is a person deeply loved by Jesus, someone the Good Shepherd is walking into the woods to find.

This is the reason many subconsciously fear the elderly, and the reason we wish to deny our own aging, quickly covering over the gray in our hair. It's the same reason we often fear children. We despise weakness. That's because we do not know who we are. Historian Will Durant mused that old age precedes death the way it does in order to gently strip us of that to which we cling. "And just as the child was protected by insensitivity on its entry into the world," he wrote, "so old age is eased by an apathy of sense and will, and nature slowly administers a general anesthesia before she permits Time's scythe to complete the most major of operations."[66]

If, though, we judge the value of our own lives by our "use-fulness" and our "independence," we will despise the revelation in those who once seemed strong and independent that things are quite otherwise. That is betrayed even in the way we speak about our old age, when we do. Sometimes in the exasperation of dealing with an aging relative, one might say, "I hope I don't live long enough to be a burden on my children!" I will admit I have said this myself, and I did repeatedly until I read an article by an ethicist I admire on why he wanted to live long enough to burden his children. Recounting the way he had stood in a hot shower with a child with croup and had run alongside the wobbling bicycle of his children, this man concluded that bearing burdens is what a family is, as opposed to a group of independent agents contracting with one another.[67]

I blushed as I recognized in my words what lay underneath them: pride. I see it even now, as I want to minister to others within the church, but am humiliated when I have to say the words, "I need you." I hesitated to even accept, much less ask for, financial help from friends when, as a poor young couple, Maria and I faced costly adoption fees for our children. I was humiliated when, in the darkest time in my ministry, I had to say to a group of friends, "I fear that I might be about to collapse and fall. Can you please help me?" I hesitate to even type that, for fear that you will find out how embarrassingly recent that was. Again, I am driven to see myself by my performance when God gave to me a church to show me otherwise, a community that is, by definition, the place not only where we can bear one another's burdens but where, by God's providence, we are often forced to the place where we must seek to have our burdens borne by others, lest we fall beneath their weight. This too is grace. Dependence is not weakness. Weakness is not failure. Failure is not fatal.

Our care for the elderly ought to remind us what we first saw at the cross. The books of 1 and 2 Samuel are filled with the exploits of David. In his heroism (as in the slaying of Goliath), in his sin (his predatory behavior toward Bathsheba), and even in his sorrow (the death of his son Absalom), David was always a blur of activity. Saul had killed his thousands, but David his tens of thousands. Moses had written his songs here and there, but David the Psalms. And yet, the book of 1 Kings opens with a very different picture: David, "old and advanced in years," shivering beneath the covers of a bed, unable to be warmed even by a young woman in the bed with him (1 Kings 1:1–4). The mighty warrior was humiliated in his frailty, in the collapse of his kingdom. And yet, the final act of the warrior-king of Israel was to point from his bed to another, to his son who was to follow him onto the throne; David received his mortality as a gift. When David's servants said to him, "May your God make the name of Solomon more famous than yours, and make his throne greater than your throne" (1 Kings 1:47), David did not chafe with envy, as Saul had done a generation earlier with David. Instead, he bowed himself down on the bed, and gave thanks: "Blessed be the LORD, the God of Israel, who has granted someone to sit on my throne this day, my own eyes seeing it" (1 Kings 1:48). In this, David gazed beyond his immediate son to his descendant he could see from afar. He modeled centuries before what John the Baptist did when he said that he must decrease that the Son of David might increase (John 3:30), when he pointed away from himself to the Lamb of God who takes away the sin of the world (John 1:29). This is not humiliation but glory—the glory of the cross.

Care for the elderly in your family, and in your church, not grudgingly but out of love and a sense of privilege. Where they are walking, you will walk too. Simon Peter prized his strength and independence. He was the swashbuckling would-be protector of Jesus, assuming he would save Jesus from the cross (Matt. 26:47-56). This bravado would not stand. After his resurrection from the dead, Jesus encountered Peter, now humbled by the exposure of his denial of Jesus. Commissioning Simon Peter to "feed my sheep" was grace. The one-time coward would proclaim the apostolic message. But this is not a comeback story. "Truly, truly, I say to you, when you were young, you used to dress yourself and walk wherever you wanted, but when you are old, you will stretch out your hands, and another will dress you and carry you where you do not want to go" (John 21:18). Peter's life would end not in the applause of a great old man, but in the humiliation of one carried away to crucifixion. After all of this Jesus repeated to him the words he had said to him at the beginning, "Follow me" (John 21:19). We do not know how or when, but if we are following Jesus, we too will walk the way to our cross. Or, rather, we will be carried there. The life cycle, starting and ending in help-lessness, ought to drive us back to where our new life started, where it will end, and where it will begin again—the cross.

* * * *

Taking a break from writing this chapter, I stopped in the hallway to watch my son Samuel walk past me. Twelve years old now, he looks more like the man he will be than the toddler I mentioned before. I can't help but wonder what burdens await him, dealing with me at the end of my story. Will I be insisting on keeping all my books after I'm too frail to walk up the stairs to my library? Will he have to tell me I can't have a library in my little apartment at the senior-care center? Even worse, will he have to wipe the drool from my chin, as I lie in a hospital bed somewhere? Will his last memories of me be of emptying my bedpan or changing my colostomy bag? I don't want him to remember me like that. I want him to remember me as the father who would sit in the floor and pretend to be a dinosaur when he was little, or as the whirl of activity who was preaching and teach-ing and debating important issues on television. I don't like those thoughts, because they betray my pride and selfishness. It just may be that in those moments of my gasping for air, my son will see the real me better than he ever has. He will see there the one who, like a crucified robber, can only look to the seemingly helpless man on the other side of me, and say, as I spit the welling blood from my mouth, "Jesus, remember me, when you come into your kingdom."

Maybe he will remember as he watches the life drain out of me what I tried to teach him about the life that is to come. And, maybe, he will watch me learning about it right in front of him. It could be that I, like so many I have watched die, will spend those last moments reliving my childhood, seeing the faces of those who loved me. Perhaps I will, in the kaleidoscope of images from my utter dependence in infancy until then, see how God was at work in ways I never even saw enough to be grateful. Maybe I will recognize that God's goodness to me—those little moments of comfort and flashes of grace—were his ways of preparing me for a kingdom that is not the end of a story, but the continuation of an old way, in a new way. Perhaps Samuel will see his father finally let go of the relentless drive to performance and approval, as I see that I was loved all along, just as I am. Maybe in that moment, my son will imagine me not as he sees me there, helplessly shrinking beneath the bed-sheets, but young again, happy again, walking into the uncreated light of the future God has prepared for me. Perhaps there, as he hears the heart monitor's beeping turn flat, he will picture that rejuvenated father of his, turning around with a smile on my face and maybe, just maybe, a little cloth owl in my hand.

CHAPTER FOURTEEN
Free to Be Family

WE TEND TO REMEMBER THE storms that threatened our lives more than the rains that saved them. In the same way, we tend to remember the big crises and turning points in our lives more than those routine, ordinary graces that sustained us along the way.

As a preacher, I don't like to think about how few sermons I remember from over the course of my life. I remind myself that preaching isn't about memorable epiphanies, but the slow, plodding formation of a psyche around the constant confrontation with the Word of God. Whether I remember them or not, they are still there, somewhere within me. But there's just one particular sermon. I heard, over twenty years ago now, a Welsh pastor preaching from the text on the thief on the cross, and his words haunt me still. Pointing to Luke's account of the repentant robber, crucified next to Jesus, the preacher said, "If that thief on the cross had any family members who were God-fearers, they probably expected that he went to hell." After all, the worst place one could end up in this life was on a Roman cross, and that cross was probably the end-point of a long, hard, rebellious life. "If there were such believing family members, they were probably shocked, upon waking up in the presence of God, to find the last person they ever expected to be walking in the light of God's eternal grace." I'm not sure why these handful of sentences arrested me so. I suppose it was because I never thought of the thief on the cross as having a family, and because it reminded me of just how often I am close to giving up on people I think are, somehow, too far gone for the mercy of God.

That sermon has persisted with me over the years. Those funerals I mentioned earlier still annoy me, those affairs in which we all pretend that the deceased, whoever the deceased is, was a faithful Christian, no matter the evidence to the contrary. And yet, my cynicism is bounded in by the echoes of that old sermon. In every situation, there's the possibility that, just as that thief on that cross, this person grasped, maybe even in the final seconds of breath, the good news he had heard somewhere back there in a Sunday school class or at a revival meeting or in the pages of a Bible read trying to go to sleep in a hotel room. We can never know, this side of Judgment Day. But we can know that God often surprises us and often appears in the moments that seem the most desperately hopeless. "Jesus, remember me when you come into your kingdom," the dying thief gasped (Luke 23:42). He gave up his illusions that he somehow could stand on his own. He confessed that his sentence was just, but, even so, he looked up for the possibility of mercy. And he found it. "Truly, I say to you, today you will be with me in Paradise," was the response he heard from the blood-soaked Galilean (Luke 23:43).

Nowhere could seem further from Paradise, there at the Place of the Skull. And yet, Jesus could see it from there. In the brokenness and horror of the cross, this thief found the glory of a gracious God. In order to find it, though, this man had to toss aside all the strategies he would use to protect himself. The other thief, after all, still postured, maintaining his own rightness, sarcastically demanding that Jesus save himself, and them. The broken thief saw, though, what the defiant thief could not. Paradise could not be found by displays of power. Paradise could only be found by turning his face away from the crowds, away from himself, and toward this One they said that just might be the Christ of God. After a life of searching for God-knows-what, he found life and peace and freedom by crying out to God knows Who. That's our story too.

* * * *

Some of you are reading this book because you've been hurt by the family. Maybe you're a scarred child, a failed parent, an unfaithful spouse, a bitter sibling. You've invested your sense of self and maybe your sense of worth in who you are as part of the family, and you've come up disappointed. Some of you are reading this book because your family is the animating figure of your life. You have not yet been hurt or disillusioned or disappointed. One day you will be. That is nothing to fear. It's impossible for any of us to see the full spectrum of our lives, but sometimes, looking backwards, we can see little ways that God made himself known to us, always in his mysterious hiddenness, that felt at the time as if they were mere coincidence or randomness or fate. Much of these have to do with family. Maybe you are who you are because someone, in your family of origin or in the family of the church, poured themselves into you, loved you, believed in you. Maybe you are who you are because you survived those—in your family of origin or in the family of the church—who did just the opposite. Yet, you are here.

In our charged time, the family is often the subject of fiery public debate. We speak of those who "value" the family, or those who would "deconstruct" the family. And yet, as important as all those conversations are, the basic reality is that all of us, at some level, fear the family. We know that family can bring love, but also the risk of hurt. Those of us with strong families often fear that something could happen, and they could be gone. Those without healthy families often fear that they will never have a people to whom they can belong. And those who weathered awful families often fear that they won't escape the damage done, or, even worse, that they will repeat it. We find ways to protect ourselves—either by grasping our families tightly, or by finding ways to run away from the duties of being family to one another. We put up protections by seeing ourselves only as the sum of our family relationships and responsibilities, or by trying to abandon those things. In either case, we are called to the place we don't want to look—the cross.

C. S. Lewis, looking back over his life, summed all of it up as being "surprised by joy." If we see "joy" only in the way the word is used most often around us, we might surmise that what Lewis meant by "joy" was what most people call "happiness" or "contentment." For him, though, joy was a sense of longing, something bittersweet, having a sense of home but not really finding it. The awakening of joy is what led him, the long way around, to the God and Father of the Lord Jesus Christ. In this, Lewis perceived pointers to the world beyond the one he could see. "When we are lost in the woods the sight of a signpost is a great matter," he wrote. "He who first sees it cries, 'Look!' The whole party gathers round and stares. But when we have found the road and are passing signposts every few miles, we shall not stop and stare."[68] The Bible tells us that one of these "signposts" of the kingdom is the family—not just "the family" in abstract in the big, broad world but your family story, particularly, in the story of your life. If we ignore the signpost, we can easily find ourselves lost in the woods of the universe around us, pretending somehow that we do not need a Father, that we do not need a home. On the other hand, we can turn the signpost into an altar, looking to the family to be not just a blessing to us but a god. Whatever the case, we will be, at long last, disillusioned.

This disillusioning is not God's judgment, but his mercy. We are all worshippers. "An idol is an object invested by your attention with the hope of transcendence," one philosopher put it. "An idol is an object turned mirror."[69] At some point, we will be disenchanted with the idol's false promises. "This moment when it looks like your worship has failed is the religious moment," he writes. "This is the revelation."[70] The disappointment is the epiphany. It's not just the one who prizes the family too much who idolizes it, but also the one who counts it as too little. Indeed, the latter often does so even more, spending a life focused on his family, in order to prove that he doesn't need them, or that they don't need him. When we come to the end of all that, though, however we get there, we can find freedom.

Family is not the gospel. If you think that family is the source of ultimate meaning in your life, then you will expect your family to make you happy, to live up to your expectations. You will then come to perceive that a dysfunctional family background or a spouse who leaves you or a child who walks away to a far country of rebellion has ruined your life. And, when you fail your family, as you inevitably will, you will spend your life trying to atone for your sins, and you will never find the peace you seek. But if you hold your family gently, you can find the freedom to see your family flourish. When you do not need to be your family's Messiah, or they yours, then you can pour yourself out for those God has placed around you. In order to find freedom and joy, you must see that family is more important even than you think—so important that it is a place of spiritual warfare, a warfare that sometimes leaves us groaning in sighs too deep for words. No matter the brokenness, there can be joy. This requires, though, what Martin Luther called a theology of the cross, not a theology of glory. "The 'theologian of glory' calls the bad good and the good bad," he confessed. "The 'theologian of the cross' says what a thing is."[71] We see this theology of glory in those who would say "the family" is itself a social construct, and that we can ignore or reconstruct it. We see it also, though, in those who, in defending the family, would idealize it to the point of denying how difficult it in fact is.

The cross-shaped life, though, frees us to neither idealize nor demonize the family. We do not resent our families as burdens to us when we see that, in the cross, burden is blessing. We do not expect our families to meet our every need or longing because we have an eternity of glory in front of us. This can only happen, though, in the kind of universe we find ourselves in: the sort of universe in which

God has joined us in our humanity, has offered up his own Son in a sacrifice of both perfect justice and perfect mercy. If family is not the ultimate source of meaning, or ultimate wound of hurt; if my life is more than my family, then I have the freedom not to cling to the family or to repel them from me. As I follow Jesus in the way of the cross, I can see every day as an opportunity to lose my life—sometimes in the ordinary rhythms of hugging a grandmother, changing a diaper, walking in the park, or singing in a choir. Knowing that my life is already over, crucified at the cross, and my life is waiting to burst into action, ascended at the right hand of God, I can gladly lose my life for my family, knowing I need not protect myself from love. I can be free to serve, free to love.

* * * *

I started this book noting that the cross was a family crisis. There we see the hidden presence of a faithful Father, the visible presence of a human mother, the background of a life lived out with an infancy, a childhood, and a hometown. There we see a Groom fighting for his Bride. The thief on the cross, though, as far as we know, was all alone. One would not expect that family members, even if he had them, would show up for someone so reviled. They would probably, after all, have been ashamed of him. They wouldn't have wanted to admit that their family was connected to someone who was both executed by the empire and cursed by God. And yet, he was not without family. "This day you will be in Paradise" is not just a promise of a solitary reunion between these two men. No, Paradise is not lonely but vibrant and alive and brimming with people. "In my Father's house are many rooms," Jesus told his disciples (John 14:2). With one word, he promised this wretched criminal that one of them would be his. In short, whatever this thief had heard from his own family, whatever he had said to his own family, Jesus' words to him were words he had learned long ago on a riverbank: "You are my beloved Son; with you I am well-pleased" (Mark 1:11).

Family is crucial, a signpost pointing away from us to the very meaning of the universe itself. Your family, whatever it is, will bless you, maybe in ways you don't even notice in the blur of busyness at the moment. Stop and notice these blessings. Listen to what God is telling you through them. Precisely because of its crucial importance, family can scare us. Perhaps you are afraid. You may be afraid of failing your family. You may be afraid of losing your family. This, too, is grace. As he lay in a hospital bed near death, John Updike noted a telephone call from his minister, and wrote: "A clergyman—those comical purveyors of what makes sense to just the terrified."[72] The most important things only make sense to the terrified. But they also only make sense on the other side of that terror. We learned that at the Place of the Skull, where we could see both the horror of our sin before a holy God and the exuberant love with which he came looking for us, even to the cross itself and beyond. Your family might bring you pain. What of it? To love is to suffer. But you have learned that suffering is not a sign of God's absence but his presence. You learned that at the Place of the Skull. You learned that when you first heard the words calling out to you, from somewhere on an ancient Galilean shore, "Take up your cross and follow me." Do not be afraid. Your family will lead you where you never expected to go. But this is no reason for fear. The path before you is the way of the cross.

The way of the cross leads Home. The Light shines in the darkness, still, and the darkness has yet to overcome it. Whatever storms you may face now, you can survive. If you listen carefully enough, even in the scariest, most howling moments, you can hear a Galilean voice saying, "Peace. Be still." If you give attention to more than just the wind and the waves, you might see some hands reaching out for you. In fact, you may notice that those hands already have you, holding you safely above the waters below. You are not as tossed about as you think you are. If you stop to recognize it, you just might notice that those hands holding onto you have spike-holes. Do not be afraid. The scars remain, but the storm has passed.

Acknowledgments

WRITING A BOOK ON THE family would be impossible, were it not for my own family. My wife Maria, as always, has strengthened this book by her example of love and sacrifice, as well as by reading and critiquing parts of it, sometimes with the words, "I don't believe I would tell that." Believe it or not, all of those sections are gone, so what you read here has been through the censoring filter of a wise woman I trust with my life.

My parents, Gary and Renee Moore, gave us love and stability such that we took such things for granted, as I wish all children could. The same is true for my grandparents—Ken and Betty Summy and Agnes Moore—two of whom are now gone, one dying as I was working on this book.

My children—Ben, Timothy, Samuel, Jonah, and Taylor—contributed to this book if for no other reason than because I never stopped realizing as I was typing away in some lonely room that I would rather be with them. Their personalities—each one very different—brim with a life and joy that I never could have imagined before they were here. I know they will all bear scars from something in this life, as we all do, but I pray that with those scars they will know that Jesus loves them and longs to be with them always. And so do I.

As I argue in this book, though, "family" for those who follow Christ is never confined to bloodlines. I could not have written this, or done anything else in recent years, if not for my family at the Ethics and Religious Liberty Commission, and, before that, at the Southern Baptist Theological Seminary. In the writing of this book, I am especially grateful to Joshua Wester, who pored with me over the initial drafts, providing much-needed advice and commentary. Nothing would get done here if not for my senior colleagues Phillip Bethancourt and Daniel Patterson, who long ago started with me as interns proofing drafts of *Adopted for Life*, and who are now, respectively, my executive vice president and chief of staff. Their ingenuity, expertise, and trustworthiness are unparalleled, and I know it. I also am indebted to my pastor Scott Patty, and also to Ray Ortlund, David Prince, Andrew Peterson, and Ken Barbic without whom I would have stopped writing last year, about everything.

I am also grateful for my literary agent Andrew Wolgemuth for shepherding this book along from the beginning, and for the unbelievable brilliance of the editorial team at B&H Publishers. I am particularly grateful for the encouragement and insight of Jennifer Lyell, and for the razor-sharp work of Devin Maddox, trade book publisher at LifeWay Christian Resources (who also, oddly enough, started out as my intern, proofing book projects back in the day). Now he's my editor, and there's not a more skilled, more imaginative one that I know of in the publishing world.

Thank you.

Notes

1. Martin Luther, *Luther's Commentary on the First Twenty-Two Psalms*, trans. John Nicholas Lenker (Sunbury, PA: Lutherans in All Lands Co., 1903), 124.

2. Christopher J. H. Wright, *Old Testament Ethics for the People of God* (Downers Grove, IL: InterVarsity, 2004), 208.

3. C. S. Lewis, *Reflections on the Psalms* (New York: Harvest, 1964), 132.

4. Walker Percy, *Lost in the Cosmos: The Last Self-Help Book* (New York: Farrar, Straus & Giroux, 1983), 78–79.

5. Jane Jacobs, *Dark Age Ahead* (New York: Vintage, 2005), 5.

6. Gerard Jones, *Men of Tomorrow: Geeks, Gangsters, and the Birth of the Comic Book* (New York: Basic, 2004), 207.

7. Les Daniels, *DC Comics: Sixty Years of the World's Favorite Comic Book* (Boston: Little, Brown, 1995), 58.

8. Christopher Matthews, "Parenthood," *The New Republic*, May 20, 1991, 15–16.

9. Wendell Berry, "The Body and the Earth," in *The Art of the Commonplace: The Agrarian Essays of Wendell Berry*, ed. Norman Wirzba (Washington, D.C.: Counterpoint, 2002), 110.

10. Ibid.

11. Rudyard Griffiths, ed., *Are Men Obsolete? The Munk Debate on Gender* (Toronto: Anansi, 2014), 9.

12. W. Robert Godfrey, "Headship and the Bible," in *Does Christianity Teach Male Headship? The Equal-Regard Marriage and Its Critics*, eds. David Blankenhorn, Don Browning, and Mary Stewart Van Leeuwen (Grand Rapids: Eerdmans, 2004), 88.

13. Jonathan Sacks, *Radical Then, Radical Now: On Being Jewish* (London: Bloomsbury, 2000), 84.

14. Rodney Stark, *The Rise of Christianity: How the Obscure, Marginal Jesus Movement Became the Dominant Religious Force in the Western World in a Few Centuries* (New York: HarperCollins, 1996), 95.

15. John Shelton Reed, *Minding the South* (Columbia: University of Missouri Press, 2003), 170.

16. See, for instance, Stephanie Coontz, *Marriage, A History: How Love Conquered Marriage* (New York: Penguin, 2005).

17. Pascal Bruckner, *Has Marriage for Love Failed?* (Cambridge: Polity, 2010).

18. Charles Murray, *The Curmudgeon's Guide to Getting Ahead: Dos and Don'ts of Right Behavior, Tough Thinking, Clear Writing, and Living a Good Life* (New York: Crown, 2014).

19. Andrew J. Cherlin, *Labor's Love Lost: The Rise and Fall of the Working Class Family in America* (New York: Russell Sage Foundation, 2014), 138–39.

20. Leon R. Kass, *The Beginning of Wisdom: Reading Genesis* (Chicago: University of Chicago Press, 2003), 106–7.

21. Frederica Mathewes-Green, *At the Corner of East and Now: A Modern Life in Ancient Christian Orthodoxy* (New York: Putnam, 1999), 92.

22. William Loader, *Making Sense of Sex: Attitudes Toward Sexuality in Early Jewish and Christian Literature* (Grand Rapids: Eerdmans, 2013), 56–57.

23. Ibid., 13.

24. The best study of this theme in the Old and New Testaments is found in Raymond C. Ortlund Jr., *God's Unfaithful Wife: A Biblical Theology of Spiritual Adultery* (Downers Grove, IL: InterVarsity, 2002). The original title of this book—*Whoredom*—put the case far

more directly right in the title but was therefore far more embarrassing to read in an airport or a train station.

25. Thomas Merton, *Conjectures of a Guilty Bystander* (New York: Doubleday, 1965), 142.

26. Christine J. Gardner, *Making Chastity Sexy: The Rhetoric of Evangelical Abstinence Campaigns* (Berkeley: University of California Press, 2011).

27. Mark Regnerus, *Forbidden Fruit: Sex and Religion in the Lives of American Teenagers* (New York: Oxford University Press, 2007).

28. Ibid.

29. Mark Regnerus and Jeremy Uecker, *Premarital Sex in America: How Young Americans Meet, Mate, and Think About Marrying* (New York: Oxford University Press, 2011), 35.

30. Tom Shachtman, *Rumspringa: To Be or Not to Be Amish* (New York: North Point, 2006).

31. Esther Perel, *The State of Affairs: Rethinking Infidelity* (New York: Harper, 2017).

32. Esther Perel, "Why Happy People Cheat," *The Atlantic*, October 2017, 46.

33. See, for instance, the virtually dead-on description in Elizabeth Landers and Vicky Mainzer, *The Script: The 100 Percent Absolutely Predictable Things Men Do When They Cheat* (New York: Hyperion, 2005).

34. Deborah Solomon, "The Professional Provocateur: Questions for Noam Chomsky," *New York Times Magazine*, November 2, 2003, 13.

35. Alan Wolfe, "The Culture War That Never Came," in *Is There a Culture War? A Dialogue on Values and American Public Life*, eds. James Davidson Hunter and Alan Wolfe (Washington, D.C.: Brookings Institute Press, 2006), 41–73.

36. Jennifer Glass and Philip Levchak, "Red States, Blue States, and Divorce: Understanding the Impact of Conservative Protestantism on Regional Variation in Divorce Rates," *American Journal of Sociology* 119.4 (January 2014): 1002–46.

37. For a contrast of evangelical perspectives on this question, see Mark Strauss, ed., *Remarriage After Divorce in Today's Church: Three Views* (Grand Rapids: Zondervan, 2006).

38. W. Bradford Wilcox, "Conservative Protestants and the Family: Resisting, Engaging, or Accommodating Modernity," in *A Public Faith: Evangelicals and Civic Engagement*, ed. Michael Cromartie (Lanham, MD: Rowman and Littlefield, 2003), 58.

39. Andrzej Franaszek, *Milosz: A Biography* (Cambridge: Belknap, 2017), 456.

40. Neil Postman, *The Disappearance of Childhood* (New York: Vintage, 1994), 148.

41. This line is attributed to Kate Michelman, formerly of National Abortion Rights Action League. Elizabeth Achtemeier cites it in an address to the Presbyterians Pro-Life meeting at the General Assembly of the Presbyterian Church (USA), June 3, 1993.

42. Will D. Campbell, *Forty Acres and a Goat: A Memoir* (Oxford, MS: Jefferson Press, 2002), 136.

43. Eli J. Finkel, *The All-or-Nothing Marriage: How the Best Marriages Work* (New York: Dutton, 2017), 97.

44. Russell Moore, *Adopted for Life: The Priority of Adoption for Christian Families and Churches* (Wheaton, IL: Crossway, 2009).

45. Flannery O'Connor, "Introduction to a Memoir of Mary Ann," in *Flannery O'Connor: Collected Works*, ed. Sally Fitzgerald (New York: Library of America, 1988), 822.

46. As one OT theologian points out, the mother-father-child relationship was still fundamental in the context of the extended family. The extended family in Israel was not "a dormitory full of double-beds." Christopher J. H. Wright, *Old Testament Ethics for the People of God* (Downers Grove, IL: InterVarsity, 2004), 355.

47. As ethicist Paul Ramsey argued years ago, the very mode of reproduction shows us that love, not the will to power, is at the heart of who we are. We reproduce in the ecstasy of a man and a woman not, in Ramsey's words, in "a cool, deliberate act of man's rational will." Paul Ramsey, *Fabricated Man: The Ethics of Genetic Control* (New Haven: Yale University Press, 1970), 37.

48. "Once we have produced the next generation, or passed the age when we might have done so, nature does not work very hard to keep us alive," notes one bio-ethicist. "We can, it seems, work to secure our own future, or we can commit ourselves to our children and others of

their generation." Gilbert Meilaender, *Should We Live Forever? The Ethical Ambiguities of Aging* (Grand Rapids: Eerdmans, 2013), 58.

49. One Jewish writer rightly observes: "Paganism often (always?) involved the readiness to sacrifice one's own children for one's own good." Norman Podhoretz, *The Prophets: Who They Were, What They Are* (New York: The Free Press, 2002), 353.

50. Anthony Hoekema, *The Bible and the Future* (Grand Rapids: Eerdmans, 1979), 267.

51. Jennifer Senior, *All Joy and No Fun: The Paradox of Modern Parenthood* (New York: Ecco, 2015).

52. Frederick Buechner, *Now and Then* (New York: HarperCollins, 1983), 55–56.

53. Eugene Peterson, *As Kingfishers Catch Fire: A Conversation on the Ways of God Formed by the Words of God* (New York: Waterbrook, 2017), 240.

54. Neil Postman, *The Disappearance of Childhood* (New York: Vintage, 1994), 129.

55. Robert Bly, *The Sibling Society* (New York: Vintage, 1977, 1996), 230.

56. E. Randolph Richards and Brandon J. O'Brien, *Misreading Scripture with Western Eyes: Removing Cultural Blinders to Better Understand the Bible* (Downers Grove, IL: InterVarsity, 2012), 14–15. The experiment cited is from Mark Alan Powell, "The Forgotten Famine: Personal Responsibility in Luke's Parable of 'the Prodigal Son,'" in *Literary Encounters with the Reign of God*, eds. Sharon H. Ringe and H. C. Paul Kim (New York: T&T Clark, 2004).

57. C. S. Lewis, *The Lion, the Witch, and the Wardrobe* (New York: HarperCollins, 1950), 139.

58. John. R. W. Stott, *The Cross of Christ* (Downer's Grove, IL: InterVarsity, 1986), 335–36.

59. Frederick Buechner, *Wishful Thinking: A Seeker's ABC* (New York: HarperCollins, 1993), 120.

60. Christian Wiman, "Lord Is Not a Word," in *Hammer Is the Prayer: Selected Poems* (New York: Farrar, Straus and Giroux, 2016), 124.

61. Humphrey Carpenter, ed., *The Letters of J. R. R. Tolkien* (New York: Houghton Mifflin, 2000), 393.

62. Fleming Rutledge, *The Crucifixion: Understanding the Death of Jesus Christ* (Grand Rapids: Eerdmans, 2015), 174–75.

63. Christopher J. H. Wright, *Old Testament Ethics for the People of God* (Downers Grove, IL: InterVarsity, 2004), 355.

64. David Whyte, *Crossing the Unknown Sea: Work as a Pilgrimage of Identity* (New York: Riverhead, 2001), 118.

65. William B. Irvine, *A Guide to the Good Life: The Ancient Art of Stoic Joy* (New York: Oxford University Press, 2009), 191.

66. Will Durant, *Fallen Leaves: Last Words on Life, Love, War, and God* (New York: Simon & Schuster, 2014), 28.

67. Gilbert Meilaender, "I Want to Burden My Loved Ones," *First Things*, October 1991, 12–14.

68. C. S. Lewis, *Surprised by Joy: The Shape of My Early* Life (New York: Harcourt, Brace, 1955), 238.

69. Adam S. Miller, *The Gospel According to David Foster Wallace: Boredom and Addiction in an Age of Distraction* (London: Bloomsbury, 2016), xii.

70. Ibid.

71. Martin Luther, "Theses for the Heidelberg Disputation," in *Martin Luther: Selections from His Writings*, ed. John Dillenberger (New York: Anchor, 1962), 503.

72. John Updike, *Endpoint and Other Poems* (New York: Knopf, 2009), 24.

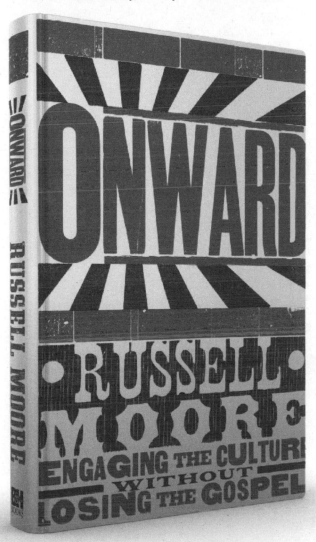

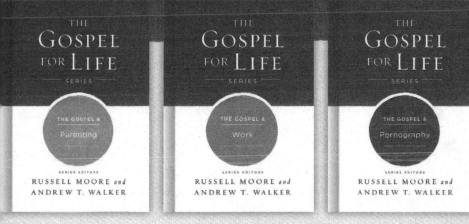

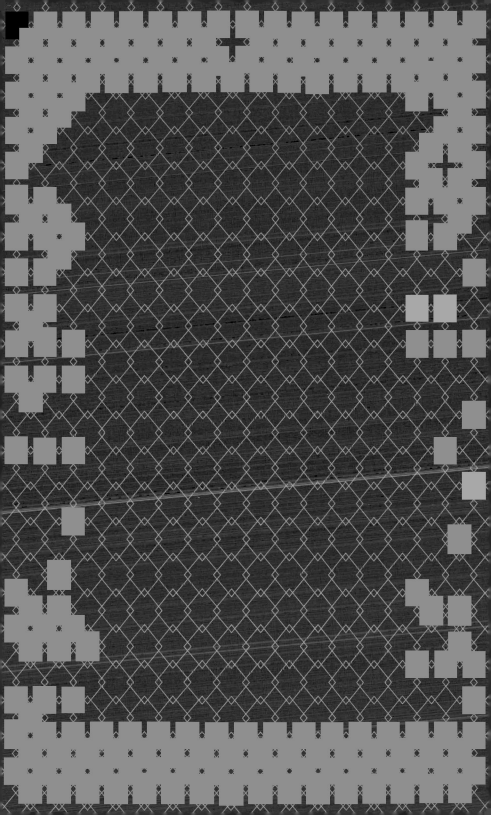

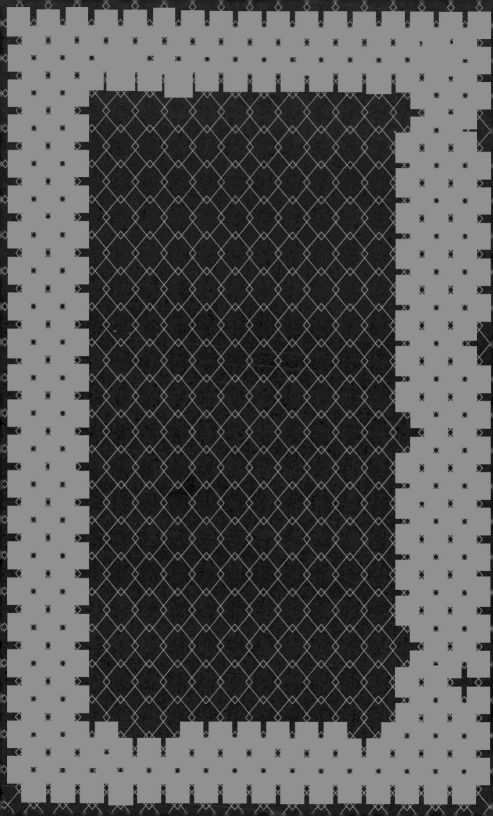